The Devil,
The Gargoyle,
and The Buffoon

KENNIKAT PRESS

NATIONAL UNIVERSITY PUBLICATIONS

SERIES ON LITERARY CRITICISM

General Editor

EUGENE GOODHEART

Professor of Literature, Massachusetts Institute of Technology

LEMUEL A. JOHNSON

The Devil, The Gargoyle, and The Buffoon

The Negro as Metaphor in Western Literature

NATIONAL UNIVERSITY PUBLICATIONS
KENNIKAT PRESS
PORT WASHINGTON, N. Y. • LONDON

Library of Congress Catalog Card Number: 76-139355
ISBN 0−8046−9006−5

Manufactured in the United States of America

Published by
Kennikat Press, Inc.
Port Washington, N.Y./London

For Marian, Yma and Yshélu

ACKNOWLEDGMENTS

I would like to express my sincere gratitude to Professors Frances Weber, Otto Graf, Robert Neiss and Marcel Muller for their invariably kind and properly demanding assessments when this study was first undertaken as a doctoral thesis in Comparative Literature at the University of Michigan in Ann Arbor.

For much of the impetus to expand and reorganize the work for publication, I am most grateful to Professor Eugene Goodheart of the Massachusetts Institute of Technology, who was willing to be helpful and to be impressed.

PREFACE

Part II of this study is introduced by way of the following observation from "The Outpost of Progress," one of Joseph Conrad's short stories:

> The contact with pure unmitigated savagery, with primitive nature and primitive man, brings sudden and profound trouble into the heart. . .excites the imagination and tries the civilised nerves of the foolish and the wise alike.

It is primarily the "profound trouble in the heart and the civilised nerves of the foolish" that concerns this study. Insofar as the Negro was "discovered" in the heart of darkness, he was seen to fit the category of "unmitigated" savage. Insofar as he was black, he posed problems to the excited imagination of the West. Since neither God nor Plato could be presumed to have made a mistake in not unequivocally fixing the place of blackness in human form, there was room for involuted speculative thought aimed at revelation. In the attempt to accommodate the suspicion that some element of human nature might lie trapped in that blackness lie some of the most extraordinary scandals to which the human capacity to invent and to devise would be subjected. To the comic frightfulness of medieval inventions would be added the stimulating dynamism of renaissance curiosity and the ethnocentrism of pre- and post- nineteenth-century Darwinism. But in all this expense of energy in English, Spanish and French literature there was much in deliberate sarcasm and enthusiastic inexactitude that was near surrealist in effect.

I had just conceived of the idea of this study when Barbara Tuchman's *The Proud Tower* and Hannah Arendt's *Eichmann in Jerusalem* were published. A number of perspectives in these chapters were perhaps influenced as a result. Insofar as Mrs. Tuchman details the feverish comedy that resulted in the disasters of war and, insofar as Hannah Arendt suggests that there is some indefinable edge to the banality of evil, they offered avenues into which these chapters willingly enter. There is something altogether unreal in the comedy and the malice of human misbehavior. It is this quality of the unreal which perhaps accounts for the inevitablity of *foolishness* as opposed to *sinfulness*. If Eichmann and the Great War are monumentally unreal, it becomes easier to transcend them and, unfortunately, easier to once again dash one's brains against them.

The aforementioned may in part explain the structure and ideas in this study. I begin in Part I with an assessment of the Sierra Leone Creole, showing the forces at work creating his precarious identity as an "African Jacobin," and also illustrating Graham Greene's literary apprehension of that parodic identity as it had become fossilized in the Thirties. Part II examines the malignant and benign literary caricatures through which the "civilised nerves" of English, French and Spanish fiction attempted to accommodate to the idea of blackness in human form. All these accommodations are traced through to the Negrophilism of the first two decades of this century. This was a period during which the intellectual, artistic sensibility found eschatology and apocalypse inseparable from awareness of Western civilization. It was a period in which "a large and enthusiastic number of people were crazy about Negroes"—a period during which iconoclastic brilliance "chose savage artists as its mentors." These too were the years that formed the "opulent pause" between the approaching disaster of World War I and the insanity of World War II.

The works chosen for analysis in Part III are all chronicles by Negro poets of that period. They relate sequentially to the assessments in Part II. Langston Hughes' *The Weary Blues*, published in 1926, is a chronicle of the Negro's sense of agony and exile and of the aberrant intoxications of the Harlem Renaissance. Nicolás Guillén's *West Indies Ltd.* (1934), with its hispanic rather than English ancestry, concerns itself with the Caribbean for the most part. Aimé Cèsaire's surrealist, symphonic poem *Cahier d'un Retour au Pays Natal*, 1939, in a profound way demonstrates its French ancestry. All three works represent a coincidence of energies by which a race of erstwhile Africans, now inadequately Negroid and inadequately Caucasoid, sought to define itself in a world that was white and antithetical to human manifestations of blackness.

CONTENTS

The Devil,
The Gargoyle,
and The Buffoon

PART I

INTRODUCTION TO A PROCESS OF SYNCRETISM

"The land of Zanj is vast," wrote Suleiman the Merchant. *"Its plants are all black in colour."*

CHAPTER 1

THE SIERRA LEONE CREOLE

I have indicated in the Preface that a high degree of psychological and cultural insecurity is inevitable in Negro-White relationships. The suggestion will be further amplified in this and subsequent chapters by discussing the fundamental antitheses in the manner in which Caucasian Europe apprehended Negro Africa. The Negroes who now inhabit the Americas are the products and embodiments of these antithetical apprehensions. The sense of agony and exile, the indecorous exasperations of the Sierra Leone Creole and of the New World Negro expressions to be studied in Part III are therefore illustrative of my intent. My purpose then is to trace the beginnings and the precarious existence of a peculiar, hybrid race, a people inadequately Negroid and inadequately Caucasian.

I begin with the Sierra Leone Creole experience because its history and artistic expression are symptomatic of those of the Negroes one finds in Haiti, Cuba and the United States. The "Negro" or Creole in this historical and "ethnological" sense is, in effect, the pathogenic product created by unintelligent contacts between Negro tribes from the African Continent and Caucasians from Europe. The resulting union may be manifested primarily in the creation of a hybrid or generally mongrelized culture, or it may be in actual biological miscegenation. Invariably, the evidence tends to indicate, be it in Sierra Leone or the Americas, a union that is both biological and cultural. I am therefore interested in the Negro insofar as he fulfills the role of Creole, with the attendant psychological and psychic precariousness. My interest in Europe will be determined primarily by the roles that England, France and Spain played in producing and maintaining the precarious identities against which the Creole will react in Sierra Leone, in Harlem, in Camaguey and in the Surrealist salons of Paris and Haiti.[1]

One significant feature is characteristic of this process of creolization. Pathological consequences are inevitable for several reasons. In the earliest instances, perception of the Negro was shaped by a naive, exotic and science fiction reductivism. In this respect, fifteenth- and early sixteenth-century perceptions of the Negro seem to me to have been

3

shaped by the peculiar fusion of an inadequately emancipated medieval approach to the excitement and curiosity of a Renaissance expansion of human horizons. In the late seventeenth through early nineteenth centuries, it was determined by an essentially pathological reductivism, the product of economic enthusiasm, extraordinary cultural ethnocentrism and a capacity for human perverseness that reached its near surrealistic zenith in the Slave Trade. The major reason for all these negative reactions is specifically that the Negro's racial and cultural attributes represented a symbolic and actual contradiction of values that Europe was either unable or unwilling to re-evaluate. The tragedy was that this was in the face of the demands of a world that made enlightened, syncretistic behavior the prerequisite for civilized coexistence. The result was that the negativism inherent in these contradictions came to function as an integral aspect of the new identity conferred on the Negro-Creole. As a consequence, we have a precariously synthetic race caught between a distorted past and an apparently unprofitable future. Agony and exile become inseparable elements in the defining artistic expressions that merge. In the final analysis, disease, whether esthetic, moral or physical, is what characterizes the Negro-Caucasian syncretism.

A direct relationship exists, nonetheless, between the psychological or even geographic distance from Africa which the creolizing force can effect in the Creole, and the intensity of the exilic consequences. The effect is, for example, quite minimal when the Negro can appeal to an inviolate or nearly inviolate African cultural talisman of his own. For this is one way of escaping the reductive antitheses of European contact. Thus, we find a lyrical mildness in "The Snowflakes Sail Gently"; the poet, Gabriel Okara, is not a Creole in the sense in which I intend to use the term. He is actually and culturally an Ijaw tribesman from Nigeria. The sense of exile in the poem is therefore temporary and the agony attenuated:

> The snowflakes sail gently
> down from the misty eye of the day
> and fall lightly lightly on the
> winter weary elms. And the branches
> winter-stripped and nude, slowly
> bow like grief-stricken mourners
> . . . .

To awaken from this contact is to become not only nostalgically conscious, but also to be faced with potentially antithetical elements:

> . . .I awoke
> to the silently falling snow
> and bent-backed elms bowing and

swaying to the winter wind like
white-robed Moslems salaaming at evening
prayer, and the earth lying inscrutable
like the face of a god in a shrine.[2]

But, significantly, the perception of the contradictory elements never becomes disturbingly acute. There is instead a gentle, perhaps nearly saccharine, sublimation of the two cultures in the poem. The appeal in the last stanza to "salaaming Moslems" and to the "god in a. shrine" are empirically and accessibly vital talismans to which a reenergizing return can be made. There is thus little danger of spiritual or psychological petrification among the "winter-weary elms." The problem here does not involve a psychological crisis of identity; instead of that more intense dislocation, we have a decidedly milder problem of artistic identity. The medium of expression is English; it is therefore subject to identification within a literary tradition that has no fixed or definite place for a Negro-African artist, and even less so for the instantaneous identification of an Ijaw poet. It is thus impossible to read the poem and to find in it spontaneous means of identifying a West African voice independently of the English literary vehicle. But the significant point is that this *artistic* precariousness is more than adequately compensated for by the inviolability of Okara's West Africanness or of his Nigerianness. This fact, to which Okara can point with a degree of comfort, prevents the kinds of permanent disorientation that one finds in the Sierra Leone Creole.

In this case, we find a dramatically different series of problems. The crises here are of greater intensity and of a more pervasive dimension. The Sierra Leone Creole thus finds a more relevant counterpart in the New World Negro than in the Ijaw of Nigeria. The displacements and dislocations involved are indeed so severe that appeals to gods in tribal shrines are psychologically and spiritually impossible. When these appeals do occur they are likely to be romantically simplistic or hysterically desperate. The curative power of these reductively remembered "shrines" are rendered ineffective by the complexity and the radical nature of the disease. The remedy lies elsewhere. The syncretistic mold in which the Sierra Leone Creole was and is being fashioned must be destroyed; and yet, the Creole lacks the dynamism to effect change on an absolute scale.

Graham Greene, in *Journey Without Maps*, has one of the most vivid descriptions of the physical and esthetic deformities which this kind of creolization can cause:

Freetown, the capital of Sierra Leone, at first was just an impression of heat and damp; the mist streamed along the lower streets and lay over the roofs like smoke.... One could see the Anglican Cathedral, laterite bricks and tin, with a square tower, a Norman Church built in the nineteenth century, sticking out of the early morning fog.

But what should be normal when supported by a vital and relevant culture becomes, in Freetown, grotesquely surrealistic in its deformities:

> Where there wasn't a tin shed there were huge hoardings covered with last year's Poppy Day posters (the date was January the fifteenth). On the roof's the vultures sat nuzzling under their wings with horrible tiny undeveloped heads; they squatted in the gardens like turkeys. . . .This was an English capital city; England had planted this town, the tin shacks and the Remembrance Day posters, and had then withdrawn up the hillside to smart bungalows, with wide windows, and electric fans. . . .[3]

But England's withdrawal was never complete enough to avoid certain kinds of unenlightened intercourses, especially the variety Greene records with crude succinctness in *Heart of the Matter:*

> Captain want jig jig, my sister pretty girl schoolteacher, captain want jig jig.[4]

I shall demonstrate later that poems to the Negress or to *dames creoles* in the *pays parfumé* of the Americas were little more than somewhat melodramatic versions of this libidinous relationship.

In many respects, the Creole population of Freetown was itself a human duplication of the physical deformities and incongruities of the city. Freetown was first settled by "liberated Africans" from the streets of London and later from the West Indies. On occasion, the settlers came from slave ships intercepted by the British Navy on West African waters. The city, built against hills overlooking the Atlantic Ocean on the West Coast of Africa, is the focal point of a one-hundred-square-mile peninsula. The British Government bought the land from local chiefs for the agreed-upon price of:

  8 muskets
  1 barrel of gunpowder
  2 bags of lead balls 1 cwt
  3 dozen hangers with red scabbards
 24 laced hats
  5 small Nicones
  4 cotton Romals
  1 cask of rum containing 10 gallons and 3/4
 34 lb of Tobacco (manufactured)
 25 iron bars
 10 yards of scarlet cloth

117 bunches of beads
13 pieces of Britannias
1 puncheon of rum containing 120 gallons.[5]

I mention these items in detail for two reasons. First, even a cursory glance at the list will suggest that the groundwork is being laid, voluntarily, not for parody, satire or mere buffoonery. It is not so much that sympathetic treatment would *in toto* be impossible; it is my impression that the above items are predicated upon a kind of unenlightenment too serious to allow the participants any lasting dignity. The second reason for the list is to more conceptually link the physical transaction above with the human drama of the Slave Trade. This trade was vital in the genesis and fate of the Sierra Leone Creole. On August 18, 1789, it was possible to buy a "Prime Man Slave" for:

4 Dane Gunes
2 Half-barrells powder
2 fine Chintss
2 Patna Do
4 Bajudepants
2 Necanees
6 Romauls
3 Half Cottons
3 Two Blues
1 Half Taffaty
4 Lead Barrs
2 Small Brass panns

On August 21, "a Stout Man" cost:

5 Half Barrells powder
6 Guns
2 Bajudepants
2 Necanees
2 Green Ells
2 Romauls
1 Two Blue and 1 Half Cotton
1 Patch 3 Kegs Tallow
3 lbs Pewter Basons.[6]

In lamentable, even if praiseworthy, reaction against the extraordinary aberration in the above transactions, Freetown became "an English city" in 1787. The name was deliberately symbolic; the hope was that it would be prophetic. The city and its people were to be symbols of Christian enlightenment over the inhumanity of the past. The inhabitants were returned "exiled sons of Africa." They had originally come from tribes up and down the Slave Coast. To get the population underway, "By a convenient arrangement. . .some sixty white prostitutes were shipped along with them in the same transport."[7] The new names of the Creole, Wellesley-Cole, Tregson-Roberts, Davies-Cole, Deveneux, or Eliseo do Bomfin (Brazil), Toussaint Louverture (Haiti) signified rebirth and enlightenment. That was the hope as sanctified in "a constitution, bound by social contract, rooted in history, in the institutions of the Anglo-Saxon monarchy, and of Israel under the judges."[8] Lieutenant-Governor Temple, "sincere Christian (Father and grandfather of Archbishops of Canterbury) who approved highly of the efforts made on the recaptives' behalf" writes in his dispatch no. 53 of June 10, 1834:

> The Liberated African so degraded and debased on his first arrival gradually assumes another station. His charms are superseded by an outward observance of the forms of Christianity. The lax intercourse of the Sexes gives way to the obligations of marriage and the consequent reciprocal duties of Parents and Children. . . .And in a few years the former savage is found in useful Artesan. . . the old consoling themselves for the loss of their country in the freedom of their children and the children exulting in their freedom as their first Birthright."[9]

There is an earnestness and dedication here that I find astonishing, particularly in the light of the pathological situation being created. The tone is confidently idyllic; it is excellent in its capture of the esthetics and ethics of eighteenth-century interest in bucolic piety and simplicity. Lietutenant-Governor Temple's dispatch is vitally related to Thomas Gray's synthesis of that tradition of bucolic naiveté which made spontaneous equations between romanticized poverty and saintliness:

> Let not Ambition mock their useful toil
>   Their homely joys, and destiny obscure;
> Nor Grandeur hear with disdainful smile
>   The short and simple annals of the poor.

In Freetown, this naiveté and evangelical sincerity, as bucolically exquisite as they were stupid, created the "short and simple annals" of a mongrel race. In actual fact, the Creole was little more than a confused mongrel African tribesman and a mongrel Englishman who, whenever he could, donned woolen frock coats ten degrees north of the equator and drank steaming cups of tea at four o'clock in the afternoon.

The Creole was educated so that he had an exaggerated inability to develop a sense of equilibrium between his African and English experiences. The Church Missionary Society Grammar School was founded in 1845 "for young men and boys requiring a sound education and the proper formation

of manners—with instruction in History, Greek, Latin, Mathematics, Music
and French if required." The aristocratically inclined Creole which resulted
was on invitation to parody.

> They have made, opined the famous Wilberforce (William) the worst
> possible subjects, as thorough Jacobins as if they had been trained and
> educated in Paris.[10]

On December 12, 1896, the *Sierra Leone Times* published the following
breathlessly elegant account of a creole wedding:

> Perhaps there has hardly been an event occurring in Freetown which
> has aroused such an intense degree of interest as have been manifested
> over the nuptial ceremony which was performed between Mr.C.C.
> Nicolls. . . and Miss Laura Henriette, daughter of J.H. Thomas, Esq. of
> Malamah House at St. George's Cathedral on Thursday, with all the
> pomp and splendor which such an auspicious occasion fully
> justified. . . .
> Scores of the weaker sex, who under any circumstances claim and
> certainly do occupy *la première place* in such matters felt it
> incumbent on them to consult their seamstresses, in order to go to see
> the much-talked about event in new and resplendent garments.
> Without perpetrating the rash *faux pas* of offering any suggestions as
> to the extent of the preparations by the *dames d'elites,* perhaps the
> leading tailors of the city might be able to give some idea as to how
> the matter "egged on" even the Lords of creation."[11]

It could have been the opening chapter in the tolerant and finely mocking
tone of a Jane Austen novel. But in the Creole experience, in the "Anglican
Cathedral, laterite bricks and tin, with a square tower" in Freetown, it is
susceptible to devastating parody. This is especially so because the "nuptial
ceremony" is caught in a perverted evolutionary cycle and yet it is
unconditionally celebrated. The Creole here cannot be Jane Austen with
any lasting degree of psychological or cultural comfort. Worse still, for
these African Jacobins to commit the *faux pas* of giving this aristocratic
sense *la première place* is quite obviously to build identity on precarious
irrelevance. It also shows a lack of awareness of a capacity for mockery that
informs the cultures of the creolizing power, be that power English, French
or Spanish. A similar Negro "nuptial ceremony" had provoked in one
Spanish poet, Quevedo, a display of unflattering and brilliant cruelty:

> Ví debe de haber tres días,
> en las gradas de San Pedro,
> una tenebrosa boda,
> por que era toda de negros.

. . . .
    Parecía matrimonio
    concertado en el infierno
    negro esposo y negra êsposa.
    y negro accompañamiento.[12]

But Francisco Gomez de Quevedo y Villegas' seventeenth-century mockery is exceptional only in its extraordinary artistry, not in the fact that it ridicules the unkind antitheses and incongruities inherent in Creoledom.

For the Creole, trapped as he was in a deformed cultural *cul-de-sac,* this parodic quality inherent in his every act came as a cataclysmic shock. Unlike Okara, the Ijaw, he had been permanently desensitized to the talismanic powers of a non-European "face of a god in a shrine." His search for a distinctive voice of his own, for metaphors peculiar to his experiences, leads to further crises. His only means of communication other than his inorganic English is creole. But to his now highly schizophrenic consciousness that too was suspect. Graham Greene's lucid observations are immediately relevant:

> . . .they had been educated to understand how they had been swindled, how they had been given the worst of two worlds, and they had enough power to express themselves in a soured way; they had died, in so far as they had been men, inside their European clothes.[13]

But express themselves they did. Part of the expression was in creole, a dialect which, like the Hispanic Negro's *disfraces negros,* the creole of Haiti, and the dialect of the plantation culture of the slaves in the United States, was a synthetic potpourri of the Creole's European and African linguistic experiences. It is in this *patois* that an anonymous Creole poet poured out his soul against the "captain-want-jig-jig" intercourse between nineteen-year-old, eighteen-year-old, and even fourteen-year-old Creole girls and the Englishman.

The poem, "For Dear Fatherland," appeared in the *Sierra Leone Weekly News* of July 1907. It is a remarkable sixteen-stanza performance that is at once a passionately evangelical expression of moral outrage and a pathetic, involuntary parody of the poet himself and his literary ancestry, English prosody.

A number of features that will distinguish the agonistic pose of this kind of poetry are observable. We find orchestrated structural parallelisms that make for a somewhat theatrical expression of pain and anger. There is the incongruous elasticity of imagery; we find metaphors and similes that are wrenched into and out of the schizophrenic dualism of the Creole's identity. Finally, no matter how artistically effective the expression, there is always a certain degree of prosodic and conceptual inelegance present. The urgency of suffering is the point of emphasis, not the vitality of an esthetic or intellectual canon. These features are obvious in "For Dear Fatherland":

> ### XIII
> O my country! − O my country
> O my dear, dear fatherland:
> I am sick, aye! I am dying;
> At the sights that meet my eyes.
> Aliens! aliens! what do ye mean;
> Thus to spoil my dearest country
> Thus to tread upon our daughters;
> Thus to sodomize our land?
> Government nor care fardin;
> Church again nor care rap,
> But de Lord will surely pay you
> Jesus will surely judge.

Anger, creolized English words and the Yoruba word, "Yooba" (vulture), a pivot for lewdness and promiscuity, are all orchestrated in dramatic, almost incoherent cacophonies:

> ### VI
> O, de Yoobas, − ah, de Yoobas
> Every day the number swell,
> Ah, me God − me fader Jesus,
> Do ya sorry for this land.

The biblical inspiration throughout the poem does credit to Jeremiah's capacity for lamentation and Hosea's uncompromising call for righteousness. The poem ends in a prayer, an appeal to a talisman. The appeal, significantly enough, cannot be directed at a corrective force independent of the origins of the Creole's dilemma. The spiritual atrophy is such that the Creole knows and can acknowledge only "Jesus of the twice-turned cheek," not the inscrutable face of Okara's god. The prayer is itself an interesting pastiche that swings with admirable flexibility between Calvary and the West African coast. The next to the last line is a fragment of an Anglican hymn, with its pivotal emphasis on the Cross. The last line's grammatical incompetence is in a sense determined by the pivotal word of that line and indeed of the whole poem, "Yooba." All these are synthesized in an appeal that cries out in despair:

> ### XVI
> Therefore pray, me dearest sisters;
> One God − me fader Jesus,

> Money sweet and free life sweet;
> But ah me God — me fader Jesus,
> Please to keep me near the Cross;
> Do not let me turn to yooba.
>   Amen![14]

There is much in this inelegant despair and melodramatic, revivalist fervor that suggests sheer caricature. But in spite of this exaggerated invitation to parody, there is pain in the expression. The degree of unsophisticated anger in "For Dear Fatherland" precludes any elegant and seductive formulation of that pain. But Aimé Césaire, *assimilé* creole from the French Caribbean, can and does formulate the pain exquisitely. Behind the gargoyle mask of deformity there is a human voice:

> . . .car la vie n'est pas un spectacle, car une mer de douleurs n'est pas un proscenium, çar un homme qui crie n'est pas un ours qui danse.[15]

The problem, indeed the defining dilemma, of the Creole is that there appears to be no exit. Lucidity is attainable, but since a happy resolution is contingent on forces beyond the Creole's apparent control this only aggravates the sense of agony and exile. To abandon the parodic ceremonies by which he is defined is to be left without identity. Not to abandon them is to become lucid and yet remain sensitively attuned to self-caricature. Thirty-eight years after the Creole "nuptial ceremony" recorded earlier, Graham Greene himself, somewhat ambivalently caught between lucid comprehension and mockery, records the following:

> . . .but they knew all the time they were funny to the heartless perfect eye of the white man. . .they were expected to play the part like white men and the more they copied white men, the more funny it was to the prefects. They were withered by laughter; the more desperately they tried to regain their dignity the funnier they became.
>
> *Fashionable Wedding at St. George's Cathedral*
> St. George's Cathedral was the scene of the first fashionable wedding to take place there this year, on Wednesday, the 11th instant. The contracting parties were Miss Agatha Fidelia Araromi Shorunkeh-Sawyer. . .and Mr. John Buxton Logan. . . .The hymn *Gracious Spirit Holy Ghost* was sung as the bridal procession moved slowly up the nave. . . .
> Before leaving them there, we wish them connubial bliss.
>
> Freetown's excitement is very English. . . .It would be so much more amusing if it was all untrue, a fictitious skit on English methods of colonisation. But one cannot continue long to find the Creole's painful attempt at playing the white man funny; it is rather like the chimpanzee's tea-party, the joke is all on one side.[16]

In summary, that which will be significantly missing in the creolized Negro's experience will be the capacity to create a permanent and salutary sense of order in his crisis of allegiance. His world, with its precarious and hostile polarities, prevents the creation of a New World Eden, such as Walt Whitman will envisage in the Americas. In much the same way, it is also impossible to return to an old world and to a convincing black "African Heaven" such as one finds in the Ghanaian poet, Francis Kobina Parkes. The Ghanaian, Fanti tribesman, not the Creole, will find talismanic gratification in the enthusiasm of the following:

> Give me black souls
> let them be black
> or chocolate brown
> color of dust —
> dustlike,
> browner than sand.
> But if you please keep them black,
> black...
>
> Let the calabash resound
> in tune with the drums...
>
> Mingle with these sounds
> the clang
> of wood on tin:
> Ken-tse ken ken ken
> ....[17]

The Creole is also unable to find relief from the antitheses of his world in the way a Yoruba poet can when the hostilities generated by that world affect him. We see something of this problem and its resolution in Wole Soyinka's "Telephone Conversation." There is quite obviously powerful enough protection in his "West African sepia" identity to make possible the sardonic performance in the poem. The *engagé* posture adopted does not prevent a healthy esthetic and emotional distance:

> The price seemed reasonable, location
> indifferent. The landlady swore she lived
> off premises. Nothing remained
> but self-confession. "Madam," I warned,
> "I hate a wasted journey — I am an African."
> Silence. . . .Voice, when it came,
> lipstick coated, long gold-rolled
> cigarette-holder pipped. Caught I was, foully

"HOW DARK?"...I had not misheard...."ARE YOU
LIGHT
OR VERY DARK?"...
Considerate she was, varying the emphasis —
"ARE YOU DARK OR VERY LIGHT?" Revelation came.
"You mean — like plain or milk chocolate?"
Her assent was clinical, flushing in its light
impersonality. Rapidly, wavelength adjusted,
I chose. "West African sepia" — and as afterthought,
"Down in my passport." Silence for spectroscopic
Flight of fancy, till truthfulness clanged her accent
Hard on the mouthpiece. "WHAT'S THAT?" conceding
"DON'T KNOW WHAT THAT IS?" "Like brunette."
"THAT'S DARK? ISN'T IT?" "Not altogether.
Facially, I am brunette, but madam, you should see
The rest of me. Palm of my hand, soles of my feet
Are a peroxide blonde. Friction, caused —
Foolishly madam — by sitting down, has turned
My bottom raven black — One moment madam! — sensing
Her receiver rearing on the thunderclap
About my ears — "Madam," I pleaded, "wouldn't you
rather
See for yourself?"[18]

It is significant here that Wole Soyinka's whiplashes have none of the
urgent desperation that would characterize the Negro-Creole's. Because he
is not victimized by a precarious self-identity, he can relish the
contrapuntal performance through which he finely tortures the landlady.
There is a calculating and inquisitorial revenge in the poem. The meticulous
selection of words, the almost sensuous delight one senses in the phrasal
pitches, offer evidence of an impish, even if deadly, self-entertainment. But
the important point is that he can psychologically and culturally afford it.
There really is no serious threat to him. A rejection would temporarily
"unhouse" him but cannot and does not constitute an effective negation
of the authentic refuge the elegant "West African sepia" offers him.
Moreover, it is an authenticity that both protects him and makes the
landlady and the threat she symbolizes less potent dangers. The sense of
exile is therefore not permanent in Soyinka. Hysterical anger such as one
finds in Leon G. Damas' *Black Label* is absent in "Telephone
Conversation," and for important reasons. Soyinka is authentically Yoruba
and therefore, as he puts it, he is a tiger who has no need to prove his
tigritude. Damas is an *assimilé* poet from French Guinea who is facing the
shock of discovery that he is not only black but also *non-white*. It is not

surprising then to find a naïve, reductive virulence in his anger:

> Jamais le Blanc ne sera nègre
> car la beauté est nègre
> et nègre la sagesse
> Car l' endurance est nègre
> et nègre le courage
> car la patience est nègre
> ....[19]

A hysterical perception of dislocation forces the creolized Negro artist into an apparently unavoidable protrayal of himself as a victim. His artistic expression, insofar as it demonstrates a confrontation with the self in a negatively polarized world, tends to become an anthology of Jeremiads. He himself becomes a most appropriate metaphor for suffering, almost always compulsively apotheosized into victimized innocence:

> I am a Negro:
> black as the night is black
> black as the depths of my Africa.
>
> I' been a victim:
> the Belgian's cut off my hand in the Congo,
> they lynch me now in Texas. [20]

So writes Langston Hughes in "Proem" to *The Weary Blues*.

As I hope to demonstrate in the chapters following, this insistent harping on disease is an inevitable consequence of the patterns I intend to trace in their English, French and Spanish literary manifestations. Moreover, so pervasive are angry hostilities in the Creole's perception of history that too insistent an optimism is apt to prove naïve or generous. Even emancipated thinking about him quite frequently has the prerequisites for generating further crises. The Sierra Leone Creole, for example, owed his liberation from slavery to the efforts of Granville Sharp, who was chiefly instrumental in the 1772 legal judgment that made slavery illegal in England. The aberrant undertones of this act of ethical enlightenment may be gauged by the fact that Sharp was obliged to seek scientific evidence as to whether the Negro was a human being. This was necessary to combat somewhat more persuasive convictions such as Long's *History of Jamaica* (1774) expressed with epigrammatic succintness: "I do not think that an Orang Outang husband would be any dishonour to an Hottentot female." Prince Hoare makes the following observation in his *Memoirs of Granville Sharp (1820):*

It is surprising, and to posterity will appear hardly credible, that the force of prejudice was so great in the enlightened nations of Europe at the time of these events that the advocate of an oppressed race, separated only by the sea and distinguished from them only by a darker tinge of the skin, thought it requisite to institute a regular inquiry *whether the natives of Africa were men*. (Hoare's emphasis)[21]

Hoare's surprise at the ignorance of Sharp's times and his expectations of "posterity" are generous. Creoledom would appear to suggest that inelegant prejudice consistently results in ineradicable caricatures.

The following observations by Graham Greene, almost a century after Hoare, clearly suggest a problem of perceptual imbalance. What we have are perceptions of creatures that are not quite human. The caricatures are erotically grotesque. There is in these perceptions a rather peculiar absence of concern with the thoughts and desires of the objects of caricature. Greene's descriptions make the Africans here little more than targets for clever mockery:

> The train stopped at every station, and the women pressed up along the line, their great black nipples like the centre point of a target. I was not yet tired of the sight of naked bodies (later I began to feel as if I had lived among nothing but cows).
>
> . . . .
>
> Natives came stooping along the path, bowed under green hammocks of palm nuts; they looked liked grasshoppers in a Silly Symphony. [22]

The next few chapters will concern themselves with evaluations of these kinds of observations about the Negro and about his place of origin, especially the Africa of the Equatorial Forest Belt. Precisely what was there in the nature of the African and of Africa that rendered both so susceptible to caricature?

NOTES

[1] Ambiguity is doubtless generated by the term. See from Webster's: "Cre.ole (Krē-.ōl) on (Fcréole, fr. Sp. *criollo*, fr. Pg. crioulo white person born in the colonies) 1: a person of native birth but of European descent – used esp. in the West Indies and Spanish America 2: a white person descended from early French or Spanish culture 3: a person of mixed French or Spanish and Negro descent speaking a dialect of French or Spanish 4a: the French spoken by many Negroes in southern Louisiana b: Haitian."

To the extent that the Sierra Leone Creole is not adequately covered above, it is incomplete. As will become obvious, my use of the term derives its value from the cultural and psychological history of the Sierra Leone Creole. To that extent the term will be used as a generic one to cover what is implicit in the hyphenated identity of Afro-Cubans, Afro-Latins, Afro-Americans and the like. For the purposes of this study, Creole is synonymous with that hybrid creature which in French is called *assimilé*, *assimilaçao* in Portuguese, and which the Nigerian Assagai recognizes in Beneatha when he calls her an "assimilationist" in Lorraine Hanberry's *Raisin in the Sun*.

[2] *Modern Poetry from Africa*, eds. Gerald Moore and Ulli Beier, Penguin African Library (Baltimore, Maryland: Penguin Books, 1966), pp. 22-23. See next chapter for a structured summary of the culture to which "the face of the god in a shrine" implicitly turns.

[3] Graham Greene, *Journey Without Maps* (London: William Heineman, 1966), pp. 32-34. The "Journal," not unrelated to Greene's undercover activities, was undertaken in the Thirties.

[4] *The Heart of the Matter*, Compass Books (New York: The Viking Press, 1948), p. 4. The novel was for the most part written in Sierra Leone. Indeed, Freetown is so easily identifiable that Greene prefaces the work with an apologetic disclaimer.

[5] Christopher Fyfe, *Sierra Leone Inheritance*, West African History Series (London: Oxford University Press, 1964), p. 113. The work is an invaluable collection of documents tracing the history of Sierra Leone.

[6] Basil Davidson, *The African Past, Chronicles from Antiquity to Modern Times* (London: Longmans, Green and Co. Ltd., 1964), pp 230-231; records from a "Manuscript Book kept by one John Johnston, while on a slaving Expedition in Africa, in 1792."

[7] Kenneth Little, *Negroes in Britain* (London: Kegan Paul, Trench, Trubner & Co., Ltd., 1947), p. 184. The work is a study of Negroes in eighteenth-century Britain.

[8] Christopher Fyfe's *History of Sierra Leone* thus somewhat ambivalently restates Granville Sharp's *Short Sketch of Temporary Regulations*.

[9] *Sierra Leone Inheritance*, p. 145.

[10] *The African Past*, p. 35.

[11] *Sierra Leone Inheritance*, pp. 216-217.

[12] *Obras Completas* (Barcelona: Editorial Planete, no date), p. 850ff. See Chapter Four.

[13] *Journey without Maps*, p. 34.

[14] *Inheritance*, pp. 34-35. The line, "Jesus of the twice turned cheek" is from Countee Cullen's agonizing answer to the question "What is Africa to me?" See Chapter Six, note 27, for this most effective statement of the crisis of identity and allegiance during the Harlem Renaissance.

[15] Aimé Césaire, *Cahier d'un Retour au Pays Natal*, with a preface by Petar Guberina (Paris: Présence Africaine, 1956), p. 42. The most extensive poetic statement of the *assimilé's* crisis in the Thirties, the *Cahier* will be discussed in Chapter Eight. See Chapter Five for its genesis in *Négritude*.

[16] *Journey without Maps*, pp. 34-35.

[17] "African Heaven" in *An African Treasury*, ed. Langston Hughes (New York: Pyramid Books, 1960), p. 170. I do not ignore the suspicion that the poet "doth protest too much." But since the Sierra Leone Creole had been educated to believe that African tribes were "unto whoms" (heathens "unto whom" the gospel is preached), even this possibly excessive refuge is impossible.

[18] *Modern Poetry from Africa*, pp. 112-13. Soyinka's is, to me, the finest satiric voice in current West African literature.

[19] Leon G. Damas, *Black Label (poémes)* (Paris: Gallimard, 1956). His *Pigments* (1937) was the first articulation of the *assimilé* revolt against assimilationism. *See* Chapter Five.

[20] *The Weary Blues*, with an introduction by Carl Van Vechten (New York: Alfred A. Knopf, 1945), p. 19. For detailed treatment of the work see Chapter Six.

[21] Kenneth Little, *op. cit.*, p. 197, quotes Hoare.

[22] *Journey without Maps*, pp. 54, 66.

CHAPTER 2

GENESIS: THE IDEA OF BLACKNESS
IN HUMAN FORM

The Sierra Leone Creole and the New World Negro had originally come from African tribes geographically bounded south of the Sahara by the equatorial forests to the north and the Atlantic Ocean to the west and south-west. The peculiar energies and confusions so inseparable in the identity of the Creole are attributable in large part to two factors. First, what the Negro is physiognomically, culturally and historically; and second, the temperament and intellectual climates of Europe when he was so perceived. The earliest contact between the two is impossible to pinpoint without relying on calculated speculation. My intent in this study makes the late fourteenth through sixteenth centuries the most relevant starting dates. I am primarily interested in assessing historical and literary manifestations beginning with what appear to be definite crystallizations during the period. These manifestations most effectively show the conflict between medieval parochialism and renaissance curiosity in the European temperament. For example, I look upon the Spanish Inquisition and the extraordinary saga of the Conquistadors in South America as evidences of this violent, and to me, energetically incompetent effort to resolve the conflict. On the one hand, we have the confused ferocity of a moribund perspective on man and man's universe and, on the other hand, the excitement of an era of unparalleled human curiosity. By the time the conflict was resolved, it had lit fires under "heretical" intelligences; it had converted those hybrid characters, the Conquistadors, from daring explorers with the practical greed of merchants into violent barbarians. It was this barbarism that in part destroyed the Indian civilization of South America with such grim effectiveness. Europe was perhaps economically ready but intellectually unprepared to discover new worlds. This was then the same period in which the Atlantic Ocean to the South began to yield to the exploratory urges of the European Renaissance. In the search for alternate routes to the riches of the East, the West Coast of Africa became important, even if accidental, watering-stops for the sailors of the

Portuguese Prince Henry the Navigator and for the "Viaggi e Scoperte di Navigatori ed Esploratori Italiani". [1] And the Negro was discovered.

I would propose in this study at least three discoveries and consequently three responses to the idea of blackness in human form. First, we have the medieval-renaissance perspective; second, there is the rediscovery between the late seventeenth through early nineteenth centuries; and third, the response during the first two decades of the twentieth century. The first two perspectives were channelled into essentially exoteric aims, while the last was elitist, iconoclastic and esoteric. (In this matter of the last, Matisse and "fauvism," Picasso and cubism and the bohemian taste for the exotic will be discused in Chapter Five). The first and the second responses were highly reductive in consequences. Caricature was inseparable from perception.

> It is the high ton *(sic)* at present in this court to be surrounded by African implings, the more hideous the more prized, and to bedizen them in the most expensive manner. The Queen has to set the example and the royal family vie with each other in spoiling and caressing Donna Rosa, her Majesty's *black-skinned, blubber-lipped, flat-nosed* favorite. (my emphasis)

Published in 1834, William Beckford's *Italy: With sketches of Spain and Portugal* provides effective illustration in this matter. [2] The Negro, insofar as he was black and physically different, became an incarnation of the incongruous and the antithetical. He was seen as an apt metaphor for esthetic and ethical caricature. Insofar as he was black, he was a metaphor for darkness and for the unholy. So he became the Devil, "being hels (sic) perfect character." [3] To the extent that his features and behavior were comically different he became a Buffoon. But these same features, "black-skinned, blubber-lipped, flat-nosed," could also be perceived as uncomfortably close caricatures. Seen in this light he became as negatively decorative and as slightly obscene as a Gargoyle:

> It was unearthly, and the men were − No, were not inhuman...that was the worst of it − this suspicion of their not being inhuman....They howled and leaped, and spun, and made horrid faces; but what thrilled you was just the thought of their humanity − like yours − the thought of your remote kinship with this wild and passionate uproar, . . . this fiendish row . . . . [4]

These three modes of perception, as devil, gargoyle and buffoon, hold true for the renaissance and the later periods. But there are significant differences. It seems to me that the caricatures of the earlier period are exploited without the pathological malice of the latter. There was instead, a fascination with the outlandish, picturesque and exotic possibilities in the caricature which the Negro represented. Moreover, there was much that was quite comically erroneous in the anthropological ideas then prevalent. The seventeenth through nineteenth centuries display a somewhat more ferocious perspective. Caricature had by then become intimately connected with economic benefits. Xenophobic reductivism was playing an important role in racial, national and cultural pride that was barely distinguishable from obnoxious chauvinism. This compulsion to think of the Negro in caricature holds true for the national literatures (English, French and Spanish) to be examined in subsequent chapters. But here again, changes in emphasis appear. Insofar as England and the United States were conglomerates of Northern European ideas, the inclination will be to see the Negro as devil. France and Spain and Portugal would opt for the gargoyle and the buffoon. Differences would result, depending on the cause of the caricature—ignorant prejudice or incompetent sympathy. The literary manifestations of these perceptions will be assessed in the next three chapters.

The Negro himself needs to be assessed at this time to evaluate the degree of dehumanization he underwent and perhaps the extent to which he actively contributed to his own difficulties.

There had always been interest of some kind in the African continent as a whole and even knowledge of some kind about Africa south of the Sahara. Arab Africa, Coptic Africa, were known quite early to Europe and even earlier to the Mediterranean civilizations of Greece and Rome. However, in discussing Africa south of the Sahara in specific relationship to the intent of this study, certain specifications will be necessary. I am primarily interested in the area from the middle ages through the emergence of the Sierra Leone Creole. We can then talk about Africa south of the Sahara in terms of three specific cultural configurations. These three subdivide into two categories: the Sudanese grassland and the Coastal groups. In summary, these configurations were:

1. *The Western Sudan Axis*: We are dealing here with three merchant city empires—Ghana, Mali and Songhai—of medieval-early renaissance times. Their inspiration—religious, commercial and cultural—was primarily trans-Saharan. Hassan ben Muhammad el Wazzan es Zayyati, Leo Africanus, offers some of the most comprehensive descriptions of this axis. His *The History and Description of Africa* was first published in Latin in the renaissance Venice of the middle of the sixteenth century:

> Its inhabitants are rich merchants who travel constantly about the region with their wares. A great many Blacks come to the city bringing

quantities of gold with which to purchase goods imported from Berber country and from Europe.[5]

In Abderrahman es-Sa'di's *Tarikh es-Sudan* we have a description of one of the great commerical centers of the axis, Djenne:

> This city is great, flourishing and prosperous. . .one of the great markets of the Muslim world. Here gather the merchants who bring salt from the mines of Teghaza and those who bring gold from the mines of Bitou. . . .It is because of this fortunate city that the caravans flock to Timbuktu from all points of the horizon. . . .The town was founded by pagans in the middle of the second century after the Flight of the Prophet.[6]

Its greatest intellectual center is described by Leo Africanus:

> Here in Timbuktu, there are great store of doctors, judges, priests and other learned men, bountifully maintained at the king's cost and charges. And hither are brought divers manuscripts or written books out of Barbary, which are sold for more money than any other merchandise.[7]

In 1590, Spanish mercenary led a Moroccan army across the Sahara desert in a successful invasion. And the medieval, Muslim civilization of this axis came to an end. By 1828, René Caillié's pilgrimmage, *Travels through Central Africa to Timbuktu*, would end in disenchantment. Timbuktu was but a "mass of ill-looking houses, built of mud."[8]

2. *The Central Sudan Axis*: We deal here with a somewhat later development of another trans-Saharan muslim trading civilization. This configuration encompasses the medieval Kanem-Bornu empire and the late Hausa-Fulani states. Dixon Denham's observations hold for the entire configuration: "There are many hajjis, who have made the pilgrimmage to Mecca, and excel in writing Arabic characters, as well as teaching the art to others."[9] From Heinrich Barth's *Travels and Discoveries in North and Central Africa* we can understand the dynamism of perhaps the principal city of this axis:

> The great advantage of Kano is, that commerce and manufacturing go hand in hand. . . .There is really something grand in this kind of industry, which spreads to the north as far as Murzuk, Ghat, and even Tripoli; to the west, not only to Timbuktu, but in some degree even as far as the shore of the Atlantic. . . .And to the south maintains a rivalry with the native industry of the I'gbira and I'gbo, while towards the south-east it invades the whole of Adamawa, and is only limited by the sans-culottes, who do not wear clothing.[10]

These two axes are only indirectly connected with the genesis I am assessing. The impetus for their culture was trans-Saharan and Islamic. Racially and culturally they lacked the fascinating human dimensions that provoke the inspired errors of Richard Eden's 1555 efforts:

> It is to understande that the people which nowe inhabit the regions of the coast of Guinea and the mydde partes of Affrica, as Lybia the inner, Nubia with divers other great and large regions abowt the same, were in oulde tyme cauled Ethiopes Nigrite, which we nowe caule Moores, Moorens or Negros, a people of beastly lyvynge, without a god, lawe, religion, or common welth, and so scorched, vexed with the heat of the sonne that in many places they curse it when it ryseth.[11]

In the exuberant inexactitude of this perspective we have the medieval renaissance origins of the crises of the Sierra Leone Creole and his New World counterpart. The "I'gbira and I'gbo" to the south, "the whole of "Adamawa," "the pagan sans-culottes," "the people of beastly lyvynge" and the "black-skinned, blubber-lipped, flat-nosed" favorites of European courts constitute the configuration of the third group.

3. *The Equatorial Forest-Atlantic Axis:* This axis includes in the main the pure negroid race found in the narrow coastal belt between the northern edge of the equatorial forest and the Atlantic Ocean. It extends south into central Africa, where in the Congo it joins the Pigmy. The configuration is relevant at this time insofar as it was organized into four major kingdoms from the middle ages to the late eighteenth century. These were the Benin-Yoruba, Dahomey, Ashanti and Congolese organizations. Chief Egharevba's *A Short History of Benin* tells us that:

> The Empire of the first period or dynasty was founded about A.D. 900. The rulers or kings were commonly known as Ogiso before the arrival of Odudua and his party at Ife in Yorubaland, about the twelfth century of the Christian Era.[12]

The *Infaq al-maysur* of Muhammad Bello indicates that "the country of Yoruba is extensive and has streams and forests and rocks and hills. There are many curious and beautiful things in it. *The ships of Christians come there*.The people of Yoruba are descended from the Bani Kan'an and the kindred of Nimrud." Of the Dahomeans another writer tells us:

> The Dahomeans were formely called Foys (Fons), and inhabited a small territory, on the northeast part of their present kingdom, whose capital, Dawhee, lay between the towns of Calmina and Abomey, at about 90 miles from the sea coast.[13]

Significantly, by the end of the second decade of the eighteenth century, Dahomey had broken through to the Atlantic seacoast by conquering a number of smaller states: Jacquin, Quidah and Whydah. The configuration could be vandalistic and violent. From the *Memoirs of the Reign of Bossa Ahadee, King of Dahomey* we learn:

> To the northeast of Dahomey lies a fine, fertile, and extensive country, inhabited by a great and warlike people, called Eyoes; the scourge of all their neighbours....They invaded Dahomy (*sic*) in 1738 with an irresistible army, and laid the country waste with fire and sword to the gates of Abomey.[14]

In all cases, not excluding "the greatest inland power of the forest belt, Ashanti," this configuration was fatally linked with the Atlantic and "the ships of Christians."

It should be clear then that as I use the terms "Negro" or "tribal features" in the assessment immediately following, I do not insist upon a monolithic identity:

> We may naturally expect that belief and practices assume divergent shapes in the wide open spaces and in the dense equatorial forest. Where rains are uncertain and are accompanied by terrific thunderstorms, it seems natural that the people's theology should be affected thereby. The Ngombe...are born, they live and they die in the forest.....The dense foliage, the short field of vision, the dark recesses, the eeriness, all encourage faith in a vast number of impish spirits.[15]

I make the assessment now for two reasons. The first is to suggest the degree of reduction which the African underwent, and the second is to identify a number of entrenched features that will appear, albeit in somewhat peculiar configurations, in Cuban, *Ñañiguismo,* Haitian Voodoo and Brazilian Candomble.[16] (The significance of their absence in the emphases of American Negro Folklore will be discussed later.)

Granted the heterogeneity of the axis above, it is nonetheless possible to make coherent statements about dynamic beliefs common to the tribes involved. The acceptance of a cosmic mana is apparently fundamental to all the religious perspectives involved. This belief is quite pervasive in "the power of the elemental forces of nature," which may be embodied either in objects or persons or may exist as a dynamic essence independent of incarnation. It may be called *bwanga bua Mulopo* (God's medicine) in the pharmacopoeia of the Luba tribe; but it surfaces again in the "Nyama" of the Dogon tribe, the "Muntu" of the Bantus. It may also be couched in the pantheistic implications of the West African "Mkissi-nsi" or "bunsi," that is, the energy in things left by God when he deserted the earth. This then is a perspective which, in essence, sees man as coexisting with and permanently accessible to vital forces that infuse animate and inanimate objects. Physical and metaphysical stimuli are manifestations of forces. Thus, hunger is a manifestation of the force, hunger. The Yoruba can therefore translate "I am hungry" by denying that the stimulus is self-originated in the consciousness of the "I." It therefore becomes *Ebi 'n kpa mi: Ebi* the god of hunger, is killing me.[17]

Polytheism (generally, anthropomorphic polytheism) is another common feature. Interestingly enough, this will serve as the justification for religious caricature in the European perceptions to be discussed. The kinds of accommodation developed for Homeric polytheism would be absent. The Yoruba, for example, have a host of divinities such as: Obatala and his wife Odudua, Olukun, god of the sea, Chango, Eshu Elegba. In all cases, a definite hierarchy exists in this polytheism, the nature of that hierarchy being determined by the theogony and cosmogony of each tribe. The hierarchy also offered places to dead ancestors or tribal heroes in various levels of apotheoses.

We can look on the the belief in these disincarnate ancestral spirits and polytheistic presences as a coherent religious and social statement about the symbiotic relationship between the living and the dead, between the animate and the inanimate world. Dr. J.B. Danquah's *The Akan Doctrine of God* best summarizes the African's intent:

> Akan knowledge of God (*Nyame*) teaches that He is the Great Ancestor. He is a true high God and manlike ancestor of the first man. As such ancestor He deserves to be worshipped, and is worshipped in the visible ancestral head, the good chief of the community. . . .All ancestors who are honoured are in the line of the Great Ancestor. . . .Life, human life, is one continuous blood, from the originating blood of the Great Source of their blood.[18]

In all instances in this Forest-Atlantic Axis, we have no evidence of a written tradition, which is in clear contrast to the Sudanese configurations. Artistic expression, religious celebration and secular business were therefore dependent upon oral transmission. There is, however, a surprising degree of complexity in the media of communication in this axis. The languages are oftentimes finely tuned and pitched instruments, in fact, quite literally so in many cases. But by and large to unschooled curiosity of confused prejudice they were little more than a discordant jangle of grunts, groans and noises. It was the "infernal din" of the black race "from Fernando Po to Timbuktu." But this was simply a case of primitive anthropology confronted by inarticulate sophistication. In Yoruba, for example, a given sound may have a triple denotation depending on the tone used. "The Tonal Structure of Yoruba Poetry," B. J. Lasebikan's presentation at the First International Conference of Negro Writers and Artists (Paris, 1956), is interesting and illustrative. It is impossible to demonstrate these tones on an absolute scale. Thus the tones mentioned are relative to the next denotative point in the same sound.

> *Lo*   in low tone means "to grind" in middle tone "to go" and in high tone "to twist"

Polysyllabic words demonstrate elaborate variations

> *Agbada*   -in mid-mid-mid tones is "frying pot" in mid-high-high it means "a man's gown"

It follows then that in the poetry and prose in which the esthetic sensitivity is expressed, these linguistic elements must be effectively manipulated. This would be necessary not only for the denotative but also for the connotative values of sounds and tone colors, unless one wished to deny that this sense of value was present in the African. Lasebikan demonstrates that there are in Yoruba, for example, several categories of poetic expression. He mentions five cycles:

> *Oriki*   - praise poems to the deities. These generally use low tones.
>
> *Ege*   - Funeral rites.
>
> *Arofo*   - Lasebikan calls these songs of abstract speculation. My impression is that they are not independent of the *Oriki* cycle.
>
> *Ogbere*   - Masqueraders' chants.
>
> *Ijala*   - Hunters' chants. These generally use middle tone.[19]

The particular tone mentioned for each cycle cannot be used exclusively. The *Oriki* cycle simply requires that the low tone be used strategically, for example to begin the chant, whenever attributes of the divinity are introduced and to end the chant. The cycles mentioned also show two general categories of expressions. The first three are religiously oriented. The last two are essentially secular; but we may presume even more varieties of expression. A pluralistic system of god indicates differences in Divine attributes. Song or poem can only offer appropriate praise when the *Oriki* demonstrates the virtues peculiar to the divinity engaged. Eshu Elegba is a Yoruba god of mischief and evil. Obatala is the Supreme Being. Eshu's songs must therefore reflect *his* potential not Obatala's:

> We are singing for the sake of Eshu
> He used his penis to make a bridge
> The penis broke in two
> The travellers fell into the river.[20]

On the other hand, Chief Egharevba's recording of the fighting song of
Eredia-uwa's soldiers is exquisite in its hypnotic simplicity:

> Oya ra gb'Eyen gb'Eboide oyeye,
> Oya ra gb'Eyen gb'Eboide oyeye;
> Ai s' odion-rae rhi ovbokhan oyeye.
> Oya ra gb'Eyen gb'Eboide oyeye.
> May Eyen and Ebiode be punished,
> May Eyen and Eboide be punished;
> For a younger brother is not taken, and the firstborn left.
> May Eyen and Eboide be punished.[21]

There is a simplicity in the prosodic architecture of these and other
expressions, but there are very involved processes at work. The expressions
are communal and oral in nature. They must therefore be so structured as
to guarantee choric or tribal participation. That participation must then be of
sufficient esthetic and intentional excitation to maintain a unified
involvement. Since the expression is oral there can be no resort to the
written word. For this reason, the structural simplicity of the architecture
must also be looked at as a calculated exercise in mnemotechnics. We find
a great deal of linear, syntactical repetition. When the lead voice must take
a solo, as in line three of Eredia-uwa's fighting song, there is invariably a
strategically developed sequence of rhythms or a return to a cue sound that
reintegrates the expression. This holds true for the erotic spontaneity of a
"Girl's Secret Love Song":

> You shake the waist—we shake.
> Let us shake the waist—we shake.
> I am going to my lover—we shake.
> Even if it is raining—we shake.
> I am going to my lover—we shake.
> I am going to my lover—we shake.
> He is at Chesumei—we shake.
> Even when night comes—we shake.
> I am going to my lover—we shake.
> Even if he hits me—we shake.
> I am going at night—we shake.
> Even if there is a wild animal—we shake.
> I am going to my lover—we shake.
> A person not knowing a lover—we shake.
> Knows nothing at all—we shake.[22]

It is equally true of the song that Oba Ewuare the Great, Crowned
Oba of Benin, under the title of Ewuakpe, used to sing and play on his
native harp during times of trouble, of which he witnessed a great deal:

Iyase rhi ugigho gumwen momo
Esogban rhi ugigho gumwen momo
Eson rhi ugigho gumwen momo
Niya de atete, niya de ebo
Niya gha wa vbe ekioba Nagbado.

Iyase lend me twenty cowries
Esogban lend me twenty cowries
Eson lend me twenty cowries
To buy a basket and a bag
For marketing in the Agbado market.[23]

Chief Egharevba's mention of the native harp is apropos of our next consideration. Some mention must be made of the musical accompaniment of these songs or expressions. The portrait of this singing monarch calls to mind David, the singing king of Isreal, and, is remote from the bongo-beating buffoon into which the African would be transformed.

The drum and its influence need to be mentioned in proper perspective. Misapprehension resulted in the Negro's being associated with an orgiastic and mindless drum beat. The drum was and still is the general factotum in the African tribal orchestra. But there are obvious and subtle complexities in its use. In the first place, the matter of construction requires intelligent use of wood and skins of particular and peculiar range and quality. There are an infinite number of variations, glides, rises and falls that the drums must pitch accurately if they are not to run counter to the expressions they are supporting. True, there were perceptions which, even if they were inaccurate, did not reduce the musical architecture of the African to untutored drumming.

Alvise Ca da Mosto's records of his *Prima Navigazione* (1455) tell us something about tribal music and dancing:

Il suo ballare e molto differente del nostro. . . .In questo paese, non si usano instrumenti da sonore di alcuna sorte, salvo di due: l'una sono tabache moresche, che a modo di nostro chiameremmo tamburi grandi; *l'altra e a modo di una viola de queste che noi altri soniamo con l'arco; ma non hanno salvoche due corde; e suanano con le dita* . . . altri instrumenti non hanno. (my emphasis)

The description I emphasize may possibly be one of the earliest European references to the variety of native harp used by Oba Ewuakpe of Benin. Ca da Mosto's description of the drumming is also nonreductive for he tells us of "quattro tamburi che suonavano con molta armonia e precision.."[24]

My intent then has been to sketch out the most important aspects of African tribal life that provoked and sustained the kinds of caricature the Negro will provoke:

They dance and jump around making a deafening noise with drums and
all sorts of old iron. Among the blacks nothing is done without music,
and the more infernal the din and racket the more solemn the feast.[25]

The next chapters examine the literary expressions of that comic
frightfulness that wrung *nigra sum sed formosa* from one of the voices in
The Song of Solomon:

> I am black, but comely, O ye daughters of Jerusalem, as the
> tents of Kedar, as the curtains of Solomon.
> Look not upon me, because I am black, because the sun hath
> looked upon me. . . .[26]

This then will be the voice of the Negro in exile in a world which he finds
is white and antithetical to the idea of blackness in human form.

> I am the darker brother. . .
>
> Besides,
> They'll see how beautiful I am
> and be ashamed.[27]

This is not to be wondered at. A precariously sophisticated African
medieval-renaissance and its European counterpart did not have the
wherewithal for decorous coexistence.

NOTES

[1] Rinaldo Caddeo is general editor for a multi-volume series: *Viaggi e Scoperte
di Navigatori ed Esploratori Italiani* (Milano: Edizioni "Alpes," 1929.) The series covers
navigational activities from the twelfth through sixteenth centuries. See Volume I for
Le Navigazione Atlantiche. Also, J.D. Fage, *An Introduction to the History of West
African* for a general summary.

[2] Beckford, *Italy, etc.* 2 vols. (Paris: Baudry's European Library, 1835.)
Selection is from volume II, p. 108.

[3] See below, Chapter Three. Beaumont and Fletcher *Knight of Malta.*

[4] Joseph Conrad, *Heart of Darkness in Three Short Novels*, with an introduction
by Edward Weeks (New York: Bantam Books, 1963), p. 42.

[5] Basil Davidson, *op cit.,* prefatory selection.

[6] From the French version of the Arabic text by Octave Houdas and Edmund
Benoist, *Tarikh es-Sudan* (Paris: 1900). Rendered by Davidson in *The African Past*,
p. 94.

[7] Basil Davidson, *op. cit.,* p. 90.

[8] See Abderrahman es-Sa'di, *op. cit.,*
"I saw the ruin of learning and its utter collapse, and because learning

rich in beauty and fertile in its teaching, since it tells men of their fatherland, their ancestors, their annuals, the names of their heroes and what lives these led, I asked divine help and decided to record all that I myself could gather on the subject of the Songhay princes of the Sudan, their adventures, their history, their achievements and their wars. Then I added the history of Timbuktu from the foundation of that city. . . .
Heinrich Barth's *Travels and Discoveries in North and Central Africa,* 5 vols. (London: 1857-1878) suggest that Caillié's disappointment may have been excessive. See Davidson, *op. cit.,* pp. 341-343.

[9] In West African Explorers, ed. C. Howard, with an introduction by J.H. Plumb (Oxford: 1951).

[10] Barth, *op. cit.,*

[11] Richard Eden in Volume Six of Richard Hakluyt's *The Prinicpal Navigations, Voyages, Traffiques and Discoveries of the English Nation* (1598-1600). Eden contributed the "memoirs" of Thomas Windham's voyage to Guinea and Benin in 1553 and of John Lok's voyage to Guinea in 1554-1555.

[12] *Op. cit.,* Third edition (Ibadan: 1960), p. 1. The work was first published in 1934 by C.M.S. Bookshop, Lagos.

[13] Archibald Dalzell, *History of Dahomey,* (London: 1793), p. 60.

[14] Robert Norris, *Memoirs of the Reign etc,* (London: 1789), p. 11.

[15] *African Ideas of God,* ed. Edwin W, Smith (London: Edinburgh House Press, 1961) as summarized in *The Study of Africa,* eds. Peter J.M. McEwan & Robert B. Sutcliffe, University Paperbacks (London: Methuen, 1967), 63-78. The selection is on page 64.

[16] For discussions of Ñañiguismo and Voodoo, see Chapters Seven and Eight respectively.

> "Candomble is a system for worshipping gods or saints. The word is from the Yoruba language and means mysteries or ritual. . . .As the people are all practicising Catholics, the African gods are blurred with Catholic saints. Even Jesus is there, identified with the loveliest of the young goddesses."
> The above is from Ruth Landes, *City of Women* (New York: The Macmillan Co., 1947), p. 15.

[17] Edwin M. Smith, *op, cit.* Also, Paul Baudin, *Fetichism and Fetich Worshippers,* translated by Miss M. McMahan (New York: Benziger Brothers, 1885).

[18] E.J. Lasebikan, "The Tonal Structure of Yoruba Poetry" *Présence Africaine,* Special Issue, Nos. 8-9-10, June-November, 1956. This special issue constitutes the report on the Conference. This English version also contains Léopold Sédar Senghor's "The Spirit of Civilisation or The Laws of African Negro Culture." For the implications of this, see Chapter Five.

[19] J.B. Danquah, *op, cit.,* p. 27. Also Edwin M. Smith, *op, cit.*

[20] Joan Wescott, "The Sculpture and Myths of Eshu Elegba, the Yoruba Trickster," Vol. XXXII, (Africa, 1962), pp. 336-354. See also Leonard Doob, *Ants Will Not Eat Your Fingers: a selection of traditional African Poems* (New York: Walker and Company), 1966

[21] Egharevba, *op. cit.,* p. 44.

[22] Doob, *op. cit.,* p. 64.

[23] Egharevba,*op. cit.,* p. 39. The same techniques are true of the illustrative songs in Paul Hazoume's "The Priest Revolt," *Présence Africaine,* Special Issue:

> "yolo nihue!
> adjayi yolo nihue
> Abahe yolo nihue.
> Adjayi e!

> Abahe yolo nihue
> Adjayi e ne niedo
> Yolo nihue
> Adjayi e ne eni edo."

The songs are offered in Hazoume's discussion of Dahomean rites.

[24] *Le Navigazione Atlantiche* in *op. cit.*, p. 243. See also André Gide's journal for 1927-28, *Travels in the Congo*; and Barry Ulanov, *A History of Jazz in America*. See Chapter Six of this study for discussion of jazz and Chapter Eight for detailed treatment of the drums in Voodoo.

[25] Paul Baudin, *op. cit.*

[26] *The Song of Solomon*, King James Version, Chap. 1, vv. 5-6.

[27] Langston Hughes, *The Weary Blues*. The lines are from "Epiloque," p. 109.

PART II

THE RESPONSE TO THE IDEA OF BLACKNESS IN HUMAN FORM

. . .the contact with pure unmitigated savagery, with primitive nature and primitive man, brings sudden and profound trouble into the heart. . .excites the imagination and tries the civilised nerves of the foolish and the wise alike.

—Joseph Conrad, "An Outpost of Progress"

CHAPTER 3

RESPONSES: THE ENGLISH METAPHOR

It is unrealistic to expect that the Negro would arrive in Europe with enough dynamic residuals that would prove helpful in coping with his new environment. By the same token, no really justifiable expectation can be entertained that his new environment would offer him materials for an evolutionary development organically related to his origins. The inevitable result was that, traumatically transplanted and rendered indefensibly grotesque by circumstances, the Negro was reduced to caricature:

> ...Negros, a people of beastly lyvynge, without a god, lawe, religion, or common wealth, and so scorched, vexed with the heat of the sonne that in many places they curse it when it ryseth.

> You can dress a chimpanzee, housebreak him and teach him to use a knife and fork, but it will take countless generations of evolutionary development, if ever, before you can convince him that a caterpillar or a cockroach is not a delicacy. Likewise, the social, political, economic and religious preference of the Negro remain close to the caterpillar and the cockroach.[1]

The observations are at least three centuries removed from each other. In the first, Richard Eden's imaginative contribution in Haklyut's *The Principal Navigations, Voyages, Traffiques and Discoveries of the English Nation* (1598-1600), we have the ingenuity of exuberant curiosity and ignorance. To that extent, it illustrates the dynamic even if incomplete medieval-renaissance expansion of man's imagination. The second, Tom P. Brady's Mississippi efforts, is really a part of that extraordinary literary monument of human perverseness, which John Campbell published in Philadelphia in 1851. The work was triumphantly and authoritatively titled:

33

> *Negro-Mania: being an examination of the falsely-assumed equality of the various races of men, demonstrated by the investigations of Champollion, Wilkinson, Roselini, Van-Amringe, Gideon, Young, Morton, Knox, Lawrence, Gen. J. H. Hammont, Murray, Smith, W. Gilmore Simms, English, Conrad, Elder, Pritchard, Blumenbach, Cuvier, Brown, Le Vaillant, Carlyle, Cardinal Wiseman, Bruckhardt and Jefferson.*

To that extent, the caricature in the second quotation illustrates an ingeniousness born of a pseudo-scientific and pathological malice. This was the nineteenth century, and the emphasis in Negro caricature would be modified or exaggerated by the speculations of polygenists and monogenists, craniologists, physiognomists and phrenologists. These concerns naturally found manifestations in literary portrayals. However, the one-dimensional portrayals of the early period were unperplexed by these pathogenically weighty concerns.

The Negro had been preceded into the renaissance literary imagination of England by the North African from the "Barbary Coast," a region that extends from west of Egypt along the Mediterranean to the Atlantic Ocean and from north of the Sahara Desert. In the literature of the period, the area was actually or symbolically referred to by the mention of Morocco, Algiers or Fez. The North African himself was called a Moor. He was, by and large, the dramatic inspiration for extravagant melodramas, the stimulus for portrayals of popular myths about Moslem potentates written in the sonorous, baroque loudness of Christopher Marlowe's *Tamburlaine:*

> Well said, Theridamas! speak in that mood;
> For *will* and *shall* best fitteth Tamburlaine,
> Whose smiling stars give him assured hope
> Of martial triumph ere he meets his foes.
> I that am termed the Scourge and Wrath of God,
> The only fear and terror of the world,
> Will first subdue the Turk, and then enlarge
> Those Christian captives which you keep as slaves.
>
>   These are cruel pirates of Argier,
> That damned train, the scum of Africa,
> Inhabited with straggling runagates
> That make quick havoc of the Christian blood:
> But as I live, that town shall curse the time
> That Tamburlaine set foot in Africa.[2]

So speaks Tamburlaine, "great Lord of Africa." The eternal hostility between Moor and Christian which this and other works emphasize is doubtless medievally inherited from the Crusades.

An equally important attribute of the Moor, his color, is exploited during this period. The Duke of Moroco in Shakespeare's *Merchant of Venice* makes a florid, expansive speech and then chooses wrongly. Portia's relief is illustratively relevant:

> A gentle riddance. Draw the curtains, go.
> Let all of his complexion choose me so.[3]

That complexion was variously described as either "tawny" or "swarthy," never "black" or "negro," before the Negro became a literary fixture. The Moor, because of his complexion, was in the peculiar position of being on neutral ground in the metaphorical color spectrum between good and evil, between gentleman and buffoon. More important, he also had attributed to him in the popular imagination a seductively exotic and hedonistic culture. It was an "orientalism" that inspired visions of silks, perfumes, harems and even the forbidding magnetism of "Islam," a religion that was damned and pagan. There was even something deliciously unmanageable in names like Hassan ben Muhammad el Wazzan es Zayyati. All these constituent parts of a fantasy floated across desert sands and the Mediterranean into European courts and into poetic Xanadus. Their attractiveness endures from the fabulous origins of the wealth of Solomon's temple:

> And the navy also of Hiram, that
> brought gold from Ophir, brought
> in from Ophir great plenty of almug
> trees, and precious stones.

to the exotic richness of John Masefield's "Cargoes":

> Quinquereme of Nineveh from distant Ophir
> Rowing home to haven in sunny Palestine,
> With a cargo of ivory,
> And apes and peacocks,
> Sandalwood, cedarwood, and sweet white wine.

To this extent, the Moor in sixteenth-century English literature, especially in drama and poetry, needs to be accepted as an incarnation of the exotic. He was also a corporate Moslem personality insofar as the Crusades had obliterated differences between Arabians, Turks, North Africans and so forth. There is, therefore, much pomp and pageantry in the reductive treatment of the Moor but not much historical, psychological or geographic realism. Even in the excesses of the Moor there is something of the extravagant. He was more likely to be fanatically extreme than "realistically" cruel. Thus *Tamburlaine* acknowledges:

...Moors, in whom never was pity found will hew us to piecemeal, put us to the wheel or else invent some torture worse than that.[4]

Considering the striking visual and cultural differences between the Moor and the Negro, it is somewhat surprising that when the Negro makes his literary appearance he is not differentiated from the Moor in a more obvious manner. When the Negro appeared in Elizabethan literature, the term "moor" was simply given a double function. It was now applied to persons from both the Barbary and the Slave Coasts. This is surprising for two reasons: the Moor has a fairly aquiline nose and much thinner lips than does the Negro. The color is visibly different. Moreover, Elizabethan England had witnessed the establishing of a sea route in the West Atlantic and compilations such as Richard Hakluyt's so indicated. At any rate, for whatever the reason, because of the insistence on the term "moor" it became necessary to distinguish between the Moor as Moor and the Moor as Negro. The prefixes "black" and "cole-black" became useful. By 1601, the terms "Black Moore," "Blackmoore" and the slightly derogatory "Blackamoore" would have evolved. But the evidence suggests that these distinctions were not used with any consistent degree of exactness. It is, for example, unlikely that Marlowe was really referring to an army of Negroes when in *Tamburlaine* he describes:

> An host of Moors trained to the war
> whose coal-black faces make their foes retire
> and quake for fear.

The suspicion here is that two allusions are fused to achieve a greater measure of terror. But as late as April 5, 1669, in an entry in Samuel Pepys' diary, we find evidence of the use of "moor" plus qualification:

> (5th April, 1669) For a cookmaid we have, ever since Bridgett went, used a black a moor of Mr. Bateliers's Doll, who dresses our meat mighty well, and we mightily pleased with her.[5]

It is nonetheless true that the inertia generated by the term "Moor" was never absolute. Elizabethan literature could be quite exact (but perhaps accidentally?), in suggesting distinctions. Thomas Heywood's *The Fair Maid of the West* makes explicit use of the terms "moores" and "negroes:"

> Finde us concubines,
> The fayrest Christian Damsells you can hire,
> Or buy for gold: the loveliest of the Moores
> We can command, and Negroes everywhere.

Syphax, villain of John Marston's *Sophonisba* (1606) is to be presumed a Moor who has Negroes under his command. The combination makes for an exquisitely unholy melodrama. Syphax threatens the fair damsel in distress, Sophonisba:

> (Syphax; his dagger twon (sic) about her hair drags in Sophonisba in hir nightgowne petticoate. . . .)

> Look. I'll tack thy head
> To the low earth whilst strength of two black knaves
> Thy limbs all wide shall strain.[6]

In general, it may be said that emphasis is placed on the black Moor insofar as the literary text functions primarily as a consideration of the nature of good and evil. In that case, the Negro's color offered the most visible and dramatic means of contrastive evaluation. In Thomas Middleton's *Triumphs of Truth* (1613) The King of the Moors notes the "amazement set upon the faces of these *white* people. . .that never saw a king so *black* especially since

> I being a Moor, then, in Opinion's *lightness*
> As far from sanctity as my face from *whiteness*.

But the King indicates that the symbolism of color is only externally relevant since internally the values have been transferred. He has been redeemed by the efforts of "English merchants, factors, travellers" and therefore:

> However *darkness* dwells upon my face,
> Truth in my soul sets up the *light* of grace.

And "Error, smiling, betwixt scorn and anger, to see such devout humility take hold of that *complexion*" goes on to express disappointment in this his erstwhile "sweet-fac'd devil."

Thus the Negro, insofar as he was "cole-black," became a most apt representation or representative of the devil. As is observable in *Triumphs of Truth*, the characterizations are not far removed from the stock repertoire of the figures in morality plays. Stereotyped figures of Gluttony, Avarice, Error and the like were fortuitously and dramatically amplified in this illustrative use of the Negro's color. Lust and more is for example, clearly symbolized in Beaumont and Fletcher's *Knight of Malta* by Zanthia—black waiting-maid and rival to the Lady Oriana. Thus, Mounteferrat's accusation, which he directs at her because he believes the false rumors about Oriana's murder, is essentially a dramatic extension of the symbolic meaning of Zanthia's color:

> Bloody deeds
> Are grateful offerings, pleasing to the devill,
> And thou in thy black shape, and blacker actions
> Being hels perfect character, art delighted
> To do what I thought infinitely wicked. [8]

Shakespeare's three dramas in which the Moor-Negro plays important roles offer the most comprehensive treatment of the renaissance perspective. An interesting compendium of names, distinctions, ambiguities and quite radical treatment are evident in the three plays, *The Merchant of Venice, Titus Andronicus* and *Othello*. It is also significant that the first and last plays also demonstrate the most vital twin personalities of the period. The Pope-Monk pivot around which Western civilization had revitalized its disintegrating Graeco-Roman heritage gives way in the renaissance to the Banker-Soldier, Merchant-Othello, axis. The effect of this change on the Negro will reach its fullest expression in the Slave Trade and its aftermath. He was as yet only of importance as a literary stimulus in this early period, not as a vital economic entity.

In *The Merchant of Venice* the evidence is clear and incontrovertible that we are dealing with the Moor as Moor, although Portia's reference to his "complexion" may suggest a slight intrusive influence from the Negro. There is first of all the direct reference to the Barbary Coast; he is Duke of Morocco. The exotic bombast of his speech is more representative of the "tawny" Moor than of the Negro:

> . . .all the world desires her:
> From the four corners of the earth they come,
> To kiss this shrine, this mortal breathing saint.
> The Hyrcanian deserts and the vasty wilds
> Of wide Arabia are as thoroughfares now
> For princes to come view fair Portia:
> The watery kingdom, whose ambitious head
> Spits in the face of heaven, is no bar
> To stop the foreign spirits; but they come
> As o'er a brook, to see fair Portia. [9]

The florid exhilaration is more truly characteristic of Marlowe's "great Lord of Affrica." In the mighty spirit of that ancestry the Duke of Morocco chooses gold, and chooses wrongly to learn the important if banal, lesson that "all that glitters is not gold." To a certain extent, the sharp descent offers a parodic twist to the Marlowe tradition. The Moor is here little more than an exotic, overblown buffoon, although in all this he is Moor rather than Negro. The very fact of his arrival to court Portia is indicative of this. He is distinguished and apparently qualified for courtship by little else but exotic bombast *and* apparent wealth. The courtship between Aaron and Tamora in *Titus Andronicus* and Othello and Desdemona in *Othello* takes on different overtones.

If there is little ambiguity in the identity of the Duke, there is some about the woman referred to in Act III, scene v of *The Merchant of Venice*. There is in the reference the already noted ambivalent use of moor-negro. The relationship described suggests something of the Mountferrat-Zanthia relationship, except that Mountferrat's role is here taken by Launcelot, clown and thus of the lower class. The scene is that in which Lorenzo points out that he could easily come to terms with the state of Venice over Launcelot's charge of inflating the price of pork, "for in converting Jews to Christians you raise the price of pork."

> I shall answer that better to the commonwealth than you can the getting up of the negro's belly; the Moor is with child by you, Launcelot.

Launcelot's response, couched in outrageous puns, explicitly equates the woman with lust:

> It is much that the Moor should be more than reason; but if she be less than an honest woman, she is indeed more than I took her for.

Some of these ambiguities had received fuller treatment in an earlier "Shakespearean" play, *Titus Andronicus.*

The play is controversially attributed to Shakespeare. Edward Ravenscroft, in acknowledging his indebtedness to Shakespeare for his own *Titus Andronicus or the Rape of Lavinia* (1678), prefixed the following "idle gossip" (Kittredge) to his work: "I have been told by some anciently conversant with the Stage that it was not Originally his, but brought by a Private Authour to be Acted, and he only gave some Master-touches to one or two of the Principal Parts or Characters." Kittredge insists on Shakespearean authorship:

> Nobody would have listened to Ravenscroft but for the feeling that *Titus Andronicus* is too horrible to be Shakespeare's. But Shakespeare was always prone to try experiments, and it would be strange if he had not one out-and-out tragedy of blood when Kyd had shown how powerful such things appealed to playgoers.[10]

The play itself is a dramatic peculiarity. There is an incredible blending of farce, horror and subhuman depravity. It is at one and the same time a melodramatically extended morality play, an excessive parody, one hopes, of Senecan tragedy and a rather crude farce with quite frequent moments of poetic and descriptive excellence. Grotesque, unexpectedly violent actions are immediately followed by farcical reviews. Aaron stabs the nurse, privy to the black bastard born to Tamora and him, with the comment: "weeke, weeke! —so cries a pig prepared to the spit." He thus silences "long-tongu'd babbling gossip."[11] Act 11, scene iv opens as *"Enter the Empress's sons Demetrius and Chiron with Lavinia, her hands cut off, and her tongue cut out, and ravish'd."* In Act V, scene i the horror degenerates into grotesque farce:

> Aaron: 'Twas her sons that murdered Bassianus;
>   They cut thy sister's tongue, and ravish'd her,
>   And cut her hands, and trimm'd her as thou sawest.
> Lucius: O detestable villain! call'st thou that trimming?
> Aaron: Why, she was wash'd and cut and trimm'd, and 'twas
>   Trim sport for them which had the doing of it.

And the violence of the actions is centered around

> . . .this place
> A barren detested vale you see it is;
> The trees, though summer, yet forlorn and lean
> O'ercome with moss and baleful mistletoe.
> Here never shines the sun; here nothing breeds
> Unless the nightly owl or fatal raven.
> And when they showed me this abhorred pit,
> They told me, here, at dead time of night,
> A thousand fiends, a thousand hissing snakes,
> Ten thousand swelling toads, as many urchins,
> Would make such fearful and confused cries
> As any mortal body hearing it
> Should straight fall mad, or else die suddenly.[12]

Kittredge has effectively shown the classical inspiration of this hybrid horror in which characters "straight fall mad, or else die suddenly." He mentions Seneca's *Thyestes* and *Troades*, Ovid's Rape of Philomela in *Metamorphoses, inter alia.* These classical sources give no hint of Aaron, coal-black Moor and his "cloudy melancholy" and his "fleece of woolly hair that now uncurls even as an adder when she doth unroll." Into the volatile synthesis described above, Shakespeare introduced Aaron, instigator to perversity and lover of Tamora, Empress of Rome:

> Believe me, Queen, your swarth Cimmerian
> Doth make your honour of his body's hue,
> Spotted, detested, and abominable.

For much of the villainous excitement, indeed the topicality of Aaron, it may be enlightening to turn to a military confrontation between Moors and Christians in 1578. In that year, the Battle of Alcazar ended with the defeat by Abd-el-Malek of troops drawn from all over Europe and led by Sebastian of Portugal. Elizabethan England's participation in the disastrous "crusade" was in the person of the incompetent but later romanticized Captain Stukely. The dimension of the disaster at El-Ksar-el-Kebir may be gauged by J.F. Conestaggio's *Dell'unione del Regno di Portugallo alla Corona de Castiglia (1578-1580)*. I quote from Edward Blount's English translation, *The Historie of the Uniting of the Kingdom of Portugall to the Crowne of Castil* (1600):

> There was none in Lisbonne, but had some interest in this warre, who so had not his sonne there, had his father; the one her husbande, the other her brother; the traders and handicrafts men, who had not their kinsmen there (and yet many of them had) did venture their wealth in it, some of them for the desire of gaine, and others for what they could not call in that which they lent Gentlemen, and souldiers: by reason whereof all were in heaviness, everie one seemed to foretell the losse of such friends, and goods he had in Affrick.[13]

The death roll which Jeronymo de Mendonça will publish at the end of *Livro 1* of his *A Jornada d'Africa* (1607) gives violent testimony to the defeat sustained by the flower of European military gentry at the hand of Abd-el-Malek and his "mourous." By near universal agreement, the major cause of the debacle was the villainy and treachery, so presumed, of one Mulai Mohammed, a Moor born of a Negro mother, "who was so blacke, that he was accompted of many for a black Moore."

In addition to numerous ballads and penny pamphlets transforming Stukely into a hero, the literary response in England was dramatic in genre and effect. George Peele's play was titled *The Battel of Alcazar, fought in Barbarie, between Sebastian, King of Portugal and Abdelmelec. With death of Captain Stukely*. The protagonist-villain of the drama was Muly Hamet; the response to the work was immediate. From suggested publication and performance dates, *Titus Andronicus* and *The Battel of Alcazar* could not have been separated by more than a few years—indeed Peele's play may have been only a year older than Shakespeare's. There are reports of numerous performances of Peele's play around the suggested dates for *Titus Andronicus*.[14] This proximity, in addition to Kittredge's view, may explain the sensationalism of *Titus Adronicus* with its murders, amputations, rape, hangings, involuntary cannibalism and a coal-black/Moor villian. There is a line in Act IV, scene ii, which, as printed in the First Quarto (1594), echoes the name of Muly Hamet when Aaron says "Not far one Muli lives, my countryman."[15]

It is not surprising then that Aaron, insofar as he represents the idea of blackness in human form, should function at all levels of this extraordinary drama. His color and its implications assume the endless kaleidoscope of evil that informs the play. It is, for example, interesting that Lavinia's description of his hue as "raven coloured" might have seemed strange were it not echoed unintentionally by Tamora when she describes one of the manifestations of evil that inhabit the play's pit of depravity (literal and symbolic). As will be noted in the excerpt already offered, she mentions *inter alia*, "the nightly owl or *fatal raven*." Aside from such subtleties, the color is exploited in more obvious ways. Act IV, scene ii opens as the nurse enters bearing the illegitimate child of Aaron and Tamora. *"Enter nurse with blackamoor child."* In a dialogue of double-entendre and ironies the usual associations are developed about the implications of blackness:

> Nurse: She is delivered, lords,—she is deliver'd.
> Aaron: To whom?
> Nurse: I mean she is brought a-bed.
> Aaron: Well, God give her rest! What hath he sent her?
> Nurse: A devil.
> Aaron: Why then she is the devil's dam; a joyless issue.
> Nurse: A joyless, dismal, black, and sorrowful issue:
> Here is the babe, as loathsome as a toad.
> Amongst the fairest breeders of our clime
> The empress send it thee, thy stamp, thy seal.
> And bids thee christen it with thy dagger's point.

The association between the Negro and the devil is obvious. There is, however, a double irony here. There is, first, Aaron's unintentional identification of himself as the devil, and second, a reversal of the role of virtue imposed by the play. Tamora is far from being the virtuous Sophonisba resisting the unholy advances of a Syphax. Moreover, this fledgeling Othello-Desdemona relationship is as dramatically opposed to the real one as Troilus and Cressida are cynical parodies of Romeo and Juliet. Tamora is not the adolescent sweetness that Desdemona may be seen as. She is instead "an insatiate and luxurious woman." Aaron calls her "this queen, this goddess, this Semiramis, this nymph, this siren." The ambiguities of color as Shakespeare uses it are therefore evident in even this play.

In several passages *Titus Andronicus* also demonstrates the ambivalent distinction made between the Moor as Moor and the Moor as Negro. The illegitimate offspring of Tamora is categorically identified as a blackamoor when first introduced, but a soldier reports overhearing Aaron:

> I soon heard
> The crying babe controlled with this discourse:
> "Peace *tawny* slave, half me and half thy dam!
> Had nature lent thee but thy mother's look,
> Villian, thou mightest have been an emperor;
> But where the bull and cow are both milk-white[16]
> They never do beget a *coal-black* calf." (my emphasis)

In the next selection, there is a peculiar hybrid creature. The last line may echo Muly Hamet, especially as the last two lines are clearly Moorish "gastronomically." In the third line, however, is the conventional, Elizabethan food of the "forest." The first line contains a physical description that appears to be more clearly negroid and which will be applied to Othello:

> Come on you, thick-lipped slave, I'll bear you hence;
> For it is you that puts us to our shifts;
> I'll make you feed on berries and roots,
> And feed on curds and whey, and suck the goat,
> To be a warrior and command camp.[17]

The rough tenderness of the last two selections is most significant because of the implicit sympathetic response to the infant manifestation of blackness in human form. Aaron refuses to kill his blackamoor child and defiantly challenges the assumptions that make a positive esthetic and moral response to blackness impossible. "Zounds, ye whore! is black so base a hue?" To Chiron, white, legitimate son of Tamora who would "blush to think upon the ignomy" of the blackamoor Aaron observes:

> Why there's the privelege your beauty bears
> Fie, treacherous hue, that will betray with blushing
> The close enacts and counsels of the heart.

Aaron's "black-is-beautiful" inversion is expressed sometimes with a surprising, lyrical tenderness that is startlingly incongruous in a play that thrives on horrifying perversions. He cradles the blackamoor child who is "loathsome as a toad," refuses to kill it and murmurs "sweet blowse, you are a beauteous blossom sure." But the following selection is more representative of the synthetic nature of Aaron's personality and of the loudness of the play as a whole. We have exuberant rhetoric and farcical, flat-footed invectives that fuse into conventionally elegant metaphors all put to the service of a bombastic apologia for blackness:

Demetrius: I'll breach the tadpole on my rapier's point:
Nurse give it to me; my sword shall soon despatch it.
Aaron: Sooner this sword shall plough thy bowels up.
(Takes child from the Nurse, and draws.)
Stay murderous villians! will you kill your brother?
Now by the burning tapers of the sky,
That shone so brightly when this boy was got,
He dies upon my scimitar's sharp point
That touches this my first-born son and heir!
I tell you, younglings, not Enceladus
With all his threatening band of Typhon's brood
Nor great Alcides, nor the god of war,
Shall seize this prey out of thy father's hands.
Ye white-lim'd walls! ye ale-house-painted signs!
Coal-black is better than another hue,
In that it scorns to bear another hue;
For all the water in the ocean
Can never turn the swan's black legs white,
Although she lave them hourly in the flood.[18]

Bombastic or not, farcical or horrifying, *Titus Andronicus* is certainly one of the most extraordinary vehicles in which English literature responds to the Negro as he was conceived by Elizabethan England.

We may look upon *Othello* as the sober restatement of some of the perspectives on the Negro seen in *Titus Andronicus*. In many respects it too contains evidence of the ambiguities generated by the Moor-Negro identity. For one thing, it does continue the transformative approach to blackness, although the Duke of Venice's statement is more ethnocentric, metaphorically speaking, than Aaron's would allow:

. . .and, noble signior (Brabantio).
If virtue no delighted beauty lack
Your son-in-law is far more fair than black.

At the end of the play, there seems to be a more reasoned and enlightened perspective.

Some illuminating conclusions about the relative apotheosis which the Negro undergoes in Shakespeare's unorthodox portrayal can be gained by examining the Italian source of the play. The striking thing about the *novella* by Giovanni Battista Giraldi (surnamed Cinthio) is the fact that color, Moorish or Negroid, plays hardly any role in the narrative and development of the plot. This is all the more surprising when one reads in the preface to the *Hecatommithi* that the *novelle* were to function as edifying exempla:

vegono rappresentate, come in vaghissima scena, & in ucidissimo spéchio, le varie maniere del vieur humano: dalle quali puo imparare qual si voglia persona utilissima avvertimenti, si di preservarsi libera da infiniti inganni, che li potessero esser contra machinati in varij tempi & in diverse occasioni.

Although the intent, as in the morality plays, could easily provide justification for symbolic use of color, Cinthio's *novella* does not do so. There can be little doubt that the *Hecatommithi* (1565) was published in an age that was quite familiar with the *viaggi e scoperte...italiani* and the maps and descriptions which they provided of *i negri* and of course of the *moro*. But all this is interestingly absent from the tale, although the barely touched upon objections of Disdemona's *(sic)* parents may have been in response. For all practical purposes then the Moor in *Novela 7 della terza Deca de gli Hecatommithi* is established more as a *gentiluomo Veneziano* than as a *uomo negro* or a *uomo berretino:*

> Fu gia in Venetia un moro, molto valoroso, il quale...habbia dato segno nelle cose della guerra, di gran prudenza, & di vivace ingegno.

Care is taken to point out that the title of *capitano* conferred on him by the state was

> tal grado di dignitá (che) non si suol dare sénon ad huomini nobili & forti, & fedeli, e che habbiano mostrato in se molto valore.

The moment this is established the narrative is developed with no reference to color or physiognomy; nor are these relied on as indirect pivotal elements in the moral structure of the tale. There does come a strategic point when, after the *capitano moro* and *alfiero*, Iago's prototype have killed Disdemona, the perspective changes slightly. The *capitano* has killed his wife "per bestial gelosia" and "i Signori Venitiani" condemn "la crudelta, usata del Barbaro." Some attempt then is made to identify the origin of this cruelty. But here one ought to take issue with English versions of Cinthio's tale which do not make any attempt to translate the *geographic* emphasis of the Italian original. To simply translate the term "Barbaro" as "barbarian" is inadequate to explain the capitalization in Italian. To my mind, the capitalization shifts the emphasis away from moral unenlightement to the Barbary Coast. I take issue only in the matter of emphasis.[19]

When Cinthio's *moro* reappears in Shakespeare's Othello certain noteworthy changes are evident. If Cinthio's captain is a synthetic character, more Venetian gentleman than Moor, Shakespeare's is essentially a combination of Blackamoor and Moor in the manner in which he is most vulnerably seen at critical moments. The significant difference between *Othello* and the other Elizabethan texts mentioned is that the response to blackness is controlled by a far greater degree of psychological realism and exploration. We find in the play certain traditional elements. Again, these elements are not unrelated to the peculiar concerns of the characters who use them. This is true when Othello is referred to in Rodrigo's

> What a full fortune does the thick-lips owe
> If he can carry't thus!

It is explicitly the case in the calculated obscenities that function effectively in the opening scenes of the play. The reductive caricatures by which Othello is identified serve two very vital functions. They rightly presuppose an active hostility to Othello's blackness in Brabantio and indeed in the mileux as a whole. They also deliberately descend to somewhat cruder manifestations of that hostility to highlight the sexual act implicitly involved in Othello and Desdemona's union:

> I am one, sir, that come to tell you your daughter
> and the Moor are now making the beast with two backs.

> An old black ram
> Is tupping your white ewe!

> . . .Arise, arise
> Awake the snorting citizens with the bell,
> Or else the devil will make a grandsire of you.

Even when the ambivalent Moor-Negro is used, the same crudeness is emphasized:

> You'll have your daughter cover'd with a Barbary horse; you'll have
> your nephews neigh to you; you'll have coursers for cousins, and
> gennets for germans.

And it works effectively, especially because Desdemona, unlike Tamora of *Titus Andronicus*, is no "Semiramis," no "insatiate and luxurious woman." It is therefore easier for the prejudicial hostility of Brabantio to be intensified since it is now easier to conceive of helpless, white, feminine purity being ravished by crude, black potency. The anguished superstition and angry indignation which Brabantio breaks into when he confronts Othello shows how effectively Iago had succeeded when he aimed his crudities at the raw center of a "general" bias:

> Damn'd as thou art, thou has enchanted her;
> For I'll refer me to all things of sense,

> If she in chains of magic were not bound,
> Whether a maid so tender, fair and happy,
> So opposite to marriage that she shunned
> The wealthy curled darlings of our nation,
> Would ever have, to incur a general mock,
> Run from her guardage to the sooty bosom
> Of such a thing as thou, to fear, not delight.[20]

The accusation is remarkable for the balanced contrasts and the esthetic and moral antitheses which effectively capture Brabantio's aversion to Othello's blackness. Even more theatrically effective is the self-crucifixion that takes place when Othello is trapped in the metaphorical logic that works for Brabantio. His torment excruciatingly aggravated by Iago, Othello cries out: "Arise, black vengeance from thy hollow cell!" This cry for the forces of darkness from a thick-lipped, "sooty bosom" is most effective theater and as noted before, effective self-crucifixion. The degree to which Othello's color or race made any difference in the development of the crisis in the play is of course a matter of speculation. I am inclined to find more merit in W.H. Auden's observation below than does Eldred Jones who quotes him in *Othello's Countrymen*:

> He (Othello) does not or will not recognise that Brabantio's view of the match
>
> > If such actions may have passage free
> > Bond-slaves and pagans shall our statesmen be.
>
> is shared by all his fellow senators, and the arrival of news about the Turkish fleet, prevents their saying so because their need of Othello's military skill is too urgent for them to risk offending him.[21]

But it must be acknowledged that the deliberate exploitation of crude prejudices in the opening scenes of the play is given a twist by the end of the play. There is, much as in *Titus Andronicus*, a transformation amounting to a modest apotheosis. The transformation lacks the dynamic force of Aaron's although it is a more literate and controlled reassessment. When *Othello* ends we have an illustration of that ambivalent moral universe so frequent in Shakespeare: "fair is foul and foul is fair." Iago, "supersubtle Venetian" and white, is showered with epithets supposedly due the blackamoor. He has become "damn'd slave," "most heathenish," "demi-devil." Othello himself seems little more than a pathetically unsophisticated "erring barbarian" not a black demon.

It is nonetheless possible to see in Othello the problems of identity imposed by the cumulative negativism of the Moor as Negro and by the fantastic scale to which the Moor as Moor was drawn. The synthesis in

Othello's personality does not allow for the presentation of a convincing human personality. The crude insistence on Othello's negroidness creates a problem unsatisfactorily ignored in the description of the courtship with Desdemona. The hostility presumed throughout the play toward the Moor as Negro seems irrelevant to the fantastic, medieval-renaissance travelogue which so charms Desdemona. Part of the reason then must be that the ludicrous "science-fiction" which draws her to the "sooty bosom" has little to do with Othello as Moor-Negro or with Brabantio's apprehension of the nature of that blackness. Desdemona is seduced by the charming fantasy of "an extravagant and wheeling stranger of here and everywhere," by Othello as Moor:

> I spoke of most disastrous chances,
> Of moving accidents by flood and field,
> Of hairbreadth scapes i' th' imminent deadly breach,
> Of being taken by the insolent foe
> And sold to slavery, of my redemption thence
> And portance in my travel's history,
> Wherein of anters vast and deserts idle,
> Rough quarries, rocks, hills whose heads touch heaven,
> It was my hint to speak. Such was my process.
> And of Cannibals that each other eat,
> The Anthropophagi, and men whose heads
> Grew beneath their shoulders.
>
> She gave me for my pains a world of kisses.
> She swore in faith 'twas strange, 'twas passing strange;
> 'Twas pitiful, 'twas wondrous pitiful.[22]

There is here an obvious self-indulgence to Othello and a delicate, charming inanity in Desdemona. Two traditions are in conflict: Othello's Moorish and Negro ancestries, and they are not satisfactorily resolved. There is thus some justification and much rabid silliness in a review of *Othello* as published in *Blackwood's Magazine* in 1850. The reviewer admits that the stage conventions of the period made Othello jet black but he does not consider that the Elizabethan age was capable of drawing proper "ethnological distinctions" between a "Moor" and the "Blackamoor" and a "Negro." The marriage between Othello and Desdemona is, therefore, not to be construed as a piece of realism but as a means of "emphasizing the dramatic and poetic symbolism of the contrast." He proceeds next in a manner faithful to nineteenth-century negative response to the Negro:

> In life you cannot bear that the White Woman shall marry the Black Man. You could not bear that an English Lady Desdemona—Lady Blanche Howard—should—under any imaginable greatness—marry a Gen-

eral Toussaint or the Duke of Marmalade. Your senses revolt with of-
fense and loathing. But on the stage some consciousness that everything
is not literally meant as it seems—that symbols of humanity, and not
actual men and women, are before you—saves the play.[23]

But there is some truth to the ideas about the Elizabethan age and its
perception of the Negro. What Othello lacks, for example, is the kind of
energy and organic personality such as springs out of the uncompromisingly
Jewish indignation of Shylock. In this respect, Shylock's voice is not a
synthetic one, such is the power and insight that Shakespeare exercises in
The Merchant of Venice. Othello, on the other hand, can react to neither
"coal-black" nor "tawny" Moor because he is not convincingly either. To
say he is neither because he is more properly a human being is
unsatisfactory nor does it offer a definition of what his humanity consists
in. The fact remains that at crucial moments he is most significantly
apprehended in contradictory and unresolved terms. In truth we may say
that Othello in his confused identity is primarily a vehicle to suggest that
whiteness can be infinitely unpleasant, just as Shylock is used, with greater
effect, to suggest "what fools these Christians be." Under normal
circumstances, that is, when the Negro is seen without infusions of exotic
energy, the caricature would be different. The Moor as Negro simply did
not have the necessary fascinating dimensions which the Moor as Moor
could generate. The Elizabethan perception of the Negro thus fails to
degenerate to the intense unpleasantness of later caricatures. This was true
to the extent that the Elizabethans were seduced by *both* the negative
possibilities in the Negro and the exotic fantasies of the Moor.

The Negro was left on his own in the eighteenth century. For one
thing there is less evidence of inexact intoxication with navigational
discoveries as in the previous centuries. Moreover, the Barbary Coast was
neither as fascinating nor as important as it had been to the poetic
imagination. The Negro, far from being a literary toy, had proved to be a
most important economic discovery. Whatever he was culturally, or even in
human terms, before he became so useful was not only irrelevant but
actually was quite useless. For before the European "discovered" him
during the Slave Trade "the main body of the Africans" had had no
history, but had "stayed, for untold centuries, sunk in barbarism. . .(so that)
the heart of Africa was scarcely beating." Perceived and exploitatively
exiled thus in England and the Americas the Negro offered justification for
caricatures of a pathogenic variety difficult to predict from the exotic
Elizabethan portraits. Instead of a powerfully dramatic voice, the Negro
now demonstrates a wide-eyed, melancholic bovinity, at least in his insular
as against colonial literary appearances. The colonial representation is of

course best read in one of the most sensationally popular novels of the last years of the seventeenth century. I refer to the 1688 publication of *Oroonoko or the Slave King* by the Surinam-born Aphra Behn, the "incomparable Astrea." The Negro there is a hybrid Indian-Negro-Noble Savage who is, of course, the son of a king. We shall have cause to refer to *Oroonoko* and its influence in France in Chapter Five.[24]

Even though the Negro was a highly visible economic and social reality in England during the eighteenth century, he was only of peripheral literary significance. And yet there must have been a great number as early as 1601 to account for Elizabeth I's deportation edict of that year, which called for the transportation of "negars and blackmoores." But when the Negro did appear literary perceptions were invariably determined by social realities. Kenneth Little's economic and sociological study of Negroes in Britain during the eighteenth century gives evidence of the pathogenic basis for these later caricatures:

> The newspapers of the 18th century contain a fairly extensive record of these public auctions and private offers of sale in all parts of the country as well as descriptions of runaways. The following are examples:
>
> *London Advertiser*, 1756: "To be sold, a Negro boy aged fourteen years old, warranted free from any distemper, and has had those fatal to that colour; has been used two years to all kinds of household work. . . ."
>
> Another advertisement in the *Public Ledger* for December 31st, 1761, reads like an offer of young dogs:
>
> "A healthy Negro Girl, aged about fifteen years; speaks good English, works at her needle, washes well, does household work, and has had the smallpox."[25]

But, as indicated in Chapter 1, there were other voices, Granville Sharp's for example, which would eventually result in slavery being rendered illegal in 1772. But to read the decision by Chief Justice, Lord Mansfield is to become aware of the moral confusion that race and economics generated in English society of the period. Lord Mansfield declared for the defendant Negro slave, Somersett, all the while dropping broad hints to the merchant class to appeal to Parliament for a bill that would make slavery *legally* possible. And yet the moral repugnance is hardly feigned:

> The power of master over his slave has been extremely different, in different countries. The state of slavery is of such a nature, that it is

incapable of being introduced on any reasons, moral or political, but only by positive law, which preserves its force long after the reasons, occasion, and time itself from which it was created is erased from memory. It is so odious, that nothing can be suffered to support it, but positive law. Whatever inconvenience, therefore, may follow from the decision, I cannot say this case is allowed or approved by the law of England; and therefore the black must be discharged.[26]

William Cowper, with an enthusiasm that was more poetic than realistic, celebrated:

> Slaves cannot breathe in England: if their lungs
> Imbibe our air, that moment they are free.
> They touch our country, and their shackles fall. . . .[27]

Somewhat less enthusiastic was the response of the merchant class to Lord Mansfield's legal and moral niceties:

A Planter wrote: "The planters of course have been left as much puzzled by this Delphic Ambiguity, as the sages themselves appear to have been, in forming their judgements upon the subject. The matter having been confounded in this grand uncertainty."[28]

Part of the social problem generated was that by 1700 there were some 14,000 to 20,000 Negroes in London alone (Kenneth Little). Even if the figures are inflated (as much as C.M. Maciness' 15,000 to 20,000 for all England appear deflated) the fact remains that the substantial amount necessitating the edict of 1601 could only have been swollen by the slave trade. After the Mansfield decision, the merchants acted on his hints but failed in 1773 to get a bill through Parliament to legalize slavery. The fact that the Negro was seen as antithetical to the very meaning of English society—other than as slave or caricature—created social problems. He could not be absorbed in an enlightened manner into the equities legally implied in the 1772 decision. Negroes became conspicuous among London beggars and were generally known as St. Giles' Blackbirds. The solution which the Sierra Leone Creole represents needs then to be seen as an exquisite combination of humanitarian instincts and opportunism. Thus it was that "men of ardent passions, whose only lessons had been stripes, and whom experience had instructed to start with dread from their fellow-creatures" set sail to establish Freetown in 1787. The justification for the accompanying prostitutes was that "removal of prostitutes (and indeed other undesirables) to the Colonies was a favourite method of the age for reforming and providing for such women." This was then the genesis of that colonial, African Jacobinism that would fascinate Graham Greene.

A race thus revealed could not generate the exotic attenuations of the Elizabethan age. Caricature and inaccuracies were attended by a degree of high seriousness and solemnity. Thus, Richard Crawshaw's biblical inspiration rescues the Negro from his black skin with sober munificence:

> Let it no longer be a forlorn hope
>   To wash an Ethiope;
> He's washed, his gloomy skin a peaceful shade
>   For his white soul is made,
> And now, I doubt not, the Eternal Dove
>   A black-faced house will love[29]

This view is quite similar to Thomas Middleton's in *Triumphs of Truth* but the style is here confidently, ethnocentrically righteous. In much the same way, whereas the Moore-Negro had been subject for melodrama, to the evangelical intensity and narrowness of eighteenth-nineteenth century Christianity, he was a cause for scandal and concern:

> Yet there is a lower and still more vile being than the black fetichist, and that is the fetichist turned Mussulman (Moslem, Islamic). To his former brutishness and superstition he adds two new vices: fanaticism and pride, two great obstacles to Christianity. [30]

We may look on William Blake's "The Little Black Boy" from the *Songs of Innocence* as being more historically reflective than might be supposed. It is a rather effective portrayal of the Negro without the energizing intrusion of the Barbary Coast. But an acknowledgement is a propos here. I recognize in Blake the conjoining of two elements. At work in "The Little Black Boy" are the blackamoor's simple-minded precariousness and Blake's own peculiar style in the *Songs of Innocence*. It is significant that practically all these poems have a naïve, restrained, sometimes charming, sometimes simplistic tone. Vitality in these "songs" frequently comes expressed in childlike wonder and eagerness. This quality is so distinctive that not even the dramatic, rhapsodic mysticism of other poems are free from its influence. "The Little Black Boy" is in the *Songs of Innocence* cycle. The simple-minded, one-dimensional portrait which emerges blends easily with the tone of the cycle. That tone may best be seen in the near banal simplicity with which religious fervor is expressed in "The Lamb":

> Little Lamb, I'll tell thee,
> Little Lamb, I'll tell thee:
> He is called by thy name,
> For he calls Himself a Lamb.
> He is meek, and He is mild;
> He became a little child.

> I a child, and thou a lamb,
> We are called by his name.
> Little Lamb, God bless thee!
> Little Lamb, God bless thee!

It is easy to imagine how the social situation of the day coalesced into the creation by Blake of what may really be called the prototype of Black Sambo and that monument to religious stoicism, Aunt Jemima. It would be sheer philistinism to offer these prototypes as the primary or even secondary intent of Blake. I suggest merely that in the manner in which Blake captured the Negro and in which he introduced him into his peculiar concerns we have a reductive portrait that forms part of the Negro caricature repertoire. There is no defiant virility in the blackamoor's voice. With melancholic simplicity he expresses concern in metaphors antithetical to his blackness:

> My mother bore me in the southern wild,
> And I am black, but O my soul is white;
> White as an angel is the English child,
> But I am black, as if bereaved of light.

The Negro mother is a monument to endurance who teaches her offspring to endure:

> My mother taught me underneath a tree,
> And sitting down before the heat of the day,
> She took me on her lap and kissed me,
> And, pointing to the east, began to say:
>
> And we are put on earth a little space
> That we may learn to bear the beams of love
> And these black bodies and this sun-burnt face
> Is but a cloud and like a shady grove.

Almost a century and a half later Langston Hughes' "Mother to Son" would change the metaphors, but not the melancholic stoicism of the mother.[31] Blake's resolution to "The Little Black Boy" is in a sense, enlightened and indecorous at the same time. It bears an extraordinary similarity to the relationship which Gilberto Freyre's *Casa Grande e Senzala* will describe between *muleques de estimaçao*, favorite slave boys and their little white masters:

> Thus did my mother say, and kissed me;
> And thus I say to little English boy:
> When I from black, and he from white cloud free,
> And round the tent of God like lambs we joy;

I'll shade from the heat, till he can bear
To lean in joy upon our father's knee;
And then I'll stand and stroke his silver hair,
And be like him, and he will then love me.[32]

It remains to be emphasized again that Blake's intent and his poetic inspirations have little to do directly with the Negro as such. The intent in his poems, and this includes "The Little Black Boy," was to build symbolic expressions based on Christian mysticism and a very personal, organic sense of religion. The use of color in the poem above and in another quite similar poem, "The Chimney Sweeper," was to suggest the antithetical effects of sin and salvation. That was the intent. But a consequence of Blake's living in the eighteenth century was an exposure to the Negro and to his appearance in English society in the manner already illustrated from Kenneth Little's study. "The Little Black Boy" may thus be seen as thematically related to Blake's entire work, since his century's perception of the Negro made it easy to introduce "The Little Black Boy" into *Songs of Innocence*. The Negro's most distinctively visible attribute, his color, becomes the medium through which Blake's evaluations are made. Within the framework of Blake's work, that color becomes symbolic of the profane: "but I am black, as if bereaved of light." I would suggest therefore, that there is both similarity and dissimilarity in the way in which blackness operates in "The Little Black Boy" and in which "sootiness" does in "The Chimney Sweeper." On the other hand, Blake was also responding to the pervasive influence, even at the time, of the Industrial Revolution. In this respect, the Negro as such was peripheral to his intent. The chimney sweeper is but a profane manifestation of an unholy and dehumanizing "progress." The blackness that resulted from that spiritually atrophying "progress" was not necessarily racial but technological, industrial. It is after all about this pollutant that Blake waxes indignant in "And Did Those Feet in Ancient Time:"

. . . .
And did the countenance divine
Shine forth upon our clouded hills
And was Jerusalem builded here
Among these *dark satanic mills*[33]

It was merely the Negro's incidental lot to fall heir to a pigmentation that metaphorically made him appear satan's perfect character.

The effect of the romanticism of the late eighteenth through mid-nineteenth century was rather peculiar. Abolitionist sentiment, pre- and post-Darwinian arguments and sheer romantic exuberance all played roles in the way the Negro would be perceived. William Wordsworth's support and praise for the Haitian Revolution in the person of the black revolutionary Toussaint Louverture was an explicit indication that the Negro was every inch a human being and that a great injustice had been inflicted upon him. It is significant that the language and tone of the poem matches the sonnet in which Wordsworth had earlier celebrated the French Revolution. (Ironically, the revolution in Haiti was against the French.) Wordsworth does not directly concern himself with the Negro, but with moral principles which he implies are embodied in Toussaint's fate:

> Toussaint, the most unhappy of Men!
> Whether the whistling Rustic tend his plough
> Within thy hearing, or thy head be now
> Pillowed in some deep dungeon's earless den;
> O miserable Chieftain:. . . .
>   Thou has left behind
> Powers that will work for thee; air, earth, and skies;
> There's not a breathing of the common wind
> that will forget thee; thou hast great allies;
> Thy friends are exultations, agonies,
> And love, and Man's unconquerable mind.[34]

Not all expressions of Romantic sympathy for the Negro would be as intelligently elevated as Wordsworth's. Many others fall victim to an expression of sympathy that proceeds by way of exotic caricatures. Walt Whitman's *persona* for expressing some anti-slavery comments in "Ethiopia Saluting the Colors" is a garishly turbaned, eye-rolling Cassandra from, not surprisingly, Ethiopia:

> Who are you dusty woman, so ancient hardly human
> With your woolly-white and turban'd head, and bare bony feet?
> Why rising by the roadside here, do you the colors greet?

The response, in broken-tongued prosodic inversions, is explicitly anti-slavery:

> "Me master years a hundred since from my parents sunder'd,
> A little child, they caught me as the savage beast is caught
> Then hither me across the sea the cruel slaver brought"

The poem ends on the strange and the exotic:

> What is it fateful women, so blear, hardly human?
> Why wag your head with turban bound, yellow, red and green?
> Are the things so strange and marvellous you see or have seen?[35]

Henry Wadsworth Longfellow's "Slave Dream" is related to Jean-Jacques Rousseau in perhaps the same way that one may refer Whitman's black

Cassandra to Macbeth's witches. The nineteenth century's search for "l'homme de la nature," natural man, would push several candidates to the forefront as the Noble Savage. This is the tendency in Longfellow's poem. It relates back also to Aphra Behn's *Oroonoko or the Slave King.* Longfellow's slave is, or rather was, a king now in abject misery:

> Beside the ungathered rice he lay,
> 　　his sickle in his hand;
> his breast was bare, his matted hair
> 　　was buried in the sand.
> Again in the mist and shadow of sleep,
> 　　he saw his Native Land.

The native land is paradisiac; the slave becomes an imperial Noble Savage who charges down the banks of the Niger with Homeric pomp and pageantry:

> . . .and then at furious speed he rode
> 　　along the Niger's bank;
> his bridle-reins were golden chains
> 　　and, with a martial clank,
> at each leap he could feel his scabbard of steel
> 　　smiting his stallion's flank.[36]

The attenuation by way of Greece and exotic simplifications was necessary for the elevation of the Negro to Noble Savage. The truth was that in its European inception this return to the Natural Man was never couched in terms that would fit the Negro. German romanticism dreamed of a Teutonic hero; Rousseau of an indefinite "l'homme de la nature." The closest that Europe came to identifying him, outside the European, was the American Indian.[37] In addition to this, nature as it was popularly conceived of in Africa actively militated against the temperate and tempered habitat of the Noble Savage. The imagination that created the dark continent was incompatible with the placing of a Noble Savage in that darkness. Moreover, the cumulative overtones of the caricatured Negro militated against a workable identification. Still, the attempt was made. The caricatures would be simplified and somewhat attenuated. We may look upon William Thackeray's *Vanity Fair* and Herman Melville's *Moby Dick* as illustrations of two extreme attempts. In *Vanity Fair* the product is startlingly incongruous. George Osborne's description of Miss Swartz, "Hottentot Venus," is urbane, mockingly tolerant:

> She has diamonds as big as pigeon's eggs. . . .How they must set off her
> complexion. A perfect illumination it must be then when her jewels are

on her neck. Her jet black hair is as curly as Sambo's. I daresay she wore a nose-ring when she went to court; and with a plume of feathers in her topknot she would look like a perfect *Belle Sauvage*. . . . Her diamonds blazed out like Vauxhall on the night we were there. . . . Diamonds and mahogany my dear! think what an advantageous contrast—and the white feathers in her hair—I mean in her wool.[38]

In Melville's *Moby Dick* the tone is far from mocking. The Noble Savage stands unveiled in Daggoo, "a gigantic, coal-black negro-savage, with a lion-like tread—an Ahasuerus to behold." I find the following passage one of the most romantically symbolic treatments of a romantic subject. Flask mounted on Daggoo's shoulder is the inspiration for this rhapsodic description:

But the sight of little Flask mounted upon gigantic Daggoo was yet more curious; for sustaining himself with a cool, indifferent, easy, unthought of barbaric majesty, the noble Negro to every roll of the sea harmoniously rolled his fine form. On his broad back, flaxen-haired Flask seemed a snow-flake. The bearer looked nobler than the rider. Though trully vivacious, tumultuous, ostentatious little Flask would now and then stamp with impatience; but not one added heave did he thereby give to the negro's lordly chest. So have I seen Passion and Vanity stamping the living magnanimous earth, but the earth did not alter her tide and her seasons for that.[39]

There is certainly sympathetic transformation here. The alchemy has transformed devil and buffoon into a magnificent, superhuman Body. It will not be too far wrong to suggest that we can see Harriet Beecher-Stowe's *Uncle Tom's Cabin* (published in 1852) as the moral culmination of abolitionist sympathy for the Negro just as the portrait of Daggoo may rightly be seen as the high point of exotic perceptions of the Negro. On one hand the agony of the mindless, sympathetic darky; and on the other the glory of the Negro's non-intellect, his Body. In these we have the caricature of ignorant compassion.

The nineteenth century was also a century of exhaustive, sometimes comical, oftentimes malicious search for criteria to determine the meaning and importance of race. In this respect, the sympathetic attitudes above were counter-productive:

One drop of Negro blood makes the Negro. It kinks the hair, flattens the nose, thickens the lip, puts out the light of intellect, and lights the fires of brutal passions.[40]

I mean counter-productive in the sense that traditional caricatures now needed to be expressed with polemical urgency. It may be mere

coincidence, and again it may not be that Darwin's *Origin of Species* was
published in 1859, Harriet Beecher-Stowe's *Uncle Tom's Cabin* in 1852, and
John Campbell's *Negro-Mania* in 1851. It was a remarkable coincidence of
divergent, contradictory and yet oddly complimentary energies.

A thin veneer of scientific analysis would henceforth overlay
perceptions of the Negro. Richard Eden's flat racial landscapes give way to
the involuted plumbings of Joseph Conrad's *Heart of Darkness*. Africa is
actually and symbolically a jungle of dionysiac intensities:

> An empty stream, a great silence, an impenetrable forest. . .amongst
> the overwhelming realities of this strange world of plants, and water,
> and silence. And this stillness of life did not in the least resemble
> peace. It was the stillness of an implacable force brooding over an
> inscrutable intention. It looked at you with a vengeful aspect.

The Negro here is hardly human. He is neither devil nor buffoon. There is
a violently gargoyle-like quality about him:

> We were wanderers on a prehistoric earth on an earth that wore the
> aspect of an unknown planet. We could have fancied ourselves the
> first men taking possession of an accursed inheritance, to be subdued
> at the cost of profound anguish and of excessive toil. But suddenly,
> we struggled round a bend, there would be a glimpse of rush walls, of
> peaked grass-roofs, a burst of yells, a whirl of black limbs, swaying, of
> eyes rolling, under the droop of motionless foliage.

All the above is seductive, literate and rather profound nonsense in the
light of the reductions that must take place to arrive at such a picture. But
there is still an apotheosis of sorts. It is a kind of atavistic regression which,
significantly, is not consummated:

> It was unearthly, and the men were—No, were not inhuman. Well, you
> know, that was the worst or it—this suspicion of their not being
> inhuman. We would come slowly to one. They howled and leaped,
> and spun, and made horrid faces; but what thrilled you was just the
> thought of their humanity—like yours—the thought of your remote
> kinship with this wild and passionate uproar. . . .An appeal to me in
> this fiendish row-is there? Very well; I hear; I admit, but I have a
> voice, too, and for good or evil mine is the speech that cannot be
> silenced.[41]

Conrad, however, expresses the dilemma which the Negro has ever posed
for the European and which provoked the nineteenth century to unending
disquisitions on race, to comparative analysis in craniology, phrenology and
the like. "An Outpost of Progress" offers a fine statement of the point of
departure:

...the contact with pure unmitigated savagery, with primitive nature and primitive man, brings sudden and profound trouble into the heart...a suggestion of things vague, uncontrollable, and repulsive, whose discomposing intrusion excites the imagination and tries the civilised nerves of the foolish and the wise alike.

Because the Negro was invariably seen as a disturbingly unholy and primitive man, caricature invariably resulted in the attempts to accommodate him and resolve the "sudden and profound trouble in the heart." By and large the "civilised nerves" of the earlier periods were not quite as tried as those of the nineteenth century. There was then an unexamined set of assumptions which functioned well enough artistically. Darwinian theory, abolitionist fervor and the beginnings of anthropological analyses freed from *a priori* bias in a sense aggravated the "discomposing instrusion" of the Negro. In the attempts to determine his place in a hierarchical chain of being lie some of the most extraordinary scandals to which the nineteenth century subjected the human capacity to invent and to reason. But there was little that was really new in these scandals. Old cliches and caricatures were resurrected with solemn efficacy.[42] Campbell's *Negro-Mania* ranges from craniological profundities to hair-splitting ingeniousness:

> The genuine Negroes have very little growth of hair on the chin, or even on other parts of the body. In a full grown lad of seventeen, there was not the smallest appearance of beard, nor of hair on any other part except the head. I never saw hair on the arms, legs, or breasts of Negroes, like what is observed on those parts in Europeans.

The Othello-Desdemona relationship and the problems it generates are re-stated and resolved by a display of divinely sanctioned, calvinistic virulence:

> But the grand secret of the separation or rather the separate existence of the races is to be found in that love of the beautiful, that instinctive and innate feeling implanted by the Creator in us, will keep forever and ever the higher race always distinctive from the inferior one....the white race of men have drawn back in disgust from anything like general intermingling with the females of inferior races.[43]

And so the Negro stands in direct confrontation with God-given truths and is shown to be wanting by both human and divine standards.

William Carlos Williams' "A Negro Woman," in the twentieth century delicately softens the exile of this "ambassador from another world."

> A Negro woman
>> carrying a bunch of marigolds
>>> wrapped
>>>> in an old newspaper:
>
> . . . .
>
> What is she
>> but an ambassador
>>> from another world
> a world of pretty marigolds
>> of two shades
>>> which she announces
> not knowing what she does. . .

But in exile she remains, trapped in an exquisite pathos. With some slight modifications, William Stanley Braithwaite's assessment is applicable to all the perspectives demonstrated so far:

> . . .It was a period (in literature) when Negro life was a shuttlecock between the two extremes of humor and pathos. . . .The writers who dealt with him for the most part refused to see more than skin-deep,—the grin, the grimaces and the picturesque externalities. . . .If any of the writers of the period had possessed gifts of genius of the first caliber, they would have penetrated this deceptive exterior of Negro life, sounded the depths of tragedy in it, and produced a masterpiece.[44]

The Afrophilism of the twenties of this century involved many who possessed gifts of genius of the first caliber. It was moreover an interest in things and persons negroid and primitive that was essentially free from the pathogenic limitations of pseudo-scientific analysis. It had its own limitations, as will become evident when the period is given detailed treatment in Chapter 5. By and large, however, its penchant was inconoclastic; its interest were essentially esthetic not "anthropological" or polemical. It had minds that were apparently not seduceable by that which was exoterically picturesque. The Negro as perceived then would be intriguingly different. Montgomery Gregory in an essay of generous enthusiam quotes O'Neil:

> Eugene O'Neil, who more than any other person has dignified and popularised Negro drama, gives testimony to the possibilities of the future development of Negro drama as follows: "I believe as strongly as you do that the gifts the Negro can—and will—bring to our native drama are invaluable ones. The possibilities are limitless and to a dramatist open up new and intriguing opportunities."[45]

It was a period that promised much but brought forth in "Congo: History of the Negro Race," the orchestrated, "Boom-lay-boom-lay booms" of Vachel Linsay's art. It was a period which, in Eugene O'Neil's *Emperor Jones* also created perhaps the most magnificent parody, doubtless unintended, of *King Lear*. But perhaps O'Neil was too much of a genius for the parodic intent to be unintentional. In Act III, scene iv or *(The Heath. Before a hovel)* King Lear, to the thunder of elemental forces, disrobes his way to a profound epiphany:

> Is man no more than this? Consider him well. Thou owest the worm no silk, the beast no hide, the sheep no wool, the cat no perfume. Ha! Here's three no's are sophisticated! Thou art the thing itself; unaccommodated man is no more but such a poor, bare, forked animal as thou art. Off, off, you lendings! Come, unbutton here.
>
> *(Tears at his clothes)*

In much the same way, Emperor Jones tears at his imperial, racial and cultural lendings in search of "quintessencial" unaccommodatedness:

> Dam dis heah coat! Like a straight jacket! *(He tears off his coat and flings it from him, revealing himself stripped to the waist.)* Dere! Dat's better! Now I kin breathe! *(Looking down at his feet, the spurs catching his eye.)* And to hell wid these high fangled spurs. Dey're what's been a-tripping me up and breakin' my neck. *(He unstraps them and flings them away disgustedly.)* Dere! I gits rid o'dem frippety Emperor trappin's an' I travels lighter.
> ...*(He is well forward now where his figure can be dimly made out. His pants have been so torn away that what is left of them is no better than a breech cloth.)*

In that archetypal costume, his attendant a "Congo Witchdoctor," his storm "the insistent, revengeful, triumphant pulsations of tom-toms," Emperor Jones is metamorphosed from mongrel imperial majesty to a quaking mass of atavistic fears.[46] As Langston Hughes will laconically put it later: "It was a period when white writers wrote about Negroes more successfully (commercially speaking) than Negroes did about themselves," for "a large and enthusiastic number of people were crazy about Negroes."[47]

But in the final analysis, there is a certain joylessness in the literary response in English to the Negros. That which seems to be unholy about him is what comes readily to the mode of caricature. In this respect he is closer to the devil. He arrives in Spain, however, to be crowned buffoon.

NOTES

[1] Quoted by Carl T. Rowan, "How Racists Use 'Science to Degrade Black People," in *Ebony*, Vol. XXV, No. 7, May, 1970, pp. 31-40.

[2] *Tamburlaine*, Part 1, Act III, scene iii. In *Marlowe's Plays and Poems*, ed. by M.R. Ridley (New York: Dutton, 1963), p. 31.

[3] *The Merchant of Venice*, Act 11, scene vii. In *The Complete Works*, eds. W.G. Clark and W. Aldis Wright (New York: Nelson Doubleday, Inc., no date given), Vol. 1, p. 341.

[4] *11 Tamburlaine*, Act 1, scene iv. In *op.cit.*, p. 81. It was not only the English imagination that was so seduced. See the "turkish buffoonery" in French drama, Molière's *Le Bourgeois Gentilhomme*, for example.

[5] *Diary and Correspondence of Samuel Pepys*, 6 vols., ed. by Richard Lord Braybrooke and the Rev'd. Mynors Bright (London: Bickers and Son, 1879). The entry is in Volume Four which covers the period 1668-1669, p.46.

[6] Act III, scene i of *Sophonisba* in Vol. II of *The Plays of John Marston*, 3 vols., ed. by H. Harvey Wood (London: Oliver and Boyd, 1938). This drama of a fair Christian damsel who refuses to become the playing of a pagan potentate is thus kin to the selection quoted above in text. The speaker there is "Mighty Mullisheg, the glory of the Moores" who thus displays a catholic taste for women. See *The Dramatic Works of Thomas Heywood*, 6 vols., reissue of the 1874 edition (New York: Russell and Russell, 1964). *The Fair Maid of the West or a Girle Worth Gold* is in Vol. II, the selection on p, 313. The name of the "glory of the Moores" may not be insignificant. See discussion of Battle of Alcazar and *Titus Andronicus* following.

[7] *The Works of Thomas Middleton*, 8 vols., ed. by A.H. Bullen (Boston: Houghton, Mifflin and Company, 1886). *The Triumphs of Truth* is in Vol. VII; selection, pp. 247-49.

[8] Vol. VII, pp. 136-37 of *The Works of Francis Beaumont and John Fletcher*, 10 vols. (Cambridge, England: Cambridge English Classics, 1909).

[9] *op. cit.*, Act III, scene iii.

[10] Ravenscroft is quoted by George Lyman Kittredge in his introductory note to *Titus Andronicus*. See *The Complete Works of Shakespeare*, ed. by G.L. Kittredge (New York: Ginn and Company, 1936).

[11] *Titus Andronicus*, Act IV, scene ii,

[12] Kittredge relates this passage to one of the classical influences evident in the play, Seneca's *Thyestes*, 650 ff.

[13] *The Historie* etc (London: A. Hatfield, 1600), p. 55. See also E.M. Bovil, *The Battle of Alcazar: an account of the defeat of Don Sebastian of Portugal at El-Ksar-el-Kebir* (London: The Batchworth Press, 1952). Also Eldred Jones' comprehensive treatment of the Negro in Elizabethan literature, *Othello's Countrymen* (London: Oxford University Press, 1965).

[14] "On January 24, 1594, Henslowe's *Diary* records *Titus & Andronicus* as a new play acted by the earl of Sussex's men. On February 6th 'a Noble Roman Historye of Titus Andronicus' was entered in the Stationers'

Register by John Danter, who printed the First Quarto in the same year. The title-page professes to give the tragedy 'as it was Plaide by the. . .Earle of Darbie, Earle of Pemnroke, and Earle of Sussex their Seruants.' This identifies it with that recorded by Henslowe as 'new,' and would fix the date of composition as not later than 1593.

Kittredge, *op. cit.*

See also *The Dramatic Works of George Peele,* eds. Hook and Yorklavich (New Haven: Yale University Press, 1961) Yorklavitch's comprehensive introduction to *The Battle of Alcazar* is on pp. 218-292.

[15] The name is otherwise rendered as 'Muliteus,' Eldred Jones ,*op. cit.* p. 139, suggests textual emendation.

[16] *Titus Andronicus,* Act V, scene i.

[17] *Ibid.,* Act IV, scene ii.

[18] *Ibid.,* Act IV, scene ii.

[19] Giovanni Battista Giraldi, *Hecatommithi* (Venice: Deuchino & Gio Battista Pulciani, 1608), p. 313 ff. The evidence suggests that Shakespeare knew only the Italian original. See also Kenneth Muir, *Shakespeare's Sources* (London: Metheun and Co., Ltd., 1957); *Othello* ed. Alvin Kernan, The Signet Classic Shakespear (New York: New American Library, 1963). J.E. Taylor's 1855 translation of the Italian source will be found on pp. 171-84.

[20] *Othello,* Act i, sc. ii.

[21] W.H. Auden, "The Alienated City," *Encounter,* Vol. XVII, No. 2, August, 1961. Also Eldred Jones, *op. cit.,* p. 141.

[22] *Othello,* Act 1, sc. iii.

[23] *Blackwood's Magazine,* Vol. LXVII, 1850, p. 484. There is an element of topicality here. See Wordsworth below on Toussaint Louverture and the Haitian Revolution in the discussion of *le nègre révolté* in Chapter Five.

[24] See *The Novels of Mrs. Aphra Behn,* ed. by Earnest A. Baker (London: G. Rutledge and Son. Ltd., 1905); also, V, Sackville West's *Aphra Behn, the incomparable Astrea* (London: G. Howe Ltd., 1927).

[25] Kenneth Little, *Negroes in Britain, A study of racial relations in English Society (London: Kegan Paul, Trench, Trubner and Company, Ltd. 1947), p. 169.*

[26] *Ibid.,* p. 192.

[27] *Ibid.,* p. 192,

[28] From Prince Hoare's *Memoirs of Granville Sharp* as quoted by Little, *op. cit.,* p. 182.

[29] See The Acts of the Apostles, Chapter 8, 26-40. The conversion and baptism by Philip of "a man of Ethiopia, an eunuch of great authority under Candace, queen of the Ethiopians, who had the charge of all her treasure, and had come to Jerusalem for to worship." And so was negated the saying, can the Ethiopian change his color or the leopard his spots?

[30] Paul Baudin, *op. cit.,* p. 103.

[31]   "Well, son, I'll tell you:
Life for me ain't been so crystal stair.
It's had tacks in it.
And splinters,
And boards torn up,
And places with no carpet on the floor—

Bare.
But all the time
I'se been a-climbin' on,
And reachin' landin's
And turnin' corners,
And sometimes goin' in the dark
Where there ain't been no light.
So boy, don't you turn back. . .
Don't you fall now—
For I'se still goin', honey,
And life for me ain't been no crystal stair."

Hughes, *The Weary Bules*, p. 107.

[32] William Blake, *The Complete Writings* ed. by Geoffrey Keynes (London: Oxford University Press, 1966), p. 125. Also Freyre for description of "un menino de familia patriarcal con seu muleque, companhiero de brinquedos," *Casa Grande & Senzala*, 2 vols (Rio de Janeiro: Livraria Jose Olympio, Editora S.A., 1964). This extensive study of the Negro in Portuguese Brazil is titled *Masters and Slaves* in the English translation.

[33] William Blake, *The Complete Writings*, p. 480.

[34] William Wordsworth's "Toussaint Louverture" bears interesting comparison with Cesáire's. See Chapter Eight.

[35] Walt Whitman, *Leaves of Grass and Selected Prose*, ed. by Johb Kouwenhoven (New York: Modern Library, 1950), p. 252.

[36] Henry Wadsworth Longfellow, *The Complete Poetical Works* (Boston: Houghton-Mifflin & Co., 1922), p. 23. Anti-slavery sentiments are expressed in other poems on pp. 24-27.

[37] The attractiveness of the candidacy of the Indian may be gauged by the fact that even Voltaire was seduced. See the story "L'Huron."

[38] William Makepeace Thackeray, *Vanity Fair, A Novel Without a Hero*, introduction by Whitelaw Reid (New York: E.P. Dutton and Co., 1930), p. 193.

[39] Herman Melville, *Moby Dick*, Modern Library, (New York: Random House, 1950), p. 221. See Ramon del Valle-Inclan and Victor Hugo in Chapters Four and Five. But Melville is remarkably catholic in his Negroes. There is Fleece, the cook, who is a dialect-speaking buffoon. Pip, the cabin boy, becomes a gargoyle-like oracle and of course there is Daggoo, the Noble Savage.

[40] Carl T. Rowan, *op. cit.*, quotes from one of the post-Civil War, "best-selling novels" of "Tarheel preacher, The Reverend Doctor Thomas Dixon, Jr." For an involved, ingenious disquisition on racial identity and racial blood, see Chapter Four, note 22.

[41] Joseph Conrad, *Heart of Darkness* in *Three Short Novels*, with an introduction by Edward Weeks (New York: Bantam Books, 1963), pp. 39-41.

[42] Since neither God nor Plato could be presumed to have made mistakes in not declaratively assigning the Negro a place in a scientific manner worthy of the age inspired revelation was needed. The reference to Ourang-Outangs, apes, etc. was the key. The inanimate (stones, etc.) was trying to become animate (plants etc); obeying the same neo-platonic-divine compulsion plants strove to become animals to the level of apes and the like. It follows then that Ourang-Outang husbands wanted "black Hottentot Venuses." And in that drive toward the pinnacle of evolutionary perfection Othello would compulsively lust after the fair maid of the West, Desdemona. An

extraordinary, parodic chapter this to Lovejoy's *The Great Chain of Being.* This comedy of malice and more is what is played out in John Campbell's *Negro-Mania.*

[43] John Campbell, ed., *Negro-Mania* (Philadelphia: Campbell and Power, 1851), p. 104. In the second selection, Brabantio's ignorant superstition is replaced by Calvinistic, scientific dogma. All in all this seems a curious expense of energy in the banality of evil.

[44] William Stanley Braithwaite, "The Negro in American Literature" in *The New Negro*, ed. Alaine Locke, with a new preface by Robert Hayden (New York: Atheneum, 1969), p. 31.

[45] "The Drama of Negro Life" in *The New Negro*, p. 153.

[46] *Emperor Jones* in *Selected Plays of Eugene O'neil* (New York: Random House, no date), pp. 23-24.

[47] From Langston Hughes' *The Big Sea.* See Chapter Six.

CHAPTER 4

THE SPANISH METAPHOR

En la poesía negra, para ser auténtica habían de entrar los cuatros
principales elementos del alma negra: la desbordante alegría dionisíaca;
la sensualidad, el vago temblor de misterio, y el ritmo congénito de la
raza.[1]

Rodriquez-Embil makes "ethnological" and "anthropological" neces-
sities – and virtues – out of reductions and stereotypes. What is left
unassessed, and thus presumed inviolate, is the moral and historical
justification for the postulated attributes which identify the *alma negra*.
The issue here is to determine whether a proper human presence is
suggested in the evaluation or whether we have exotic and erotic
simplifications. To what extent then is that perception representative of the
Negro? To what extent is it an extended series of metaphors that define a
pathological condition? What degree of blindness, esthetic, moral and
psychological, is evident in this categorical attribution of *alegría,
sensualidad, misterio* and *ritmo congénito* to the Negro race? Even if these
qualities were congenital to the race, to what extent are they quintessence
or mutation? Does the perspective above suggest the possibility of
evolutionary development or does it imply a permanent identity? The
apologist and incompetent posture adopted by Rodriquez-Embil is one that
not infrequently leads to dithyrambic exaggerations, even in a Federico
García Lorca:

> El negro que está tan cerca de la naturaleza. ¡Ese negro que se saca la
> música hasta de los bolsillos! *Fuera del arte negro no queda en los
> Estados Unidos más que mecánico y automatismo....*Cuando canta un
> negro en un teatro se hace un "silencio negro," un silencio cóncavo,
> enorme y especial. (my emphasis)[2]

These perceptions are representative of the tradition which made of the
Negro a buffoon-Orpheus. It was a perception which, in all polished
sincerity, believed that the Negro "with his gay ha-ha! had turned the

round horizon into one star-belled tambourine." It would not be an exclusively Spanish or Hispanic point of view, but it would be the dominant one in that tradition. *Negro, tambor* (drum), and "gay ha-ha's" would be inseparable. The Negro would dance his way through his hispanic caricature because, as Cervantes notes, "tal es la inclinación que los negros tienen a ser músicos." The literature will be assessed in roughly corresponding periods as in the previous chapter.

The ambivalent usage of the terms "Moor" and "Negro," which played an important role in the apprehension of the Negro in England is missing in Spanish literature. And for very evident historical reasons. There was Moorish infusion in Spain of a far more pervasive and organic nature than anywhere else in Europe. There was therefore little of the exotic irrelevancies in the Spanish perception of the Moor, which are evident in Elizabethan England's. There was no necessity to invent synthetic Moorish customs or baroquely loud Moors. One went instead to Sevilla, to Córdoba; one listened for the arabic or North Africanisms in the social and everyday realities of words like "alcalde," "alhambra," or "azucar." Physiognomically different and culturally inarticulate when he appeared, the Negro was identifiably different from what had by the middle ages become a Moorish-Jewish-Spanish culture.

It is uncertain when the Negro of the Equatorial Forest-Atlantic axis first came to Spain. Contact between the Barbary coast and Iberian peninsula was evidently quite early and quite frequent. By 1573, Juan Latino, Ethiopian slave once owned by the Duke of Sessa, was sufficiently established as Professor of Latin at the University of Granada. We find Cervantes making a casual reference to him in one of the prefatory verses to the *Don Quijote*. The particular preface, the one addressed to Urganda, is written in the truncated verses, *de cabo roto*, of Alonso Alvarez de Soria. (This is to explain the apocopes.)

> Pues al cielo no le plu —,
> Que salieses tan la di —
> Como el negro, Juan Lati —,
> Hablar latines rehu —.[3]

But the fact that he was Ethiopian is significant. Ethiopia does not fall into the configuration I described earlier. It was instead, frequently used to glamorize the Negro. Thus the Ethiopian background may have been of more than incidental significance in explaining Juan Latino. For the pure Negro, the *bembon* or the *bozal*, to arrive in Spain contact had to be established with the axis south of the Sudanese configurations of the middle ages. Basil Davidson's studies, *inter alia*, indicate that the flurry of Moorish-Arabic activity in Egypt and the Sudan was actually part of the expansionist move that involved the Iberian peninsula. Gold, salt, leather goods and arabic manuscripts had formed the basis of the lively trans-Saharan, trans-Mediterranean activity which Leo Africanus so effectively records. Slave raids and other intrusive contacts had obviously taken place with areas of the Equatorial configuration. It is not unlikely that there were indeed some "hosts of coal-black Moors" in the armies that fought or invaded southern Europe. These activities probably account for contacts between the Iberian peninsula and the Negro earlier than the voyages of the fourteenth-fifteenth centuries. By 1067, the Andalusian writer al-Bakri knew of Sudanese Ghana as a large and powerful empire.[4]

When the Negro appeared in Spain he was called by a variety of names. *Negro* would be a generic term, but the *negro* most useful in literary representations was the *bozal* – a *negro* born in Africa, who spoke, somewhat laughably, in *disfraces negros*, that is, in dislocated Spanish. Another was the *bembón*, a *negro* with pronounced negroid features. He was in a sense, the "black-skinned, blubber-lipped, flat-nosed" *negro* described by Beckford in his sketches of the Iberian and Italian peninsulas.[5] In passing, it would be relevant here to mention two examples of portrayals that are not as insistently aesthetic as the dominant trend is in this Hispanic tradition. There is a somewhat ambivalent perspective in *Lazarillo de Tornes* (1544), where Zayde is described as *un hombre moreno;* but the offspring of this *moreno* and Lazarillo's mother, who is white, is referred to as *un negrito*. A didactic observation made by Lazarillo a few pages later soon explains the implications of *negrito* as used. The *negrito* runs away in fear from Lazarillo's stepfather, Zayde, who is *moreno*, crying, "Madre coco." Lazarillo then observes:

> ¡Cuántos debe de haber en el mundo que huyen de otros, porque no se ven a si mismo! [6]

The intent then is to draw a moral conclusion using color as the vehicle. A somewhat more melodramatic expression of this perspective can be found in the succinct "negros suzios que en verlos es asco e abominación" of the Arcipreste de Talavera's *El Corbacho*. But these two illustrations represent deviations from the pattern of caricature in the Hispanic tradition. This tradition will now be examined in two sequences – the peninsular and the New World manifestations. In many ways, the perception of the New World, particuarly the tropicalism of the Caribbean, affected the manner in which the Negro was apprehended.

In the discussion of the Negro in English literature a striking feature is the absence of a Negro voice. I mentioned this in relation to *Othello*. Othello does not speak an identifiable Negro English. Aaron's frequent rhetorical bombast is far from the pathetic uncertainties of a "broken tongue." This absence prevented the early exploitation of a significant element that one finds in Spanish literature. It was this ever-present feature which helped to identify the caricatured Negro immediately. In Spain, the Negro entered with his racial peculiarities and with his music. He also entered speaking:

> El culazon me cosquiya,
> quitaliyo, ¡oh, cómo suena!
> No ce que liabo ce tiene
> este modo de instulmenta
> como le tengo infición
> y tora el arma me yeva.

The song is from Luis Quiñones de Benavente's play more than appropriately titled *El Negrito Hablador (The Talkative Nigger)*.[7]   As should be obvious, this caricature Negro voice allowed for several levels of parody. First, there is the visible, physiognomical oddity, then the quality of the song and finally the precariously dislocated Spanish in which the voice sings. The linguistic caricature here may be due to the more vital reasons than might initially be assumed. The most obvious factor was, of course, an illiterate exposure to Spanish. This would lead to phonetic and syntactic distortion in any case. What gave the *bozal's* distortion its peculiar features are perhaps linguistic and artistic interferences from his origins. The Spanish caricaturist developed a fine ear for the consequences of that interference and of oral transmission in the *bozal's disfraces negros*. I have already discussed some relevant features of African tribal expressions. The evidence from the caricaturist suggests that the subculture which the *bozal* or *bembón* created in Spain showed its ancestry. When he expressed himself in song there were still the ever-present repetitions of sound patterns. In the original, these sounds obeyed tonal subtleties and the demands of an organic human vision. This kind of elevating dynamism was, not unexpectedly, absent in his Spanish. The nature of his introduction to the language and the repertoire of his experiences in it did not have the wherewithal for a decorous or elegant expression of his *alma negra*. At any rate, the percussive repetitions were seized upon in practically all literary portrayals where the Negro sang — and he was invariably shown singing. These lexically meaningless negroid percussions, *"jitanjáforas,"* as they will later be called, became indispensable adjuncts in one-dimensional representations of the Negro.[8] The net result was the emptyheaded but melancholic percussiveness of the *bembon*, or Orphic buffoon.

In Lope de Vega's *El Capellan de la Virgen* the buffoonery is due essentially to the *disfraces negros* which are used in a nonsense song. There are elements of self-mockery since "el hocico neglo de vosa mese" may be translated "the nigger snout of your lordship." This is then the nature of the song that entertains the "beautiful washerwomen of the Sagra:"

> Entrandose las hermosas
> labradoras de la Sagra,
> ellos, con disfraces negros,
> este villancico danzan:

> El hocico de vosa mesé
> he, he, he,
> me tiene periro
> de amore venciro
> ay, ay, he, ay, ay
> que me moriré. que me moriré.
> he, he, he. . . .[9]

The same buffoonery is seen in Simon Aguado, a contemporary of Shakespeare. He describes a Negro wedding using a *bembon's* voice. The *jitanjáfora* sequence is rather interesting here as it provides an extension of the meaning of the term. A legitimate word, such as "Tu" (you), could be so used as to deprive it of any meaning. The sequence in Anton's second line, whether voluntarily or not, has all the coherence of a *tonto*, an idiot. The selection is from *Entremes de los negros* (1602):

> Todos: A la boda de Gasipar
> y Dominga de Tumbuctu
> turo habemos de bailar
> toca negro

> Anton: Toca tú:
> tu, pu tu, pu tu tu, pu tu tu. . . .[10]

It is unlikely that Gasipar and Dominga were really from "Tumbuctu." The designation is, however, logically conventional in this tradition. Timbuktu, insofar as it was the center of the Sudanese configurations, had been most accessible to North Africa. To say this is to say that it was also accessible to the Iberian peninusla. In another sense, the tambor-like resonance of the word must have been irresistibly attractive to the mode of caricature. There is nonetheless, a tolerant mockery in these representations. One might almost say benign, were it possible for an essentially malignant historical process to be so described.

When Quevedo's voice intrudes into this world he sounds a jarringly discordant note. To me, this is not so much because he departs from caricature, but rather because the amount of brilliant energy expended on his caricature makes his mockery startingly deliberate and calculated. In the larger context of Quevedo's works this is not surprising. Quevedo's disgust was always deliberate, calculating and brilliantly ferocious in its expression. The thirteen-stanza poem in which he describes a Negro wedding is a *conceptista tour-de-force.* If there is a degree of "democratic" participation in the Negro's life suggested by the attitude in Aguado, Benavente or Cervantes, it is there because to the artists the Negro is little more than a literary toy. In Quevedo, the tone is uncompromisingly aristocratic in the distance it maintains from the *bembón* or *bozal*. This distance isolates the *bozal* in the much larger context of Spanish-Western culture. He is thus shown to be parodically antithetical to the very means by which he now defines himself. The caricature does not therefore result from the crude unsubtleties employed by other artists. The poem is really a series of conceits sustained by the incongruous and parodic denotations and connotations which Quevedo can generate by a thirteen-stanza punning look at the *negro*. I offer again the first and last stanzas:

> Ví, debe de haber tres días,
> en las gradas de San Pedro,
> una tenebrosa boda,
> porque era toda de negros
> . . . .
> Parecía matrimonio
> concertado en el infierno
> negro esposo y negra esposa
> y negro accompañamiento.

The contrastive, therefore inevitably reductive, juxtapositions are numerous in the poem as a whole. In the stanzas quoted there is the incongruity of the Church of San Pedro and Hell linked now by the Negro's blackness. The holy (white) sacrament of matrimony is implicitly transformed into a black mass. Poetic virtuosity and satiric conceits fuse here in a drama of the incongruous.

But if Shakespeare summarizes for me the English medieval-renaissance perspective, perhaps Góngora's Negroes in his *Romances y Letrillas* represent the most consistent illustration of peninsular caricature. It is quite evident that Gongora's Negroes are either *bozal* or *bembón*. The poems in which they appear invariably take the same forms. Two Negroes, generally female, are shown in conversation on Holy Days. The speech is in *disfraces negros*; the *jitanjáforas* are always present and somewhat more primitive, that is, the rhythmic sounds are distinctly more non-European. In general, there is a greater degree of precariousness in the dislocated Spanish. It seems to me that nowhere else is the sense of melancholic non-humanness more evident than in these vignettes of simple-minded, barely articulate, Orphic worship. There is something of Quevedo even here. These female *bembón* are incongruous, slightly parodic media through which to apprehend the Sacraments of Roman Catholicism. In the first example, Mangalena (Magdalena) and an unnamed *bembón* "contemplate" Christmas Day in "Al Nacimiento de Cristo Señor:"

> 1. — ¡Oh, qué vimo, Mangalena!
>   ¡oh, qué vimo!
> 2. — ¿Dónde, primo?
> 1. — No pórtalo de belena. . .
> 2. — Vamo aya.
> 1. — Toca instrumento
> 2. — Elamu, calambú, cambu
>   elamu. . . .[12]

As usual, the vignette is resolved in the *jitanjáfora* sequence at the end. In "En la Fiesta del Santísimo Sacramento," Juana and Craca (Clara), two *morenicas de Congo* prepare for Corpus Cristi:

Juana:	Mañana sa Corpus Crista
	mana Crara.
	alcoholemo la cara
	e lavemono la vista.
Clara:	Ay, Jesu, como sa mu trista.
Juana:	¿Que tiene, pringa señora?
Clara:	Samo negra pecandora
	e branca la Sacramenta.
Juana:	. . .Pengamo fustana
	e bailamo alegra,
	que aunque samo negra,
	se hermosa tú.
	Zambambú, morenica de Congo,
	zambambú. . .[13]

"We is black sinner/ an' de Sacrament is white. . .but let's dance happy/no matter how black we is, Zambambú, black Congo gal, zambambu. . . . " There is a pecular, melancholic vulnerability to the Negro as he is caricatured here. He is neither romantic, exotic nor evil. The representation has the pathos of the inarticulate and the simple-mindedly incongruous. Vitality or *altisonancia* (loudness) will be the distinguishing attributes when he appears next in Hispanic literature as either a magnificently sensuous beast or a bongo-beating Orpheus.

Spain, like England and France, was economically and politically involved in the New World. Consolidation and exploitation of the benefits of the discoveries of the renaissance would be dominant concerns during the seventeenth through nineteenth centuries. In the pursuit of these concerns, Spain would transport and exile the African throughout the Caribbean and the length and breadth of South America. The African thus exiled would be different from his peninsular counterpart as he appears in literature. I shall concentrate on the Caribbean, in particular Cuba, since Cuban *Ñañiguismo* will play an important role when Nicolás Guillén is assessed in Part III of this study. The New World Negro re-emerged in Hispanic representations infused with a surprising amount, indeed an excess, of energies. A large measure of vitality was fused into Gasipar and Dominga of Tumbuctu. The Negro was still one-dimensionally apprehended, but to that simplicity was added the exotic and the erotic. There are several reasons for the change.

For one thing, the conjunction of the peninsular imagination with the luxuriant tropicalism of the Americas generated a dynamism all its own. The Spanish in the New World and the *criollo* (Spaniard born in the Americas), became "inebriate of air" to a degree that out-Dickinsoned Miss Emily Dickinson. Otto Oliviera puts it effectively when he says:

> Se canta a la naturaleza por su feracidad y por sus frutos, y el canto reluce con el inevitable cromatismo que en toda esa naturaleza había.[14]

The inebriation would involve flora and fauna and the elemental forces that formed the exuberant quintessence of a tropical "delicioso Eden. . . . " The "debauchee" of tropicalism, where "prodiga/madre naturaleza en abundancia/la odorifera planta fumigable!" was not given to stinginess in his outpourings:

> ¡Oh, Cuba dulce, perla abrillantada,
> tierra del sol, Edén resplandaceiente!
> ¿Quién más bella que tú? ¡Mundo, responde!

Un sol más esplendente.
una atmósfera azul más despejada
no existe bajo el cielo
del Sur al Norte.

So writes Joaquín Lorenzo Luaces in his "Ultimo Amor."[15] This kind of exclamatory celebration substituted a passion for the brilliant heaviness of a fertile tropicalism for the dark, melancholic contemplations of Northern pastoralism. Nature was here pregnant with an exotically rich flora: "cargada de melui y tabaco/mameyes, piñas, tunas y aguacetes/plátanos y mamones y tomates." These "gastronomic excitements" would lead to that "sublimaciòn estética" which Jorge Mañach has, with appreciative ambivalence, called "el frutismo," fruitism. A prime example of this can be seen in the extended stanzas of "Las Frutas de Cuba" in which Antonio López Prieto undertook to celebrate the fruits of Cuba in stanza after stanza:

Más suave que la pera
en Cuba es la gratísima guayaba
. . . .
El marañon fragante,
más grato que la guinda si madura,
el color rozagante
¡oh, Adonis! , en lo pálido figura;
arbol, ¡oh, maravilla! ,
que echa el fruto despues de la semilla.[16]

The history of the New World was also Indian. To that extent the Muse was not invited to "lap. . .soft in Lydian airs/married to immortal verse." The poet pleaded, instead,

Contadme leyendas
de amor y contiendas
del indio de Jagua, Magón, Jiguaní,
Marien, Guamuhaya,
Bayamo, Guaimaya,
Cueibá, Marcorijes, Jiguabo y Baní.[17]

Thrillingly unpronounceable names became the basis for banal, incantatory stanzas such as we find in Francisco Pobeda:

Jaimquí, Yacuage, Guara,
Yuraguano, Jata, Tea,
Vijaguara, Cuanají,

Yamagua, carne doncella,
Hayabacana, Daguilla,
Siguaraya, Raspa lengua,
Pitajoni, Camaguá,
Júcaro, Arraigan y Ceibas[18]

To a temperament given to *"tremendismo,"* that is, to hyper-injections of energies, a sensitivity to the tropicalism described above is hardly surprising. We turn to Raman del Valle-Inclán's *Sonatas: Memorias del Marqués de Bradomin* for the best illustration of the Negro as portrayed by this excitement. His *Sonata de Estío* is vividly exotic:

¡Cuán bellos se me aparecen esos lejanos países
tropicales! ¡Quien una vez los ha visto, no los
olvidará jamas! . . . .Por mi memoria desfilan las
torres de Veracruz, los bosques de Campeche, las
arenas de Yucatán, los palacios de Palenque, las
palmeras de Tuxtlan y Laguna. . . .[19]

The apprehension of the jungles never quite matches the dionysiac intensities of Conrad. In Valle-Inclán it is slightly dionysiac but essentially decadent and vibrantly sensual:

El horizonte relampagueaba. Un vago olor marino, olor de algas y
brea, mezclábase por veces al mareante de la campina, y alla muy
lejos, en el fondo oscuro del oriente, se divisaba el resplandor rojizo
de la selva que ardía. La naturaleza, lujuriosa y salvaje, aún palpitante
del calor de la tarde, semejaba dormir el sueño profundo y jadeante de
una fiera fecundada.[20]

It is therefore hardly surprising that when Gasipar of Tumbuktu is treated he should become a conglomerate of energies in harmony with the surroundings:

Un negro colossal, con el traje de tela chorreando agua, se sacude
como un gorila en medio del corro que a su rededor han formado los
pasajeros, y sonríe mostrando sus blancos dientes de animal
familiar. . . .El negrazo musita apretando los labios elefánticos.[21]

The *bembón* has become a sensuously animalistic colossos.

If Gasipar undergoes a transformation, so does his female counterpart, Dominga. Part of the reason for the transformation of Dominga lies in the implications of the more organic syncretism between Negro and Criollo. To cover the degrees of social, political and biological union between them, finer distinctions became necessary. In addition to *bozal* and *bembón*, according to the degree of white blood in the Negro, he was called *mulato, tercerón, cuaterón, quinterón.* Sometimes with punctilious particularity he was called *tente-en-el-aire,* a faint-stain-in-the-air; sometimes with abrupt unkindness he was a *salto-atras,* a jump-backward.[22] Since the act of miscegenation frequently meant Dominga's involvement with the Criollo (as against Gasipar and the *criolla*), the Negress became a sexually exciting and a-moral creature. There would never be any moral concern expressed about the presumed erotic energy that emanates from her. After all, "it is much that the Moor should be more than reason: but if she be less than an honest woman, she is indeed more than I took her for." The libidinous quality in her is innate, inherent and to be enjoyed. Not even an expression of concern and sympathy can dull the erotic invitations generated by decadent, languid Negresses:

> Mujeres de tez cobriza y mirar dulce salían a los umbrales, e indiferentes y silenciosas nos veían pasar. La actitud de aquellas figuras broncineas revelaba esa tristeza transmitida, vetusta, de las razas vencidas. Su rostro era humilde, con dientes muy blancos y grandes ojos negros, selváticos, idolentes y velados. Parecían nacidas para vivir eternamente en los aduares y descansar al pie de las palmeras y de los ahuehuetes.[23]

The most uncompromising dedication to these attributes of the Negro either as Negress or as *mulata* is best seen in the unapologetic dithyrambs celebrating her written by the peninsular, Asturian Alfonso Camín and the Caribbean Francisco Muñoz del Monte. Camín's Negress in his "Elogia de la Negra" is a splendid creature, a "Negra, carbon celeste, carne de tamarindo." What follows in the poem is a series of passionate extravaganzas inspired by her "airosa falda," her breezy skirt:

> Negra, vigor mellizo de una raza
> hecha de miel, de lujuría. . .
>   Negra estupenda
> que te me diste como negra ofrenda
> Negra de labios gruesos y sensuales
> los ojos, amplias noches misteriosas. . . .[24]

Negress — languid energy of a race made of honey, of sensual yearnings. Negress — stupendous Negress, with thick sensual lips; your eyes, black mysterious nights. This intoxication, difficult as it may be to imagine, is matched and surpassed by the audacious passions of Muñoz del Monte's poem. It is quietly but dramatically titled "La mulata." The poem bears extensive reproduction:

¡Mulata! ¿Será tu nombre
injuria, oprobio o refrán?
¡no sé! Sólo sé que al hombre
tu nombre es un talismán. . .
. . . .
Ser mulata es ser candela,
ser mulata es imitar
en el mirar la gacela,
la leona en el amar.
Copa que embelesa y mata
si se liba hasta la hez.
Su almo encanto la mulata,
¿lo debo acaso a su tez?
. . . .
Elástico culebra, hambrienta boa,
la mulata a su víctima sujeta,
lo oprime, estrecha, estruja, enreda, aprieta,
y chupa, y lame, y muerde en su furor.
. . . .
Y crujen sus elásticas caderas,
y tocados de inmenso magnetismo,
cada ojo revela un hondo abismo,
de apetito, de rabia y de pasión.
Y su delgada y mórbida cintura
agitada de internas convulsiones,
en mil secretas circunvolunciones
se fuerce cual reptil que nos va a herir.[25]

As Otto Olivera summarizes it, "esta composición presenta el primitivismo emocional y la proverbial sensualidad de la mujer mestiza con una osadía poco frecuente. No cabe duda que en los versos de Muñoz del Monte está la más franca interpretación poética escrita en aquella epoca (1845) sobre un tipo colonial." But all this erotic extravaganza is little more than a polished version of the cruder "Captain want jig jig" succinctness in Graham Greene. And Rodriguez-Embil's apologia for the *alma negra* with its *alegría dionisiaca*, its *sensualidad*, etc., is little more than a glorification of a simplistic cliche. Small wonder that Regino Pedroso, Cuban and Negro, is moved to the indignation of asking "¿No somos más que rumba, lujurías y comparasas? "[26]

But there was also a tradition in which Gasipar and Dominga were more clearly recognizable as in their peninsular representations. Here too there was the same kind of energization I mentioned earlier. The *jitanjáforas* become more elaborate; the rhythms are extremely decorative and *altisonante*. The buffoonery is peculiarly gratuitous, even arbitrary in that the degree of craftsmanship expended on the architecture of the caricature invariably calls attention to itself rather than to the Negro *per se*. The only difficulty for Negro poets like Regino Pedroso was that the Negro was rendered highly visible thereby and rather excellently insulted in the effectiveness of the artistry.

The most illustrative architect is the Puerto Rican poet, Luis Pales Matos. In Matos' "Danza Negra" the "cro-cro-cro/pru-pru-pru" is a picturesque, tolerant, onomatopoeic mockery that syncopates the Negro's engaging mindlessness. It is picturesque primitiveness that characterizes the *raza negra* in "tierras rojas, islas de betún/Haití, Martinica, Congo, Camerún" and of course "en Tombuctu:"

> Calabó y bambú.
> Bambú y calabó.
> El Gran Cocoroco dice: tu-cu-tu.
> La Gran Cocoroca dice: to-to-to.
> Es el sol de hierro que arde en Tombuctú.
> Es la danza negra de Fernando Póo.
> El cerdo en el fango gruñe: pru-pru-pru.
> El sapo en la charca sueña: cro-cro-cro.
> Calabó y bambú
> Bambú y calabó.

As indicated before, the *jitanjáfora* sequences are more elaborate. Indeed, they may rightly be called onomatopoeic conceits. *Calabó* and *Cocoroco* besides their obvious rhythmic values are proper nouns, meaning "drum" and "supreme chief" respectively. The decorative elaboration continues as Matos builds *jitanjáfora* orchestrations to accompany the primitive dance. *Junjunes, gongos, botucos* below are, respectively, a kind of African violin, a variety of drums, and a group of lesser ranking chiefs.

> Rompen los junjunes en furiosa ú
> Los gongos trepidan con profunda ó
> Es la raza negra que ondulande va
> en el ritmo gordo de mariyandá
> Llegan los botucos a la fiesta ya.
> Danza que te danza la negra se da.

All these percussive revelries to the accompaniment of drums, African violins, the croaking of frogs and the grunting of pigs are the celebrative vibrations of the *alma africana* from Haiti to "Tombuctu."

> Es es sol que arde en Tombuctú.

Es la danza negra de Fernando Póo.
Es el alma africana que vibrando está
en el ritmo gordo de mariyandá.[27]

For this decorative, one-dimensional expending of energy, Pales Matos
has been described by Anderson Imbert as one of the most original poets of
the modern era. This generous assessment may be true to the extent that
Arturo Torres-Rioseco summarizes hispanic Negro poetry: "Negro poetry
abandons the syllabic principle of Spanish versification; musical effects are
based entirely on rhythm, and enhanced by alliteration, parallelism,
onomatopoeia, internal rhyme, endless repetition of vowel sounds, and even
instrumental devices."[28] If we accept this as entirely satisfactory in its
narrow formalist approach then Luis Pales Matos deserves the generosity of
Anderson Imbert. I choose, however, to see him as a resurrector of clichés
and an orchestrator of elaborate and exotic jingles. His inspiration and
justification is chiefly to be found in the Afrophilism of the Twenties, in so
far as the Afrophilism engaged exotically-inclined dilettantes.[29]

As in the case of the previous perception of the Negro (a la
Valle-Inclán), even when sympathy is expressed for the Negro it is not
separated from the reductive point of departure. The Uruguayan poet,
Ildefonso Pereda Valdes, recognizes the pain in what has been insistently
seen as merely decorative *joie-de-vivre* But his otherwise sensitive "La
Guitarra de los Negros" apparently finds the *Orfeo bongosero*, the
bongo-beating Orpheus, irresistible:

Los negros lloran cantando
añoranzas del candombé.
Suena el tambor de sus amas
            con un ruido seco y sordo.
            Y un borocoto lejano
            los despierta de sus sueños.

            ¡Dos negros con dos guitarras
tocan y cantan llorando! [30]

There remains to be mentioned what in my opinion is the most
powerful and literate expression to come out of the Hispanic tradition
inspired by the Negro. I refer to Federico García Lorca's poems devoted to
the Negro during his stay in the United States in the Thirties. The date and
place are not insignificant. They escape the thematic parochialism in which
the tradition had been content to remain. The place, Harlem, is the Harlem

after the negrophilism of the twenties had been exhausted by the stock market crash. The Negro is seen and treated now in the context of a European civilization not so much narcotizing itself in the slack nihilism of post World War I disenchantment, as hypnotically contemplating the "goose-stepping" insanity of Hitler. By "September 1st, 1939," W.H. Auden would describe a world on which "death looked gigantically down" (Poe):

> I sit in one of the dives
> On Fifty-Second Street
> Uncertain and afraid
> As the clever hopes expire
> Of a low dishonest decade:
> Waves of anger and fear
> Circulate over the bright
> And darkened lands of the earth,
> Obsessing our private lives;
> The unmentionable odour of death
> Offends the September night.[31]

The poems by García Lorca, "Norma y Paraíso de los Negros," "Inglesia Abandonada, Balada de la Gran Guerra," and the extraordinary "El Rey de Harlem" need to be understood against this background. They are all a part of the polyphonic, surrealist excitement with which *Négritude* responded to the "opulent pause" before World War II. There is in the last stanza of "El Rey de Harlem," a brilliant orchestration of surrealist, apocalyptic visions. In a sense, even though the Negro is highly visible in the poem, he is primarily used as a charged medium through which "waves of anger and fear" are expressed about "un gentío de trajes sin cabezas," about a headless race of people. A more literate expression of a surrealistic *danse macabre* would be difficult to imagine. This poem stands with Leopold Sédar Senghor's "A New York (pour un orchestra de jazz: solo de trompette)" as two of the finest artistic monuments about Harlem:

> Entonces, negros, entonces, entonces,
> podreís besar con frenesí has ruedas de las bicicletas
> poner parejas de microscopios en las cuevas de las ardillas
> y danzar al fin, sin duda, mientras las flores erizadas
> asesinan a nuestro Moíses casi en los juncos del cielo.
>
> ¡Ay, Harlem, disfrazada!
> ¡Ay, Harlem, amenazada por un gentío de trajes sin cabezas!
> Me llega tu rumor,
> me llega tu rumor atravesando troncos y ascensores,

a través de laminas grises
donde flotan tus automoviles cubiertos de dientes,
a través de los caballos muertos y los crímenes diminutos,
a través de tu gran rey desesperado
cuyvas barbas llegan al mar.[32]

We shall see in the next chapter the movement toward this expression. The disillusionment that preceded World War I, the discordant search for alternatives and the inevitable death march toward World War II — all these led to the angry conviction that "l'ère de métamorphose est ouverte." They helped push the Negro as a medium for reflecting upon the blond blood of Europe spilt on pavements, "Le sang blond des pavés." Interest would then be focused on the rhythms of jazz, the erotic and exotic enchantment of the trumpets of Harlem and the "non-cartesian" mysteries of Haiti and Africa.

NOTES

[1] From a speech given by Luis Rodriquez-Embil at the University of Chile in 1939. Subsequently published as *La Poesía Negra en Cuba* by the University of Chile under the auspices of the Instituto Chileno-Cubano de Cultura, p. 13.

[2] In Ramón Guirao ed., *Orbita de la Poesía Afrocubana* (La Habana: Ugar, García y Cia., 1938). p. xxi.

[3] Miguel Saavedra de Cervantes, *Don Quijote de la Mancha (Madrid: Ediciones Castilla, no date), p. 13. Also:*

> "...*Juan Latino, the best Latinist of Spain in the reign of Philip V*, incumbent of the chair of Poetry at the University of Granada, and author of Poems printed there in 1573 and a book on the Escurial published in 1576."

— Arthur A. Schomburg, "The Negro Digs Up His Past" in *The New Negro*, ed. Alain Locke, pp. 231-244.

For language and culture discussion above see good summary approach in J.B. Trend, *The Language and History of Spain* (London: Hutchinson House, 1953).

[4] Basil Davidson, *Africa: History of a Continent* (New York: Macmillan, 1966). See Chapters Three and Five in particular.

[5] The Spanish word "bembón" means "lips," but differs from *labio* in that it is derogatory.

[6] *Lazarillo de Tormes*, Anonymous, in *Antología General de la Literatura Española*, Vol. 1, ed. by Angel del Rio and Amelia de del Rio (New York: Holt, Rinehart and Winston, 1960).

[7] Luis Quiñones de Benavente, *Entremeses*, 2 vols., ed. by Don Cayetano Rosell (Madrid: Libros de Antano, 1874). *El Negrito Hablador* is in Vol. II. For selection see p. 31.

[8] The word was coined independently of hispanic negro poetry by Alfonso Reyes in his discussion of the poetry of Mariano Brull. It has since been most frequently used in discussions of Negro expression. The word is of uncertain origin though it shares or appears to share a common root with "jitar" – to vomit.

[9] Anthologized in Emilio Ballagas, *Mapa de la Poesía Negra Americana* (Buenos Aires: Editorial Pleamar, 1946), pp. 277-278.

[10] *Ibid.*, p. 279.

[11] *Conceptismo* and its esthetic manifestations parallel the conceits and juggling wit of Metaphysical artistry in English literature of the seventeenth century.

[12] Don Luis de Góngora, *Obras Poéticas*, 2 vols. (New York: The Hispanic Society of America, no date). See Volume Two.

[13] *Ibid.*

[14] Otto Olivera, *Cuba en su Poesía* (Mexico: Ediciones de Andrea, 1965), p. 76.

[15] Joaquín Lorenzo Luaces, *Poesías* (La Habana: La Moderna Poesía, 1909), p. 123

[16] Antonia López Prieto, *Parnaso Cubana* (La Habana: Miguel de Villa, 1881), pp. 21-22. Compare the Caribbean, tropical nostalgia of Claude McKay in the "Tropics in New York," in *The New Negro*, p. 135:

> "Bananas ripe and green, and ginger root,
> Cocoa in pods and alligator pears,
> And tangerines and mangoes and grape fruit,
> Fit for the highest prize at parish fairs.
>
> Set in the window, bringing memories
> Of fruit-trees laden by low-singing rills,
> And dewy dawns, and mystical blue skies
> In benediction over nun-like hills.
>
> My eyes grew dim, and I could no more gaze;
> A wave of longing through my body swept,
> And, hungry for the old familiar ways,
> I turned aside and bowed my head and wept."

[17] José Fornaris, "Nuevos cantos del siboney" in *La Floresta Cubana* (La Habana, 1856), p. 105.

[18] Francisco Pobeda, *Poesías* (Sagua La Grande: Imprenta de Antonio M. Alcover, 1863), p. 899. For a discussion of the influence of African words see "Nicolas Guillén and Afro-cubanism," Chapter Seven. The exotic words in *Ñañiguismo* (of African origins) worked more or less the same enchantment.

[19] *Ramon del Valle-Inclán, Sonatas: Memorias del Marqúes de Bradomin* (Mexico D. F.: Populibros "La Prensa," 1959), p. 130.

[20] *Ibid.*, p. 87.

[21] *Ibid.*, p. 94.

[22] Actually, in typical nineteenth-century fashion, there was a complicated

reasoning behind these designations. See the explanation of the word *"griffe"* from Victor Hugo's *Bug-Jargal* in *Oeuvres Romanesques Complètes*, ed. by Francis Bouvet (Paris: Jean-Jacques Prevert, 1962). pp. 119-20:

"Une explication précise sera peut-être necessaire à l'intelligence de ce mot.

M. Moreau de Saint-Méry, en dévellopant le système de Franklin, a classe des espèces génériques les différentes teintes que présentent les mélanges de la population de couleur.

Il suppose que l'homme forme un toute de cent vingt-huit parties, blanches chez les blancs, et noirs chez les noirs.

Partant de ce principe, il établit que l'on est d'autant plus près ou plus loin de l'une ou de l'autre couleur, qu'on se rapproche ou s'éloigne d'avantage du terme soixante-quartre, qui leur sert du moyenne proportionelle.

D'après ce système, tout homme, qui n'a point huit parties de blancs est reputé noir.

Marchant de cette couleur vers les blancs, on distingue neuf souches principales, qui ont encore entre elles des varietés d'après le plus ou le moins parties qu'elles retiennent de l'une ou de l'autre couleur. Les neuf espèces sont le *sacatra*, le *griffe*, le *marabout*, le *mulatre*, le *quarteron*, le *métis*, le *mameluco*, le *quarteronne*, le *sang-mêlé*.

Le *sang-mêlé*, en continuant son union avec le blanc, finit en quelque sorte par se confondre avec cette couleur. On assure pourtant qu'il conserve toujours sur une certaine partie du corps la trace ineffaçable de son origine.

Le *griffe* est le resultant de cinq combinaisons, et peut avoir depuis vingt-quatre jusqù'a trente-deux parties blanches et quatre-vingts sieze ou cent quatre noires." See next chapter for discussion of *Bug-Jargal*. See also Chapter Three, note 40 for a less "scientific" statement of the case by Thomas Dixon.

[23] Valle-Inclán, *op. cit.*, p. 104.

[24] Emilio Ballagas, *Mapa de la Poesía Negra Americana* (Buenos Aires: Pleamer, 1946), pp. 287-294.

[25] In José Manuel Carbonell, *Evolución de la cultura cubana*, Vol. II (La Habana, El Siglo XX, 1928), pp. 93-97. See also Otto Olivera, *op. cit.*, pp. 142-152.

[26] In *Antologia de la Poesía Negra Americana*, ed. Ildefonso Pereda Valdés, pp. 121-124. The poem is a much anthologized one. See Chapter Seven for treatment in context.

[27] *Mapa de la Poesía Negra*, p. 170.

[28] Arturo Torres-Rioseco, *The Epic of Latin American Literature* (Berkeley, 1961), p. 127.

[29] See Gerald W. Haslam's anthology, rather combatively titled *Forgotten Pages of American Literature* (Boston: Houghton Mifflin Co., 1970), pp. 165-180.

[30] *Mapa de la Poesía Negra*, p. 236. Pereda Valdes is more incisive as a sociologist-historian. See *El Negro Rioplatense* (Montevideo: C. García y Cia., 1937).

[31] W. H. Auden, *Collected Shorter Poems* (Faber & Faber)

[32] Federico García Lorca, *Obras Completas* (Madrid: Azuilar, 1954). The cycle of poem dealing with his intensely unhappy but productive stay in New York will be found on pp. 397-458. The Negro poems appear on pp. 403-408.

CHAPTER 5

THE FRENCH METAPHOR

The response to the Negro here assumes extraordinary proportions. The normal trajectories traced in the last two chapters coincide in the first two decades of this century with a burst of eclectic energies that was Paris based. Edward Fry has generously and perhaps prophetically assessed the implications of this eclecticism:

> It was a period which saw the emergence of Mann, Proust, Apollinaire, Gertrude Stein; of Gropius and Frank Lloyd Wright; of Stravinsky and Schoenberg; of Planck, Rutherford, Einstein, Bohr; and of Croce, Poincaré, Freud, Bergson, and Husserl. In painting and sculpture these same years produced Matisse, Picasso, Braque, Gris, Léger, Delaunay, Duchamp, Mondrian, Malevich, Kandinsky, Brancusi, Archipenko, Boccioni, and Lipchitz, to name only the most prominent of a brilliant galazy of artists; the aesthetic innovations and achievements of these years were fully as important and as far-reaching as the work of scientists and intellectuals. It was, as will one day be recognized, one of the golden ages of Western civilization.[1]

It would follow then that when the Negro is apprehended in the dynamic atmosphere thus generated, possibilities – "limitless," "new and intriguing" – would appear inevitable. In a sense this was the case during this period, especially in its pre-World War I manifestation, when iconoclastic brilliance "chose savage artists as its mentors." This chapter will lead up to the potential of the period by examining the French perception of the Negro insofar as it parallels what has been offered in the last chapters.

When Vautrin, in Balzac's *Le Père Goriot,* makes the following observation about Negroes, some of whom he expects to buy in America,

> Des nègres, voyez-vous, c'est des enfants tout venus dont on fait ce qu'on veut, sans qu'un curieux. . .vienne vous en demander compte.[2]

we have a cynical transformation, true to Vautrin's character, of the tradition of *Le Nègre Généreux:*

84

> Nègre est sensibl', nègre est fidèle,
> Quand maître a li n'est pas méchant. . . .[3]

Nigger's good, nigger's faithful/when massa don't treat him wrong. These
lines, from Act 1, scene iii of Béraud and Rosny's *Adonis ou le Bon Nègre*
(1798) illustrate the kind of Negro most evident in the literature of French
Romanticism.[3] Béraud and Rosny's play is itself an adaptation of J. B.
Picquenard's novel *Adonis ou le bon Nègre, anecdote coloniale*. The title,
insofar as it includes *"anecdote coloniale"* offers us a fine point of
departure in studying the Negro in such works. In general, it was the
colonial Negro who frequented the pages of French literature. There is very
little evidence of the existence in France of a Negro or slave population to
the extent found in England and the Iberian peninsula. The nature of the
perception of the Americas and the Caribbean in French literature
consequently played a major role in the dimensions of the Negro characters
treated. By and large, the Americas proved to be literarily exotic and
decadent. But it differed from the Hispanic tradition in that there was little
of the raw, unsophisticated energy expended in Spanish literature. The
exoticism of the French had much of the aristocratically decadent about it,
even in the cynical Vautrin. It may be hyperbolic but not too misleading
to say that tropicalism functioned much like the backdrop to an elegant,
precieux boudoir. This is true of Theophile Gautier's "Ce monde ci et
l'autre," with its antithetical appraisals of "l'Europe décrépite" and "la
jeune Amérique." A *négresse* appears as part of "la jeune Amérique" in a
scene that is almost silly in its elegance and decadence.

The poet's love is protected from insects by her maid:

> Et la bonne négresse aux dents blancs qui rit
> Chassant les moucherons auprès de votre lit.[4]

"The negro maid with laughing white teeth/chasing the flies from around
your bed." The same quality is apparent in the tropicalism of Baudelaire's
later celebration of his *dame créole*. The seductiveness of this "brune
enchantresse" never quite matches the celebrative rawness of either Camin's
poem to his *negra* or of Muñoz del Monte's rhapsody to his *mulata*. There
is instead a civilized sensuousness to both Baudelaire's *créole* and her *pays
parfumé*, her "palm-fringed, sun-kissed perfumed land."

> Au pays parfumé que le soleil caresse
> J'ai connu sous un dais d'arbres tout empourprès
> Et de palmiers d'ou pleut sur les yeux la paresse,
> Une dame créole aux charmes ignorés.
>
> Son teint est pâle et chaud; la brune enchantresse

A dans le cou des airs noblement maniérés;

As Baudelaire goes on to observe, she is a "belle, digne d'orner les antiques manoirs."[5] It is against the seductive attenuations of this tropical backdrop that the drama of *le nègre généreux* is played out.

We cannot ignore the influence of Aphra Behn's 1688 novel *Oroonoko or the Slave King* in discussing the generous, forgiving black slave who was capable of nobly sacrificing his life for his master's sake. The work was as popular in French as it was in English. Translated and adapted by Antoine de La Place in 1745, the "incomparable Astrea's" slim novel became a two-volume opus. Servais Etienne's *Les Sources de Bug-Jargal* indicates the popularity and influence of *Oroonoko:*

> ...adapté par La Place en 1745, et reimprimé, il est parmi les neufs romans anglais les plus lus vers le milieu du XVIII$_e$ *siècle; le Supplément du Dictionnaire* de Bayle en donne un tres bon résumé et le soin qu'il y met confirme le cas qu'on en faisait... Jean-Jacques Rousseau l'a connue; Voltaire s'est servi du roman pour le dénouement de *l'Orphelin de la Chine.*[6]

Reports, such as were read two years later in L'abbé Prévost's *Histoire générale des Voyages* (1747) gave further justification to the Negro portrait. They show in the Negro an extraordinary capacity for a dignified, melancholic stoicism under the most rabid and epileptic ill-treatment:

> D'une haute taille,... hardi, fier et vigoureux. Ce misérable semblait regarder ses compagnons avec dédain, lorsqu'il les voyait prompts et faciles à se laisser visiter. Il ne tournait pas les yeux sur-les marchands; et si son maître lui commandait de se lever, ou d'étendre la jambe, il n'obéissait pas tout d'un coup ni sans regret. Loabstone, indigne de cette fierté, le maltraitait sans ménagement à grands coups de fouet qui faisaient de cruelles impressions sur un corps nu, et l'aurait tuè. ...
> Le nègre supportait toutes ces insultes avec une fermeté surprenante. Il ne lui echappait pas un cri. On lui voyait seulement couler une larme ou deux au long des joues; encore s'efforçait-il de les cacher, comme s'il eut rougi de sa propre faiblesse.[7]

Such a figure had all the prerequisites for romantic treatment in a romantic age. And Joseph Lavallée's novel *Le Nègre comme il y a peu de Blancs* (1789) is thematically logical. The title sums up the perspective. It is all about a Negro such as has few equals among whites. The review in *Esprit des Journax*, December 1789, effectively highlights the work:

> Les èvénements sont bien choisis; les caractères bien dessinés; les noirs sont conformes à eux-mêmes; l'avidité, l'atroce insensibilité, les

> fourberies des marchands d'esclaves y inspirent une sainte horreur; la confiance, la petulance, la naiveté, le courage, la patience des noirs y sont tres bien developpés.

To this kind of imagination there was only one reason why the Negro should show so much majestic stoicism. As Servais Etienne somewhat sardonically puts it:

> Voilà, convenez-en, un nègre comme il y a peu de blancs. Et peu de nègres aussi, d'ailleurs. C'est que cet esclave est fils de roi.[8]

The *nègre génèreux* was a king's son, a prince *sans pareil* much as in Longfellow's poem. And he was on his way to being crowned Noble Savage. But as I suggested in Chapter 3, the conglomerate inelegance of perceptions of the Negro made the coronation impossible without attenuating that which made the Negro prince inviolately negroid. Not even the power of French Romanticism at its most extravagant could so transform the Negro without some kind of racial cosmetology. Victor Hugo's *Bug-Jargal* appeared in two versions, in 1820 and then in 1826. The cosmetic is as obvious as the style is inflated in the following description:

> Quelle homme! comme il était fort, comme il était nerveux, comme sa figure était belle pour un nègre! . . . Sa figure, ou les signes caractéristiques de la race noire étaient moins apparents que sur celles des autres nègres . . . offrait un mélange de rudesse et de majesté.[9]

By one of those peculiar coincidences whereby reality outruns or replaces fiction the eighteenth century had seen the appearance in Paris of the Dumas' from *les îles*. The following description from André Maurois' *Les Trois Dumas* shows how an exotic creature of fiction was transformed into living flesh in the aristocratic salons of Paris. Maurois' description is of Thomas-Alexandre Dumas:

> En 1772, la mère noire (Céleste Dumas) mourut. L'enfant fut élevé par son père à Saint-Domingue; puis, vers 1780, le 'marquis' de la Pailleterie . . . revint à Paris. La coutume était, parmi les planteurs nobles, que l'on ramenât en France les fils de sang mi-africain et que l'on laissât les filles aux Iles. Le jeune homme (Thomas-Alexandre) avait alors dix-huit ans. Son teint étaient purs; les yeux superbes, les attaches belles; les mains et des pieds de femme. Traité en fils de famille, il eut tout jeune, des succes amoureux.[10]

His strength was prodigious, an attribute he shares with Hugo's Bug-Jargal:

> Ses muscles fortement pronouncés, la largeur de ses épaules, et la

vivacité de ses mouvements annonçaient une force extraordinaire jointe à la plus grande souplesse.

In this respect, Victor Hugo, Herman Melville and Ramon del Valle-Inclán do little more than glorify the Negro by sheer physical extravagance. But insofar as the tradition of the *nègre génèreux* was connected to the New World, it carried its own negation. The action of *Bug-Jargal* takes place in the Caribbean of the Haitian Revolution. To this extent, Toussaint Louverture cancelled the generous celebration of *le nègre comme il y a peu de blancs*. The dark vitality of Voodoo negated the transparent seductions of a sun-kissed Caribbean. Hugo represents that dark vitality in the person of Bissaou in *Bug-Jargal*. But even in the earlier period, it needs to be understood that the *nègre génèreux* did not exist in literature independently of the *nègre révolté*. The Haitian Revolution merely brought the latter to the forefront. There had been early rumblings of discontent before the revolution broke out in 1791. But as early as 1775, Doigny du Ponceau had entered his *Discours d'un Nègre à un Européen* in an *Académie francaise* contest. The protagonist is uncompromisingly *révolté* and the melodramatic violence promised would be fulfilled in reports about the revolution in Haiti:

> Du moins ne te plains pas, si, marchant sur ta trace,
> Ma vengeance t'imite et même te surpasse. . .
> D'Africains soulevés une foule heroique
> Fait déjà retenir les forêts d'Amérique
> Du cri de la vengeance et de la liberté.
> Ils marchent; rien n'arrete un courage irrité
> Point de pardon pour vous, tremblez, maîtres barbares!
> Prodigues de leur sang, de leur bonheur avares,
> Terribles, s'elançant du fond de leurs deserts
> Et vous redemander leurs mères et leurs femmes
> Instruments méprisés de vos plaisirs infames.
> Cent mille malheureux, courbés sous les travaux
> A leur puissante voix deviendront des heros! [11]

"Do not be surprised, do not complain, if . . .a hundred thousand unhappy wretches rise up to demand satisfaction for their mothers and wives abused by your licentious desires." So speaks the Negro to the European in du Ponceau's drama. Between 1791 and 1802 the battle would be enjoined. To Hugo's imagination in *Bug-Jargal* it becomes "un si immense sujet: la révolte des noirs de Saint-Domingue en 1701, lutte de géants, trois mondes interéssés dans la question, l'Europe et l'Afrique pour combattants, l'Amérique pour champ de bataille." The melodramatic and inflated style of *Bug-Jargal* was to do justice to that battle of three continental giants.

The immediate repercussions of the uniquely successful black revolution were not literary. The revolution and its success were explicit threats to all European nations whose economy depended on slave labor. The United States, itself barely established in its revolutionary victories, reacted with measures that would have repercussions in the late flowering of its Negroes' artistic expression:

> Two questions are likely to occur to the reader introduced for the first time to the poetry of the American Negro. What happened after the death of Phyllis Wheatley to the impulse represented by her poetry? . . .The answer is simple enough, once the history of the period is recalled.
>
> Legal restrictions on the education of slaves were introduced after Phyllis Wheatley's time. The purpose, of course, was to keep from slaves news and propaganda likely to incite a lust for freedom. During the era of the French Revolution and the Haitian Insurrections this was regarded as a serious matter, and slave uprisings, or attempted uprisings, in Virginia, South Carolina, and elsewhere in the United States added to the anxiety. Penalties were imposed on people who violated the restrictions.[12]

In France, the repercussions were of sufficient magnitude to justify an official and comprehensive statement:

> Rapport sur les troubles de Saint-Domingue, fait au nom de la Commission des colonies, des Comités de Salut public, de législation et de marine. . .imprimé par l'ordre de la Convention nationale et distribué au corps législatif (1795).

In 1820, the *revolution nègre* was still of enough popular interest to account for an unofficial and more dramatic publication. From a Monsieur Randeynes et Fils came the following report:

> Débarquement de la flotte française à Saint-Domingue, faisant suite aux revolution de ĉette île; révolte des nègres, évènements deplorables de la guere désastreuses qui suivit le débarquement; second incendie du Ĉap par les Noirs; massacre et destruction presque générale de l'armé et des colons; avec un précis historique de l'érection de cette île en royaume d'Haiti.

In Haiti, the success of the revolution meant the early, and to some extent permanent, disruption of any possibility of a balanced syncretism between the *nègre révolté* and his Africanism and the elements of French culture created by seventeenth- and eighteenth-century *planteurs nobles*. The exposure to French culture had been short, severe and pathogenic. By the same token, there had not been time enough for the African influences, consolidated in Voodoo, to be extensively eroded. But there had been enough time for all these features to develop into peculiar and distorted configurations, which will be further complicated by the United States in one of its numerous intrusions into the Caribbean.

In any case, the success of the revolution led to the establishment of a monarchy on the island. The fall of that monarchy and the emergence in the late nineteenth century of a francophile elite coincided with the proclaimed manifest destinies of Europe as a conglomerate of expanding, colonizing states. The process of intense creolization would be seen by England's Rudyard Kipling as the divinely sanctioned undertaking of the "White Man's Burden." France would undertake in Martinique, Guadaloupe, Guayana, Senegal *et al* its *mission civilisatrice*. The francophile elite of Haiti then became umbilically attached to things, persons and ideas French at the same time that its ties to the Voodoo subculture were atrophied by embarrassment and estrangement. Thus was created in Africa and the Caribbean, from Senegal to Haiti, the *assimilé*, whose energies will coincide in the late Twenties and early Thirties with the latter day manifestations of the intellectual ferment described in the opening paragraphs of this chapter.

We come therefore to the "third" discovery of the idea of blackness in human form and its manifestations. It was essentially esthetic and little concerned with evangelical justifications for creolization. It had little in common with the kind of frank greed that Belgium's King Leopold II shows in his 1877 letter to Baron Solvyns: "We must lose no chance of winning a share in this magnificent African cake." This esthetic discovery and the integrative use of its consequences was Paris based. Given the nature of the period, this was perhaps inevitably so:

> No other city in the world in the early years of the twentieth century could boast of a comparable century-long history of outstanding artistic activity; and the relatively central location of Paris in western Europe served only to facilitate the migration of the most gifted young artists and writers from Spain, Italy, Germany, Russia, and the Low Countries toward this cultural mecca. Paris offered them not only the challenge of their most gifted contemporaries, but also its great art museums; it offered a tradition of moral and intellectual freedom, and an artistic bohemia in which they could live cheaply at the edge of society without suffering the ostracism inflicted by the

bourgeoisie in smaller, more conservative, and less cosmopolitan European cities. . . .Paris contained an astonishing number of young men of genius, whose presence constituted an intellectual 'critical mass' that soon produced a series of revolutionary cultural explosions.[13]

This was before the frightful comedy in the rumblings of World War I, the war itself, and the "opulent pause" that led to the second world conflagration, converted much of this energy into apocalyptic and eschatological cynicism.

It remains to be added that since she was the cultural center of the French *mission civilisatrice*, Paris was also the mecca for a colony of French *assimilé* geniuses. The nature of assimilationism meant the creation of the French counterpart of the African Jacobin in Freetown. It meant the emergence of a Parisian who happened to be Negro. No obstacle is placed in his path when he has so thoroughly accepted the credo of the *mission civilisatrice*, "nos ancêtres, les Gaulois," that it raises no crisis of allegiance, suggests no incongruity and no mongrelization of identity. He was, however, entitled to a seat in the French Parliament. He could legally, and theoretically, become President of France. The late Twenties and early Thirties will transform the *assimilé* into a *nègre révolté*. The artistic ferment of that revolt will offer us in the Guyanan, Leon G. Damas' *Pigments* a succinct statement of the process of assimilationism in all its irrational incongruity:

> Mes amis, j'ai valsé
> valsé comme jamais mes ancêtres
> les Gaulois
> au point que j'ai le sang
> qui tourne encore
> à la viennoise

My friends, I have waltzed, and waltzed as never did my ancestors the Gauls. I have waltzed so long my blood still circulates in Viennese, three-quarter time. Thus the 1930's find, among other *assimilés*, the Senegalese Léopold Sédar Senghor and the Caribbean Aimé Césaire in Paris.

To the eclectic quickness of the pre-World War I, Paris-based esthete, the masks and fetishes from Africa and Oceania were not merely things such as men in the temperate zone see "and that but dimly in their dreams." To Henri Matisse and other "fauve" painters, especially Vlaminck and André Derain, who studied them sympathetically, they provoked interest in the Negro as a sculptor of concepts. Maurice de Vlaminck and

André Derain would ponder on the eidetic nature of the primitive sculptures which had heretofore provoked either religious indignation, ethnocentric mockery or evangelical crusades. Dérain marveled "at the art with which the image-makers of Guinea and of the Congo managed to reproduce the human figure without using any element taken from direct vision." In 1907, Guillaume Apollinaire offered what may be called the manifesto of the period's literate and creative syncretism:

> Consequently the artistic 'handwriting' of all kinds of styles — those of the hieratic Egyptians, the refined Greeks and the voluptuous Cambodians, the works of the ancient Peruvians, the African statuettes proportioned according to the passions which have inspired them — can interest an artist and help him to develop his personality.[14]

To artists of such temperament, the masks from the Ivory Coast and other African colonies housed in the then *Musée Trocadéro* may suggest apparently contradictory ideas. To some, African art had the gift of combining "twenty forms into one"; Carl Einstein's *Negerplastik* may argue that comparatively speaking Negro sculpture would be found to be out and out realism from a formal point of view. Still, the language and perceptions of this period did avoid the silliness or malice of other exoteric ideas of the Negro. Eventually, in Picasso particularly, the period would produce in cubism what Edward Fry insists "is still today the greatest single aesthetic achievement of the century."

On the other hand, Barbara Tuchman's excellent study of the European scene between 1890 and 1914 suggests a strange, aberrant capacity for comic frightfulness on which death looked gigantically down. It is to the societies of *The Proud Tower* that one must turn to understand the degeneration into picturesque and slack nihilism of the energies Edward Fry describes. The decadent "cabaret" excitements of the Harlem of Langston Hughes' *The Weary Blues*, the mongrel constipation of Guillén's *West Indies Ltd*. and Aimé Césaire's clarion call "ecoutez le monde blanc/horriblement las de son effort immense" (listen to the white world, horribly exhausted by its immense exertions)—all these have been effectively captured in their genesis by R. M. Albérés' *L'Aventure Intellectuelle du XXe Siècle:*

> Au débouché d'une civilisation qui avait ·voulu comprendre et organiser le monde selon la parfaite raison se présenter un spectacle de massacre, de guerres coloniales, du conflit à venir, de dissensions interieures.

That the reaction should be a distrust of reason is not surprising, even if that distrust is actually quite illogical. It is hardly debatable that the disasters of war depended on irrational behavior such as Mrs. Tuchman records. An unenlightened application of bad reasoning would hardly seem to be justification for an indictment of rational thought. All the same, as Albérés puts it, a consequence was that "tout ce qui était réel cessa d'être rationnel." But there may have been a perversely logical dimension to the irrationality. The world that Fry's "golden age" disintegrates into has something of the surrealistic about it, as the artists capture it. The War had been an insanity in which Ezra Pound says "There died a myriad/and of the best among them

> For an old bitch gone in the teeth
> For a botched civilization.[15]

In the place of energetic vitality there was "The Waste Land" with

> Cracks and reforms and bursts in the violet air
> Falling towers
> Jerusalem Athens Alexandria
> Vienna London
> Unreal

Eschatology and apocalypse appeared inseparable from any kind of intelligent sensitivity. Much of the disenchantment would be expressed with the lamentation of Jeremiah and the cynicism of Ecclesiastes.   They perfectly match the fears of Oswald Spengler's *Untergang des Abendlands* and Arnold Toynbee's fear of cyclic catastrophes. Carl Sandburg's "Four Preludes on Playthings of the Wind" is as eschatologically-minded as Eliot's "The Waste Land," only less esoteric; it is as apocalyptic as W. B. Yeats' "The Second Coming," only less lyrical and less artistically inventive. But it does not betray the spirit of the age:

> It has happened before.
> Strong men put up a city and got
> a nation together,
> And paid singers to sing and women
> to warble: We are the greatest city,
> the greatest nation,
> nothing like us ever was.
> And while the singers sang
> and the strong men listened
> and paid the singers well,
> there were rats and lizards who listened
> . . .and the only listeners left now

. . .are. . .the rats. . .and the lizards.
And there are black crows
crying, "caw, caw,"
bringing mud and sticks
building a nest
over the words carved
on the doors where the panels were cedar
and the strips on the panels were gold
and the golden girls came singing:
    We are the greatest city,
    the greatest nation:
    nothing like us ever was.[16]

Archibald Macleish may have been insightful when in "Hypocrite Auteur: mon semblable, mon frère" he accuses the age of self-indulgence:

our epoch takes a voluptuous satisfaction
in that perspective of the action
which pictures us inhabiting the end
of everything with death for only friend
not that we love death
. . . . Our taste is for the opulent pause
Before the end comes.

Whether faddishly in love with "easeful death" or not, the period between 1914 and 1939 was eloquent with despair for Western civilization.

The perception of the Negro was naturally affected by these concerns. Where the Negrophilism of the first decade and a half had been a creative, artistic and intelligent enterprise, it now became charged with excesses. By and large, the war had disrupted the iconoclastic community of artists in Paris. Appreciation of Negro cultures now lacked the guiding intellect of genius.[17] Much of that appreciation is quite enthusiastically silly but it becomes less so when read against the background of the eschatological concerns just presented:

The most important element to be considered is the psychological complexion of the Negro as he inherited it from his primitive ancestors and which he maintains to this day. The outstanding characteristics are his tremendous emotional endowment, his luxuriant and free imagination and a truly great power of individual expression. He has in superlative measure that fire and light which, coming from within, bathes his whole world, colors his images and impels him to expression. The Negro is a poet by birth. . . . Poetry is religion brought down to earth and it is the essence of the Negro

soul. . . .The white man in the mass cannot compete with the Negro in
spiritual endowment. . . .The Negro has kept nearer to the ideal of
man's harmony with nature and that, his blessing, has made him
a vagrant in our arid, practical American life.[18]

The Negro was Body, he was Non-Intellect, he was exotically Natural, and
he was therefore good and beneficial since all the stated attributes are
congenital to the race. By an irony of fate, the concerns of the age had
inverted the very means of denigration, transforming them into the
attributes of a Messiah. Clearly, here was an alternative: non-European,
non-cartesian and presumably beyond Spengler and Toynbee's apocalypse.
It is appropriate that Spengler himself should prove the flexibility of his
vision. Ramon Guirao somewhat indignantly reports on Spengler's reaction
to the Negrophilism generated by France. At a news conference, Spengler
warns about the "black peril," a peril far worse, he feels, than the
"yellow" peril that was threatening Europe. The blood of Europe was
being poisoned by France's perverse miscegenation:

> Spengler, el filósofo del prusianismo, resentido por la participación de
> los ejercitos coloniales en la derrota germana, señaló a los
> corresponsales de la prensa internacional, un peligro negro, más
> amenazador que el amarillo que, a su juicio, avanzaba sobre Europa.
> 'Francia, nos dice, ha traicionado la cultura europea. En nombre de su
> propia impotencia ha despertado al continente africano. La horda
> negra no es aparición. La sangre de Europa está envenenada por la
> perversa miscegenación de Francia.[19]

But, like his earlier disquisition on the health of Western civilization,
Spengler's diagnosis of the power of this negrophilism was more
apprehensive than accurate.

Insofar as Blaise Cendrars was functioning as the *vulgarisateur*
(populariser) of the interest in African primitivism, the intelligent, even
erratic brilliance of Guillaume Apollinaire had been replaced by a
one-dimensional taste for the exotic and the picturesque. It was
nevertheless the fate of the *assimilé* Negro that his crisis of identity
coincided with this change in the perception and value of primitivism. The
result, against the backdrop of Western civilization's "opulent pause,"
would be one of the most intensely productive crises of
Negro-Creole-Assimilé identity. To the group of *assimilés* involved in trying
to organize their crisis into a dignified even if elaborate and imitative
statement of *Négritude*, there must have been something uncomfortable
about the picturesque primitivism of Luis Pales Matos, Vachel Lindsay and,
in Paris, of Blaise Cendrars. The genre used by Cendrars for *Petits Contes*

Nègres pour les Enfants des Blancs is significant. The justification is transparently profound.

> Un homme raisonnable ne peut parler de choses sérieuses à un autre homme raisonnable; il doit s'adresser aux enfants.

But the genre, coincidentally, functioned well enough for the exotic simplification which interest in the Negro now involved. Some two years or so before Césaire and Senghor launched the term *"négritude"* as the life-bouy for *assimilés* drowning in French-European culture, Cendrars published *Comment les Blancs sont d'anciens Noirs*. The work is charmingly picturesque. Manipouta, the Father of all, had two sons, Zonga and Manicongo, both black. Who are the whites? Well, they were all original blacks:

> Qu'est-ce que les Blancs, le savez-vous, vous autres? ... Non? ... Eh! bien, ce sont tout simplement d'anciens Noirs, oui, des Noirs, des vieux frères à nos aïeux, les cousins de nos grandpères!

The reasons for the change in color are ascribed, somewhat ambivalently, to the dynamic insensitivity of the soon-to-be white Zonga:

> A l'aube, la poule se mit à chanter. Zonga partit en courant. Il vit un lac et y entra. Il remarqua alores avec étonnement qu'à mesure qu'il entrait dans l'eau, il devenait blanc,

and, second, to the phlegmatic naturalness and spontaneity of Manicongo who remains unchanged:

> Manicongo rejoignit bientôt son frère. Il s'était arrêté en route pour dire bonjour à la Terre, bonjour aux cailloux du chemin, bonjour à l'herbe des prairies et il avait conversé avec la poule.
> Quand il entra à son tour dans l'eau, il resta tout noir.[20]

In the description of Manicongo's reaction to his failure to turn white in the waters of the lake, the single-minded drive toward assimilationism could hardly have been more unconsciously and indelicately portrayed: "il avait beau se tremper, se frotter, plonger au fond du lac, il restait noir." And this in a city where a colony of *assimilés* was awakening to the pangs of 'desimilation.' The evolutionary consequences go beyond cosmetic change of course. Manipouta offers gifts to his two sons. What they chose is of self-evident implications: for Zonga, the attraction of pen, paper, telescope, gunpower and gun; for Manicongo, bracelets, iron, spear, bows and arrows. "Zonga prit du papier, des plumes, une longue-vue, un fusil, de la poudre. Manicongo préféra, lui, des bracelets de cuivre, des cimmeterres en fer, une lance, des arcs, des flèches." It is hardly surprising that when Cendrars renders the song of the Negro the song should be rhythmic, exotic, and mindless, much like Pales Matos. Drunk, frenzied, the black race tries to cross a river to the whites' land of riches. But because of a session with "le vin de palme" (palm wine) they cannot and begin to sink. They retreat "et les Noirs s'assirent découragés sur la rive même du fleuve." All this takes place to the orchestrated buffoonery of:

> Clic, clac! clic, clac!
>   Alou bengan.
> Clic, clac! alou Bishour.
> Meshong a si, megnian eyo.
> Clic, clac! sem-ge bengan!
> Clic, clac! nbem a se mbeng,
> Mis, menou, meshong!
>   Cric, crac! cric, crac!
>   Le jour des crocodiles.
>   Cric, crac! le jour des Noirs!
> Des dents en bas, misère en haut.
> Cric, crac! venère le crocodile!
> Cric, crac! mon coeur n'est pas gai,
> Des yeux, des bouches et des dents! [21]

The White race succeeds in making the crossing, inheriting a *pays des richesses*. Among other things, they had avoided palm wine; "ils n'ont pas bu de vin de palme." The blacks sit in envious contemplation of the tantalizing land of riches. People say that to get to the land of the whites takes days, weeks, months. And that is too much for the blacks! They'll never leave and get there! Poor blacks! ". . .contemplant avec des yeux avides cette Terre des Richesses que jamais ils ne devaient connaître! "

> On dit que, pour la traverser aujourd'hui et pour s'en aller chez les Blancs, voir ce Pays des Richesses, il faut des jours, des semaines, des mois. Cela est beaucoup trop loin pour les Noirs! Il ne partiront jamais! Pauvre Noirs.[22]

This exotic fantasy may have been grotesquely true in the case of the tragic and brilliant *assimilé* poet, Jean-Joseph Rabéarivelo. So effective was the creolizing influence of *la mission civilisatrice* on him that he committed suicide when his efforts to go to France were constantly thwarted.

But the *pauvre noir* insofar as he was Leon G. Damas, *assimilé*, Aimé Césaire, *assimilé*, and Léopold Sédar Senghor, *assimilé*, did make the crossing to the mecca of his *pays des richesses*—Paris. And whatever might have been the intent of Blaise Cendrars, be his portrayals a series of exaggerated ironies to fit the taste for primitivism or merely a mannered estheticism, he and others like him presented the *assimilé* with serious inconveniences. And yet the pervasive eschatological mood of the time demanded identities, realignments and redefinitions. The frenzy of a "low dishonest decade" (Auden) posed questions for the *assimilé:* In what way did he belong to that decade? To what extent did he belong to the West? Was Caucasian Europe Eden or Babylon? What was the meaning of his blackness, which so dramatically contradicted his erstwhile "ancêtres, les Gaulois?" Out of that confrontation with blackness in an apparently disintegrating white universe came the idea of *Négritude*, defined in a general phenomenological sense as "ce que l'homme noir apporte." The attempt to define *Négritude* in qualitative and quantitative terms would be the responsibility of Césaire and Senghor. It would provoke the surrealist intensities of Césaire's *Cahier d'un Retour au Pays Natal* (1938). (This will be discussed in Chapter 8.) Senghor will develop his exegesis into an elaborate, imitative, pseudo-mystical and pseudo-philosophical search for black dignity. Chronologically speaking, Leon G. Damas' *Pigments* (1937), angry, virulent and disenchanted, was the first articulation of the *assimilé's* dilemmas. The mecca of the *mission civilisatrice* reacted with flexibility. The spirit of civilization was replaced by the demon of vandalism. The work was destroyed by the French police. The resurrection of the *nègre révolté* in Senghor was doubtless just as intense but more decorous, more intellectual and more expansive in scope. As he later explained:

> Nous ne vivions plus sous les Askia du Songhai, ni même sous Chaka le Zoulou. Nous étions des étudiants de Paris et du XXe siècle dont une des realités est, certes, l'éveil des consciences nationales, mais dont une autre, plus réelle encore est l'interdependence des peuples et des continents. Pour être vraiment nous-même, il nous fallait encarner la culture negro-africaine dans les realités du XXe siècle. Pour que notre négritude fut, au lieu d'une pièce de musée, l'instrument efficace d'une libération, il nous fallait la débarraser de ses scories et l'insérer dans le mouvement solidaire du monde contemporain.[23]

Negro-African culture had to be defined and made functional in the light of the contemporary realities. Senghor's first and perhaps most serious problem was the state of health of the *monde contemporain*. The dialectics of *Négritude* coincided strangely with the diagnostic rhetoric and the curative prescriptions for European civilization.

We can generally note a disenchantment in the age, from the turn of the century, actually, with rationalism of the cartesian variety. By and large, empirical awareness of human behavior and institutions, such as were portrayed in Barbara Tuchman's *The Proud Tower* hardly justified the rationalist and optimistic position that "the natural light of reason suffices to establish basic axioms of universal import, and therefore permits us to deduce specific consequences from them." For a world intent on apparent suicide, the somewhat juvenile revolt of dadaism and surrealism, its adolescently intelligent outgrowth, would seem more relevant phenomena. The obvious empirical outrage but intuitive epiphany of Paul Eluard's surrealist landscape ("le ciel est bleu comme une orange" or the sky is blue like an orange) finds a complementary phenomenon in that use of color with "unprecedented freedom, intensity and arbitrariness," which had earned for Matisse and his followers the derogatory label "fauvism." Even if the rational instuitionism of Edmund Husserl's *Ideen* (1913) seems closer to cartesian meditations we can still see it as a development from the popular sensuous intuition of Henri Bergson.[24] World War I would, of course, shatter the belief in the possible perfection of a rational *homo sapiens.*

In all, it is not too far wrong to suggest that the period was temperamentally inclined toward iconoclasm by way of spontaneity—absolute, organized or Freudian. The expression of fears of cultural disasters was not unrelated to a conviction that the European temperament and spirit had been atrophied by an excess of mechanistic intellect. The Virgin had in essence lost out to the Dynamo. Quite clearly then the road to health involved a retreat from mechanism and a return to vitalism of some kind.

To read Senghor's qualitative assessment of *Négritude* is to be exposed to a series of echo effects. I intend no perverse insinuations here. I intend no denial of the *assimilés'* crisis at the same time that I record coincidences of diagnostic and remedial prescriptions. Senghor's most articulate and comprehensive statement of the premises on which *Négritude* operated would be offered quite late, in 1956, at the First International Conference of Negro Writers and Artists held in Paris. The title of the presentation is somewhat pretentious: "The Spirit of Civilization or The Laws of African Negro Culture." Lilyan Kesteloot's *Ecrivains Noirs de Langue Française* is a comprehensive albeit essentially descriptive study of what I would call *assimilé* literature. What follows is a summary of her broader coverage of Senghor's exegesis on *Négritude*. Senghor noted profound distinctions between the Negro's world view and the Caucasian's. *Négritude* was "intuitive par participation"; the Graeco-Roman tradition was "analytique par utilisation." It was the exploitative insistence on utility in a cold, cartesian, mechanistic manner which had led the West to dehumanize itself, to become a dying civilization. This is what Césaire was calling attention to in his "écoutez le monde blanc/horriblement las de son effort immense." In art, *Négritude* sensibility involved a new esthetics. Its expression is triumphantly vitalist, dionysiac:

> Répondre, consonner au rythme des choses est le plaisir le plus intense, la joie du Nègre, sa raison de vivre.

The poetry of this kind of sensibility "a besoin de se perdre dans la danse verbale, aux rythme du tam-tam, pour se retrouver dans le Cosmos." The cartesian epigram "Je pense, donc je suis" is replaced by the *eureka* of *Négritude*—"Je sens l'Autre, je danse l'Autre, donc je suis."[25]

There was much in all this *tam-tam verbal* that fused the *assimilé's* de-similation process with the concerns of the age. It is hardly surprising then to find in it the basis for a magnificent apotheosis. *Négritude* became messianic. The Negro was coincidentally offered by both white and *assimilé* as a savior. The age was of such temperament that the offering was logical and acceptable. But it had its moments of artistic splendor. When the lyrical elegance and evangelical fervor of Senghor's *tam-tam verbal* turn to Harlem as a *Négritude* symbol we have one of the most seductive moments in his poetry. The last stanza of "A New York (pour un orchestre de jazz: solo de trompette)" is an exquisite symphonic coda which restates the pretentious pronouncements of the exegete in the metaphors of a brilliant artist:

> Ecoute au loin battre ton coeur nocturne, rythme et sang du
> tam-tam, tamtam sang et tamtam
>   111
> New York! je dis New York, laisse affluer le sang noir dans ton sang
> Qu'il dérouille tes articulations d'acier, comme une
>   huile de vie
> Qu'il donne à tes ponts la courbe des croupes et la souplesse de
> lianes.
> Voici revenir les temps très anciens, l'unité retrouvé la
>   réconciliation du Lion du Taureau et de l'Arbre
> L'idée liée à l'acte l'oreille au coeur le signe au sens.
> Voilà tes fleuves bruissants de caimans musiques et de lamantins
>   aux yeux de mirages. Et nul besoin d'inventer les Sirènes.
> Mais il suffit d'ouvrir les yeux à l'arc-en-ciel d'Avril
> Et les oreilles, surtout les oreilles à Dieu qui d'un rire de
>   saxophone créa le ciel et la terre en six jours.
> Et le septième jour, il dormait du grand sommeil nègre.[26]

New York! , New York, I say to you let black blood flow into your blood/let it, like the oil of life, remove the rust from your steel joints/....And no need to invent the Sirens/But it suffices to open the ears, especially the ears to God who out of the laugh/of a saxophone created the heavens and the earth in six days/and on the seventh day, he slept the great sleep of the Negro. We see the Negro on one of his most lyrical pedestals: a representation of salvation offering transfusions of pulsating blood to a mechanistic wasteland. The most definitive anthology of *Négritude* poetry was presented by Senghor in 1948. Sartre wrote a preface to the *Anthologie de la nouvelle poésie nègre et malgache de langue française* and he wondered "le grand fleuve noir colorera-t-il malgré tout la mer dans laquelle il se jette? " Gerald Moore and Ulli Beier in summing up the influence of *Négritude* suggest an answer:

> In the last few years there have been signs that the well-spring of *Négritude* is running dry....Césaire, Damas and Senghor have all been notably unproductive....
>
> It is no coincidence that the word itself was coined by a West Indian (Césaire), or that he should have written the most extended poetic exposition of it *(Cahier)*. The black man in Haiti, Cuba, Puerto Rico, Martinique, or Jamaica grew up in a permanent state of exile. He had no name, no tolerated religion, and scarcely any distinct culture of his own, yet until recently he could not expect any position of power or influence in the new mixed societies which had been built upon his labours. Without even knowing, in the vast majority of cases, from which part of Africa his ancestors came, he was obliged to build a romantic, idealized vision of "Guinea," a kind of heaven to which all good negroes go when they die.[27]

It is nevertheless true that the conjoined energies of the *assimilé's* identity crisis, the eschatological interests of Europe and the romantic nihilism of the age proved most productive. They gave the saga of the Negro intrusion into "the civilized nerves of the wise and the foolish alike" one of its most extraordinary manifestations. It offered a harmonized musical romanticism in the place of the discordant jangle of cruel caricatures. The problem was "How could a large and enthusiastic number of people be crazy about Negroes forever? " Langston Hughes colloquially voices the question that Jean-Paul Sartre had asked about "l'être-dans-le-monde du noir."[28]

NOTES

[1] Edward F. Fry, *Cubism*, (New York: McGraw-Hill, no date), p. 9. For details of the framework of this chapter see also Ortega y Gasset, *The Dehumanization of Art and Other Writings on Art and Culture* (New York; 1956); Gertrude Stein, *Autobiography of Alice B. Toklas* (New York, 1933); Maurice Mandelbaum, Francis W. Gramlich and Alan Ross Anderson, *Philosophic Problems* (New York: The Macmillan Press, 1964), in particular, the selections on "Rationalism, Intuitionisn and Pragmatism," pp. 114–146. The selection from Langston Hughes' autobiography *The Big Sea* in *The Langston Hughes Reader* (New York: George Braziller, Inc., 1958), especially "When the Negro was in Vogue," pp. 317–398.

[2] Honoré de Balzac, *Le Père Goriot* (Paris: Gallimard, 1961), p. 177.

[3] Béraud and Rosny, *op. cit.* (Paris: Clisau, 1798).

[4] Théophile Gautier, *Poésie Complète*, 3 vols., ed. by René Jasuiski (Paris: Firmin-Didot, 1932).

[5] Charles Baudelaire, *Les Fleurs du Mal*, ed. Antoine Adam (Paris: Garnier Frères, 1959), p. 68. When Baudelaire comes to express a genuine sympathy *aux captifs, aux vaincus* by way of a tuberculosed Negress, "Le Cygne" suffers from exotic simplification:

> "Je pense a la negresse, amaigre et phtisique
> Pietinant dans la boue, et cherchant, l'oeil hagard
> Les cocotiers absents de la superbe Afrique.
> . . . .

[6] Servais Etienne, *Les Sources de Bug-Jargal* (Bruxelles: Académie de Langue et de Litterature francaise, 1923), p. 24.

[7] *Op. cit.*, pp. 218–220.

[8] Etienne, *op. cit.*, p. 13.

[9] Victor Hugo, *Oeuvres*, Vol 1 (Bruxelles: J. P. Méline, 1836); Bug-Jargal, pp. 9–71.

[10] André Maurois, *Les Trois Dumas* (Paris: Hachette, 1957), p. 14. And so the word became flesh for this was the age of Oroonoko whose head, "à l'exception de la couleur, c'était une des plus belles têtes que l'on put voir."

[11] See *Les Sources de Bug Jargal*

[12] Arna Bontemps, ed. *American Negro Poetry* (New York: Hill and Wang, 1965), pp. xvii–xviii.

[13] Edward Fry, *op. cit.*, pp. 11–12.

[14] *Ibid.*, p. 46. Fry quotes in translation from Guillaume Apollinaire in *La Phalange*, Paris, 15 December 1907, pp. 483–4.

[15] Ezra Pound, *High Selwyn Mauberley*.

[16] Carl Sandburg, *Smoke and Steel* (New York: Harcourt, Brace & Co., 1920).

[17] "With the outbreak of war in 1914 there inevitably came a sharp break in the artistic life not only in Paris but of all Europe. Of the principal cubists, only Picasso and Gris, being Spaniards, were not mobilized. . . ." Edward Fry, *Op. cit.*, p. 32.

"(Apollinaire) enlisted when War was declared, was seriously wounded in 1916 and was removed to Paris, where after a partial recovery and a resumption of this literary activities he succumbed to influenza in the epidemic of 1918." *ibid.*, p. 47.

[18] Albert C. Barnes, "Negro Art and America" in Locke, *The New Negro*, pp. 19-20. This extraordinary, exclamatory essay opens the anthology-manifesto of the Harlem Renaissance. It coincides with similar pronouncements by Rodriquez-Embil and García Lorca as in the opening pages of the previous chapter.

[19] Ramón Guirao, *op. cit.*, p. xviii.

[20] *Comment les Blancs Sont d'anciens Noirs* (Argenteuil: R. Coulouma, 1930), pp. 1; 19-20.

[21] *Ibid.*, p. 118.

[22] *Ibid.*, pp. 122-3.

[23] *Rapport sur la doctrine et la propagande du parti*, Congres constitutif du Parti du Rassemblement Africain, 1959. In addition to the eschatological concerns of Europe, the *assimilé* was also stimulated by the discoveries and translations into French of almost all the arabic texts quoted in Chapter Two. Much of this translation was made by Octave Houdas with Edmund Benoist and Maurice Delafosse between 1900 and 1915. Senghor shows influence from Mahmud Kati's *Tarikh al-Fettash* which among other topics deals with Askia Muhammad, emperor of Songhay in 1498. All these and other archaelogical discoveries led the *assimilé* to the suspicion that the African continent might be more than the "dark continent" of prejudice and ignorance.

[24] Henri Bergson, *L'Evolution Créatrice* (1907). Husser's *Ideen* (1913) was further developed in *Meditations Cartesiennes* (1931). See Ortega y Gasset, *op. cit.*, and Mandelbaum *et al*, *op. cit.* Also Richard Ellman and Charles Feidelson, Jr., eds. *The Modern Tradition: Backgrounds of Modern Literature* (New York: Oxford University Press, 1965).

[25] Lilyan Kesteloot, *Les Ecrivains Noirs de Langue Française* (Belgium: Universite Libre de Bruxelles, 1963). In addition to pp. 111-123. See especially Chapter Nine, "La Négritude." For a full expression in Senghor's direct speech, see "The Spirit of Civilisation etc," in *Présence Africaine*, Special Issue, June-November, 1956. For an elegantly cynical reaction see James Baldwin's "Princes and Powers" in *Nobody Knows My Name* as also Eldridge Cleaver's furious reaction to Baldwin in *Soul on Ice*.

[26] Léopold Sédar Senghor, *Poèmes* (Paris: Editions du Seuil, 1964). (This collection contains his major works *Chants d' Ombre, Hosties Noires, Ethiopiques*. "A New York" is from *Ethiopiques*), p. 115. See Moore and Beier, *op. cit.* for a good introduction in effective translation to Senghor.

[27] Preface to Moore and Beier, *op. cit.*

[28] From Sartre's preface "Orphée Noir", to the *Anthologie de la nouvelle poésie nègre et malgache de langue française* (Paris: Collection Colonies et Empires, 1948). The preface provoked a bitter response from Frantz Fanon. See *Peau Noire, masques blancs* (Paris: Seuil, 1952), Chapter Five "L'experience vécue du noir," pp 113-41.

PART III

ALLEGIANCES AND IDENTITIES

Black consciousness really begins with the shock of discovery that one is not only black but is also *non-white,*

--Lewis Nkosi

CHAPTER 6

LANGSTON HUGHES AND UNITED STATES NEGRO FOLKLORE

The rhythm of life
Is a jazz rhythm,
Honey.
The gods are laughing at us.[1]

The lines are from Hughes' "Lenox Avenue: Midnight" in *The Weary Blues* and they offer a fine comment on the precarious excitements which the negrophilism of the Harlem Renaissance partly generated and partly sustained. *The Weary Blues*, written in 1926, may best be seen as a chronicle, both esthetic and moral, of that first period of European elitist interest in things and persons African and negroid. This interest, as I have tried to demonstrate, was multifaceted. The search for conceptual, creative alternatives spear-headed the esthetic discovery of Africa in the inconoclastic elitism of Picasso, Modigliani, Apollinaire. On the other hand, it also led a great number of other European dilettantes on a somewhat less inconoclastic but no less exotic argosy to the New World. Three places perhaps best represent the New World and the kinds of alternatives it was presumed to provide. Out of Cuba comes the decorative *joie de vivre* of Afro–cubanism. Haiti offered mystery and the dark vitality of dionysiac paganism. In Harlem, the emphasis would be on celebrating an intoxicating bacchanalia.[2]

The Harlem of this period as captured in *The Weary Blues* is in a sense the dramatic coincidence of two energies. On the one hand, there was that energy caused by the transformation of an oral, peasant, slave culture into jazz and blues, the oral expressions of the city. But equally important was the compulsive hedonism of the negrophiles who flocked to the "cabaret civilization" of Harlem. Jazz and the Blues then became rhythms for "chansons vulgaires," for "nymphs" and "wild fauns." In "Young Singer" Langston Hughes again suggests the excesses and the fatal blindness of this apocalyptic orgy:

107

> One who sings "chansons vulgaires"
> In a Harlem cellar
> Where the jazz-band plays
> From dark to dawn
> Would not understand
> Should you tell her
> That she is like a nymph
> For some wild faun.[3]

Even if it was only for a brief span of time, "a large and enthusiastic number of people were crazy about Negroes:"

> It was a period when local and visiting royalty were not at all uncommon in Harlem. And when the parties of A'lelia Walker, the Negro heiress, were filled with guests whose names would turn any Nordic social climber green with envy. . . .It was a period when white writers wrote about Negroes more successfully (commercially speaking) than Negroes did about themselves. It was the period (God help us!) when Ethel Barrymore appeared in black face in *Scarlet Sister Mary!* It was the period when the Negro was in vogue.[4]

Many Harlemites, especially upper-class Harlemites, and the "local and visiting royalty" thought the millenium had arrived. The Devil, the Gargoyle and the Buffoon had been apotheosized into talismans for the times. The age demanded and created an image worthy of itself. Hottentot Venuses and bass-plucking Negroes, "long-headed jazzers," became the erotic messiahs for a "botched civilization." Nowhere else in *The Weary Blues* do we have a more vivid description of the effects than in "Harlem Night Club":

> Sleek black boys in a cabaret.
> Jazz-band, jazz-band,
> Play, plAY, PLAY!
> Tomorrow . . . who knows?
> Dance today!

The saturnalian excitement is crude, enthusiastically animalistic and integrated:

> White girls' eyes
> Call gay black boys.
> Black boys' lips
> Grin jungle joys.

> Dark brown girls
> In blond men's arms.
> Jazz-band, jazz-band, —
> Sing Eve's charms!

But Hughes is never far from suggesting in *The Weary Blues* that the excitements of the period have something of the eschatological about them. "Harlem Night Club" indicates that its intensities are essentially narcotic. Such is the degree of precarious rhapsody that a moment of hesitant, reflective questioning makes the opiate all the more imperative:

> White ones, brown ones,
> What do you know
> About tomorrow
> Where all paths go?

> Jazz-boys, jazz-boys, —
> Play, plAY, PLAY!
> Tomorrow . . . is darkness.
> Joy today![5]

These moments of questioning finally crystalize in *The Weary Blues* into an expression that may best be understood if we make an assessment of the folkloric dimensions of the inspiration of Hughes and the era. In a very real sense, what was unheard in the collective madness of the cabarets, and which Hughes records in *The Weary Blues*, is the voice of the Negro transforming a primitive, plantation expression of exile into another statement of exile in an erstwhile postulated urban paradise. Indeed, so excruciating and unending appeared the disenchantment that it was apparently only bearable when transformed into the suicidal frustrations in the lyrics of Jazz and the Blues — even if these lyrics were expressed in what appeared to be outrageous hyperboles:

> Want to lay my head on de railroad line
> let de train come along and pacify my mind.[6]

An understanding of the impact of the controlling influences is necessary to establish the nature of the folklore that inspired Hughes' *The Weary Blues*. Here, the influence of Protestantism cannot be underestimated in explaining the radical differences that one finds in the Negro subcultures of the Americas under the Southern European temperament and those under Northern European influence. On the one hand, we have Candomble in Bahai (Brazil, Portuguese), Ñañiguismo in Cuba (Spanish), and Voodoo in Haiti (French). On the other hand, there is the mongrelized but intense Christianity of the Sierra Leone Creole (British), and of the Negro in the United States. Of the four Negro subcultures in the Americas mentioned in this study, that of the United States Negro is the least African. The influence of Protestantism cannot be underestimated in this area. One of its most beneficial consequences, politically and economically, is that it succeeded in neutralizing the tribal heterogeneity of a very large slave population. In this respect, it may not appear to differ much from near similar consequences under Roman Catholicism. But the significant difference was also a profoundly reactionary, calvinistic one. The new identity developed by the now manageable homogeneity of the slave class was never allowed to define itself outside the boundaries of Northern European Protestantism. There were, of course, modulations and changes in emphasis, but nothing like the effect which African tribal religions had on Roman Catholicism.

The result is that despite having the largest Negro population in the New World, there developed only two minimal islands of non-protestant black identity in the United States. The first is in Louisiana, where in 1755 some 4,000 of 18,000 Acadians and Negro-Creoles sought refuge under what was really Spanish-French Roman Catholic protection. This was after they had been expelled by the British from the Acadian peninsula (Nova Scotia).[7] The other island, and it is the one that shows the strongest and most vital survivals of African elements, is Gullah. Lorenzo Dow Turner's *Africanisms in Gullah Dialect* illustrates just how organic the survival is. Here we have an island free from Protestant and urban intrusions primarily because of extreme isolation. The Gullahs are ex-slaves settled on the Sea Islands and coastal regions of South Carolina, Georgia and north-eastern Florida.

In examining the dominant Negro subculture and its role in the Harlem Renaissance, there will therefore be two areas of emphasis: the subculture created by slavery and Protestantism and that subculture as it was transformed by urbanization and the formation of ghettos. The first area is dominated by sermons, spirituals and folktales; the second by Jazz and the Blues. The representative artistic voices are the preacher, the storyteller and the singer. Eventually, we will illustrate by way of *The Weary Blues* the influence of Europe on Harlem and vice versa and the use to which Hughes puts his excursions into folklore.

The dominant trajectories of the plantation-slave-folk culture were determined by the historical, religious and artistic sensitivity of the "gentlemen and other" pioneers of the seventeenth and eighteenth centuries. This is useful in understanding why the slave culture showed a preponderance of certain elements having very little to do with the perspectives that dominated European, particularly English, folklore:

> The colonizing Englishmen of the seventeenth century had largely lost the folk art of storytelling. They had retained vivid legends of witches, ghosts, and the Devil, but they had ceased to relate magical fictions of stripling heroes and enchanted castles. In the American colonies and the new republican states, a mobile class of independent farmers replaced the communal peasants of Europe.[8]

But given devil, ghost and witch, the Negro slave added to them the dislocations and incongruities of his precarious existence and the vague but perhaps spontaneous resurgence of his Africanness. These elements were synthesized into a culture that fixed spiritual and temporal boundaries to the harsh realities of a world that must have seemed inexplicably chaotic to the imported slave.

The Negro subculture was oral and I propose two dimensions in assessing it as a slave-plantation heritage.

The Mythological Dimension

The power and intensity of this dimension owed much it seems to me to the nature of revivalist Protestant belief in sin and the devil. For the revivalist camp meetings, neither Hell nor Heaven were vaguely or abstractly conceived or described. The sermons were fire-breathing in the best traditions of innocent and melodramatic belief. The urgency of the need for salvation and punishment demanded a highly anthropomorphic God. Metaphors and similes were shaped by a compulsion to selectively intensify immediate experiences. The rhetoric was uncompromisingly righteous; it became theatrical because it had to be self-evidently urgent. All this evangelistic fervor did not exclude the slave. Even as his body was being exploited with economic enthusiasm, his soul was being delivered from the "valley of the shadow of death" with an equal show of Protestant dedication. This was the immediate background. Out of these disparate and actually hostile experiences, the mythological dimensions of the plantation culture evolved. The perspective on the condition of man, as interpreted through the Negro's experiences, was influenced, and almost completely resolved within the myths and history of the Judaeo-Christian tradition. In rather interesting parallels, the slaves, like the Sierra Leone Creoles, would see themselves as "Lost tribes of Israel." The peculiarities of Judaism and Christianity formed the basis for an intensely dionysiac expression of agony, exile and salvation. The general framework of the operating metaphor is as follows: the Old Testament of the Bible provides the basic metaphors for the drama of persecution and suffering insofar as it represents the vivid agonies of exilic Jewish expression. Hence the equation: The Black Slave-Slavery-Slavemaster and The Jew-Exile-Diaspora-Pharoah. The poetry here can therefore say:

> Go down, Moses,
> Go down, Moses,
> Tell old Pharoah
> Let my people go.

For the slave, like the Jew, was symbolically in "Egypt's land," like the Jew, he was "oppressed so hard" he could not stand. But the influence of the New Testament is quite strong when once this fundamental framework is established. What is singularly missing in the subculture's use of the Jewish imagination from the Old Testament is the ardent wish for violent retribution on the oppressor. It is "Jesus of the twice-turned cheek" to whom the imagination of the black expression is directed, not to the "jealous Jehovah, visiting the iniquity of the fathers upon the children unto the third and fourth generation of them that hate me." There is thus in the original Jewish perspective an extraordinary union of exquisite, lyrical agony and a militantly revengeful spirit. The exilic poetry of Psalm 137 begins with unparalleled lyricism:

> By the rivers of Babylon, there we say down, yea, we wept, when we remembered Zion.
> We hanged our harps upon the willows in the midst thereof.
> For there they that carried us away captive required of us a song; and they that wasted us required of us mirth, saying, Sing us one of the songs of Zion.
> How shall we sing the Lord's song in a strange land?
> If I forget thee, O Jerusalem, let my right hand forget her cunning.
> If I do not remember thee, let my tongue cleave to the roof of my mouth; if I prefer not Jerusalem above my chief joy.

All this is exquisite nostalgia and catastrophe, exquisitely felt and expressed. The ending of the Psalm is therefore all the more extraordinary in its outrage and violence:

> Remember, O Lord, the children of Edom in the day of Jerusalem; who said, Rase it, rase it, even to the foundation thereof.
> O daughter of Babylon, who art to be destroyed; happy shall he be, that rewardeth thee as thou hast served us.
> Happy shall he be, that taketh and dasheth thy little ones against the stones.

What the New Testament offered the slave was the drama of

Salvation. The setting of the drama, insofar as it was Calvary, commanded the trembling and eager devotion of the poetry here. A devotion to Africa as vital and demanding of affection as the Jerusalem or Zion of Psalm 137 would doubtless have led to a similarity in response, but it was not to be. The Crucifixion, the Resurrection and the Apocalypse become the icons of this expression. True, man is invariably inhuman to man in "this lonesome valley" which "you've got to walk all by yourself/for nobody else can walk it for you." True, there is a kind of human indifference or insufficiency for "nobody knows the troubles I've seen/Nobody knows but Jesus." But, precisely because of the drama played out by that Jesus "when they nailed him to the cross," (a drama that causes the slave "to tremble, to tremble"), precisely because of that, pain, no matter how intense, will come to an end. So the poetry here can fuse two traditions together and say:

> Swing low, sweet chariot,
> Swing low, sweet chariot,
> Coming for to carry me home.

And Home is neither Jerusalem, nor Guinea, nor Timbuktu but rather a Christian heaven where

> I've got shoes. . .
> I've got robes. . .
> I've got wings. . .
> I've got a harp. . . .

Heaven is freedom for "before I be a slave/I'll be buried in my grave/. And go home to my Lord and be free." The New Testament offered the seemingly inaccessible and yet guaranteed escape from suffering.[9]

   Towering over these allegorical visions of the dramas of persecution, suffering and salvation, stands a personality at once theatrical, pathetic, profound and ridiculous: The Black Preacher, Son of Thunder, God's Thunder, God's Trombone. His formal education began and ended with the Bible. His informal education was determined by his experience as a slave. His artistry was fashioned in several ways. He patterned himself after the revivalist preacher, but significant changes in emphases and style appear. The most distinctive element in the style was the way in which all his precarious attributes would be transformed into a singularly effective voice. He fashioned his uncertain English into a finely tuned, rhetorical instrument of theatrical proportions. The glides and dialectal timbre of plantation Negro speech were used, consciously or not, to create a compelling, metrical substratum. His uncertainties about the proper lexical values of words of "thundering length" resulted often in theatrical but emotionally effective malapropisms. And all these were put to use in sermons that were at one and the same time expressions of intense conviction and sheer theatrics. He was a man of God and he was also a Man. The folktales and blues claim to know him when he was away from the pulpit: "a sealskin brown will make a preacher lay his Bible down." The titles of his "sermons" ranged from the dramatic simplicity of "De Sun do Move" to the hyperboles of

> Train Sermon: The Black Diamond Express, running between here and hell, making thirteen stops and arriving in hell ahead of time.

But the hyperbole does not prevent accomplishment — at least to the preacher's satisfaction. He could and did fuse disparate metaphorical and experiential allusions. Out of the unlikely synthesis would be constructed a religious and emotional rhetoric which offered hope, release and entertainment in cathartic proportions to his congregation:

> There is the story of one who after reading a rather cryptic passage took off his spectacles, closed the Bible with a bang and by way of preface said, "Brothers and sisters — I intend to explain the unexplainable — find out the undefinable — ponder over the imponderable — and unscrew the inscrutable."[10]

But the total effect was never a comic one. The organic, emotional ties between preacher and congregation, the nature of the dislocations common to both created an intense antiphonal union. For, in reality, this was what the "sermons" should more properly be called: *intense antiphons in a liturgical drama between preacher and congregation.*" Emotions of such dionysiac and corrosive a nature could not but leave their mark even after the preacher lost relevance and authority. The influence and seductive hysteria of this antiphonal drama are evident in Negro writings from the confessions of Nathaniel Turner to the confessional essays of James Baldwin. Ralph Ellison's *Invisible Man* shows a multifaceted inspiration. His protagonist "descended like Dante, into its (music's) depth . . . and heard an old woman singing a spiritual as full of *Weltschmertz* as flamenco." And then at a lower level of his Dantean descent, Ellison captures what, in my opinion, is the most effective recording of the antiphonal drama between Negro preacher and Negro congregation:

> I found a lower level and a more rapid tempo and I heard someone shout:
>   "Brothers and sisters, my text this morning is the 'Blackness of Blackness."
>   And a congregation of voices answered: "That blackness is most black, brother, most black. . . ."
>   "In the beginning . . ."
>   "At the very start," they cried.

"... there was blackness ..."
"Preach it ..."
"... and the sun ..."
"The sun, Lawd ..."
"... was bloody red ..."
"Red ..."
"Now black is ...," the preacher shouted.
"Bloody ..."
"I said black is ..."
"Preach it, brother. ..."
"... an' black ain't ..."
"Red, Lawd, red: He said it's red!"
"Amen, brother...."
"Black will git you ..."
"Yes, it will ..."
"... an' black won't ..."
"Naw, it won't"
"It do ..."
"It do, Lawd ..."
"... an' it don't."
"Hallelujah ..."
"... It'll put you, glory, glory, Oh my Lawd, in the
WHALE'S BELLY."
"Preach it, dear brother ..."
"... an' make you tempt ..."
"Good God a-mighty!"
"Old Aunt Nelly!"
"Black will make you ..."
"Black ..."
"... or black will un-make you."
"Ain't it the truth, Lawd?"[12]

Thus by intoned prayer, by rhythmic cry and by chanted phrase the preacher both ameliorates and aggravates the harshness of being black in a world antithetical to blackness. Melvin B. Tolson's *Lento Grave* movement in his poem "Dark Symphony" effectively summarizes the consistent attunement to pain in this mythological dimension:

Black slaves singing "One More River to Cross"
In the torture tombs of slave ships,
Black slaves singing "Steal Away to Jesus"
In jungle swamps,
Black slaves singing "The Crucifixion"
In slave pens at midnight,

Black slaves singing "Swing Low, Sweet Chariot"
In cabins of death.
Black slaves singing "Go Down, Moses"
In the canebrakes of the Southern Pharoahs.[13]

Urban civilization and modern institutions were working changes on "the centuries-old pathos" in these voices by the end of the nineteenth century and during the first decade of the twentieth. William Sperry's *Religion in America* raises relevant questions about the direction of change. These questions were answered in part during the period "when the Negro was in vogue," that is, during the Harlem Renaissance.

> The emancipated Negro, like the modernist Protestant, has foreshortened the picture and has attempted to restate his hope of heaven in the terms of an earthly Utopia. We can hardly blame him for so doing. The symbolism remains the same: bondage, flight, freedom, wanderings, arrival in a land of milk and honey. These transactions now take place in the terms of present life. Thus a brilliant Negro journalist, writing of his people today, takes the title for a recent book from one of the old, familiar spirituals, *Good Times A-Coming*. The question is how long the old symbols will last, wanting the depth of earlier faith and feeling. They were in the first instance religiously conceived; they have less expectation of life when restated economically and politically. Can they survive indefinitely the subtle erosion of secularism?[14]

The answers provided by the Harlem Renaissance will be assessed after the second dimension of the plantation subculture is evaluated.

The Secular Dimension: The Folktales

If what we have in the mythology is a sublimation of pain by religious speculation and expectation, the folktales offer a different picture. The perspective on man's inhumanity to man is here satiric. One transcends persecution by developing an ironical shrewdness. Satire, laconic understatement and sometimes self-mockery serve as the vehicles by which a somewhat more empirical awareness of exile is expressed. Thus, if what we have in the mythological dimension is the triumph of the dionysiac over the intellect, we may cautiously see this non-mythological expression as a peculiar triumph by wit over the stupidity and comedy that much of human wickedness demonstrates. In one of the several cycles in which the folktales are grouped, (The John and Massa), John (the name is used as a generic one for a black slave with all the attributes traditionally ascribed *vicariously* to Brer Rabbit), expresses discontentment with the harshness of his life with Massa (master). The upshot is that John retreats to a secluded spot where he daily asks God to "kill all white folks." Massa eventually hears of John's activities in this regard and decides to teach him a lesson. So he climbs up a tree with a prepared noose.

John's next visit to the spot runs true to form — complaints about the beatings etc., with the request that all whites be killed. This time Massa swings the noose over John's head. As he hangs there, John turns his eyes to heaven; in the true laconic style of this tradition he asks: "Lawd, can't you tell black folks from white folks?" The remarkable element here is the accommodation that is made to precisely the same brutality that inspired the near hysterical pain of the antiphonal dramas and the spirituals. It was an accommodation that frequently involved self-mockery. There are cycles explaining why Negroes have flat noses, why Negroes have "fat mouths," why Negroes have kinky hair. (The reason for the last is that when fine hair was being offered, the "niggers was too busy having a watermelon party.") But perhaps the most celebrated feature of these folktales is the extensive and rich symbolism of the bestiary cycle. There was powerful Brer Wolf, stupid Brer Bear, shy Brer Fox, etc. The most important animal, for both those who interpret the tales as vicarious symbolism and those who do not, was Brer Rabbit. He has come to be seen as a synthetic portrayal of hopes and failures; the only animal in the cycle who matches the complex capability of John. Brer Rabbit was braggart, glutton, wit, trickster, and lady's man. But perhaps his most significant attribute was that he represented the triumph of weakness over strength. In Brer Rabbit's invincibility we may have the secular equivalent of the religious expectation of heaven.

These fables depended entirely on oral transmission. The slaves were uneducated and could therefore develop no written tradition. Moreover, plantation life demanded an immobile peasant class. Entertainment and, in some cases, information depended on these folktales. Out of this condition evolved the storyteller and his art. His artistry was as multi-faceted as the preacher's. It was the use to which it was put which marked the difference. Storytelling demanded the kinds of drama and personality that would make the fables vivid and easily recalled. This was one way of guaranteeing their immortality since resort to the written word was impossible. The quality of the human voice and its evocative potential played major roles in the narrative technique. The storyteller became an exact temporal duplicate of the preacher. Indeed, preachers who did not have regular congregations frequently functioned as storytellers. These preachers ("jackleg preachers") thus combined in one person the principal twin personalities of the plantation subculture. Richard Dorson's introduction to his anthology of *American Negro Folktales* captures a storyteller at work:

In a barber shop in Mound Bayou, Mississippi, I heard an old, portly "jackleg" preacher, Reverend J. H. Lee, his voice thick and rumbly with age, suddenly turn clear and sharp as he imitated the fowls with uncanny realism, adding one call new to me, the hen shrieking in panic,"Good God,good God look *out*, good God,good God look *out*" — telescoping the first five words and shrilling the last, with a feverish snap, in startling likeness of a fluttering hen's cackle.[15]

But this tradition and the religious one, as William Sperry suggests, could not function effectively in an urban environment. The emancipated Negro became mobile and this mobility destroyed the old communal sense upon which the plantation culture depended. The center of expectation and identity shifted from the plantation to the city. In a way, the metaphors of the spirituals were too historical and too conceptually limited to relate effectively or satisfactorily to the new experiences mobility offered. The northern city, and the optimism it initially generated meant a belief in the City of Man. This perspective was a negation of the expectations of the City of God such as the Negro-Slave had felt compelled to await. A new voice was needed to express this kind of perspective. Langston Hughes' "Bound No'th Blues" is compulsively "mobile":

> Road, road, road, O!
> Road, road. . .road. . .road, road!
> Road, road, road, O!
> On the no'thern road.
> These Mississippi towns ain't
> Fit fer a hopping toad. [16]

True, there was suffering still in the cities but these were sufferings that provoked responses different from those which the naked brutality of slavery had aroused. The preacher became ineffective. In the first place, the Son of Thunder needed clearly defined and simplified stimuli for the simple-minded "omnipotence" of his abilities. Moreover, the peculiar inadequacies of his education, which had played so important a role in his art, could not work under a generally more permissive society. Better education meant in his case an awareness of the impracticality of depending merely on a capacity to "unscrew the inscrutable" for curative purposes. A mobile, urban Negro congregation meant a general weakening of the antiphonal unity between preacher and church. "God's Trombone" was therefore pathetically isolated in "The Kingdom of Harlem." Rudolph Fisher's short story, "Vestiges: Harlem Sketches," effectively captures his irrelevance and emphasizes the hysteria and psychic violence of the antiphonal union between preacher and congregation. The entire passage bears reproducing:

> Where you running, sinner?
> Where you running, I say?
> Running from the fire —
> You can't cross here!

The preacher stood waiting for the song to melt away. There was a moment of abysmal silence, into which the thousand blasphemies filtering in from outside dropped unheeded.

The preacher was talking in deep, impressive tones. One *old patriarch* was already supplementing each statement with a matter-of-fact "amen!" of approval.

The preacher was describing hell. He was enumerating without exception the horrors that befall the damned: maddening thirst for the drunkard; for the gambler, insatiable flame, his own greed devouring his soul. The preacher's voice no longer talked — it sang; mournfully at first, monotonously up and down — a chant in minor mode; then more intensely, more excitedly; now fairly strident.

The amens of approval were no longer matter-of-fact, perfunctory. They were quick, spontaneous, escaping the lips of their own accord; they were frequent and loud and began to come from the edges of the assembly instead of just the front rows. The *old men* cried, "help him, Lord!" "Preach the word!" "Glory!" taking no apparent heed of the awfulness of the description, and the *old women* continuously moaned aloud, nodding their bonnetted heads, or swaying rhythmically forward and back in their seats.

Suddenly the preacher stopped, leaving the *old men* and *old women* still noisy with spiritual momentum. He stood motionless till the last echo of approbation subsided, then repeated the text from which his discourse had taken origin; repeated it in a whisper, lugubrious, hoarse, almost inaudible: "In — hell —," paused, then without warning, wildly shrieked, "In hell —" stopped — returned to his hoarse whisper — "he lifted up his eyes. . . .(my emphasis).

The preacher was in fact shrieking impotently and irrelevantly to

> The Kingdom of Harlem. Children turned into mockers. Satan in the hearts of infants. Harlem — city of the devil — outpost of hell.

The atrophying of the heretofore umbilical relationship is so complete that the final response is a cruel "that old bird would' a' coughed up his gizzard in two more minutes. . . ."[17]

The first two decades of this century marked the turning point in the transformation of the plantation culture into an urban and ultimately into a ghetto expression. And here we recognize two developments. There was first what may be described as a natural, historical evolution from slave, preacher, spiritual singer to urban-ghetto dweller, jazz musician and blues singer. In this case, the esthetic expression of this development demonstrates a consistent awareness of suffering and exile. Jazz and the Blues were not adopting a public posture. On the other hand, this same evolutionary process was energized and given a decadent twist by the European intervention in Harlem in the period covered by *The Weary Blues*. The following selections from Hughes' autobiography, *The Big Sea*, best illustrate the processes at work. The Twenties offered in Rev. E. Clayton one last look at the preacher with the near superhuman aura of the old manner. Hughes describes his presence at the funeral of Harlem hostess, A'lelia Walker:

> We were startled to find De Lawd standing over A'lelia's casket. It was a truly amazing illusion. At that time *The Green Pastures* was at the height of its fame, and there stood De Lawd in the person of Rev. E. Clayton, a harlem minister.[18]

But this period was also turning the preacher's art and his congregation's responses into circus shows:

> It was a period when Charleston preachers opened up shouting churches as sideshows for white tourists.[19]

We turn away now from the recording of processes of disintegration for a brief assessment of what was created as an alternative. The urban ghetto culture which, was in effect the dynamic substratum of the Harlem Renaissance, evolved from the plantation songs and the preacher's and storyteller's artistry. The easiest connection to trace is perhaps the storyteller's art, which created the *cante fable*. The rhythmic discourses, imitated cries and sometimes chanted syllables created stories that were really more songs than straight narratives. This gave rise in part to the talking blues, also called *cante fable* and meaning singing plus talking. The quiet control of the Spirituals presumably fused with the strong syncopations of work songs to create the insistent rhythms of gospel songs. The work songs also influenced secular music and in their lyrics demonstrate social and economic changes. The demands of physical labor in the cotton fields required a compulsive, sustaining rhythm:

> Hoe down niggers, hoe down quick –
> Hoe down the weeds where they done grow thick,
> The sun am hot and the nigger might drop –
> But the cotton must grow and the nigger musn't stop.[20]

The chain gangs demanded muscular energy and imposed new rhythms on the form of expression:

> Take this hammer – huh!
> and carry it to the captain – huh!
> You tell him I'm gone – huh!
> You tell him I'm gone – huh!
>
> If he asks you – huh!
> Was I runnin' – huh!
> You tell him I was flying – huh!
> You tell him I was flying – huh![21]

These "syncopated syncopations" undoubtedly conjoined with other currents to create Jazz. The development of Jazz itself is clouded in controversy – mainly between the school for White origin and that for Black. I find the general thesis of Barry Ulanov's *A History of Jazz in America* useful and intelligent: several currents, African, European and American, conjoined in musical experimentation. Attempts at isolative particularization soon degenerate into unsatisfactory polemic or speculation. There is quite clearly an insistent rhythmic core to Jazz around which are built essentially non-lyrical structures. In this sense, Jazz differs rather significantly from the quieter, melodic, lyrical lines of the Blues. In general, the Blues lack the percussive excitements that one finds in Jazz. But the varieties of Blues suggest a variety of sources and hence of musical emphasis. There are Chain Gang Blues, Prison House Blues, Ball and Chain Blues, Cottonfield Blues, Backwater or Mississippi Blues, Talking Blues, and the more commonly heard Love Blues or Broken-hearted Blues.

One of the major differences between these urban expressions and the religious songs from which some of them originate lies in the matter of despair versus hope. The emphasis in these urban-ghetto expressions was on dislocation. To use Sperry's words again, "the symbolism remains the same: bondage, flight, freedom, wanderings." What was impossible, since neither history nor personal experience appeared to justify it, was the "arrival in a land of milk and honey." For this reason, the blues always showed a tragic sense of life:

> De worry blues ain' nothin' but de heart disease.
> De worry blues ain' nothin' but de heart disease.
> De worry blues ain' nothin' but de heart disease.[22]

Even in the Love Blues, which will form the decadent inspiration for the *"chansons vulgaires"* in Harlem cellars, the expression was invariably one of frustration:

> I hear my daddy callin' some other woman's name.
> I know he don't mean me; I'm gonna answer jes de same.[23]

Ralph Ellison has said of the Blues that they are:

> An autobiographical chronicle of personal catastrophe expressed lyrically. Their attraction lies in this, that they at once express both the agony of life and the possibility of conquering it through sheer toughness of spirit. They fall short of tragedy only in that they provide no solution, offer no scapegoat but the self.[24]

I agree with the effective and comprehensive literacy of the definition offered. But the implied prescription for what is tragic is rather puzzling, rather esoterically irrelevant to the very tragedy explicit in the history of the Negro. But Blues lyrics can show a fine even if sardonic awareness of this pathological ambiance:

> Did you ever see a one-eyed woman cry?
> Says, did you ever see a one-eyed woman cry?
> Jack, she can cry so good out of that one old eye.[25]

It is against this background that the energies of the Harlem artists of the Twenties were stimulated. The prolific creativity of the period of *The Weary Blues* can therefore be seen as the esthetic climax of some of the major issues raised by the excellence and limitations of the "racial heritage" described above. The Harlem Renaissance did not solve these issues in any definitive sense. This was in itself a most fortunate situation for it resulted in the expansive, artistic activities with which the "New Negroes," as they called themselves, are associated. It was precisely in the attempt to offer an effective definition or manifesto of what the "newness" and "negroness" constituted that the difficulties and stimuli resided. What was the "old" like? What were the collective and individual racial responsibilities to the old Negro? Disruption and unchartered optimism were almost inseparably bound in the exploratory search of the Harlem Renaissance.

The turn of the century migratory movements had resulted in the disruption of the near-absolute plantation-slave-peasant identity heretofore associated with the Negro. That identity became at once important but essentially irrelevant to the exigencies of life in the city. The spirituals were important but did not appear to count; the preacher and the antiphonal celebrations he led were important but again did not seem to count. The folktales were stimulating, historical, esthetic documentations of a racial response but appeared to have been rendered pointless by the peculiar demands of urban settlement. Very often urban settlement was:

> . . .a close-built, top-heavy city. . .baring the mangy backs of a long row of One Hundred and Thirty-ninth Street houses; disclosing their gaping, gasping windows, their shameless strings of half-laundered rags, which gulp up what little air the windows seek to inhale.[26]

Another contradiction was the fact that the race had optimistically migrated from hell in the plantation only to discover, in the main, that the presumed "land of milk and honey" was like "Harlem, this city of Satan. . .this great noisy, heartless, crowded place where you lived under the same roof with a hundred people you never knew." But then the very freedom from the crippling psychological and intellectual limitations of slavery opened to blacks the possibility that the world and man were fundamentally bigger and more expansive than the metaphors and similies of the "heritage" said they were. All these issues brought a number of crises to a climax. What was a Negro? Who was a Negro? Why is the Negro? Is the American Negro a black man? What did blackness consist of? Could a man be biologically a Negro and psychologically colorless? Was the Negro perhaps an African? If so, in what sense — first, inorganically by way of nostalgic memories? Or perhaps, even more vitally, more organically — did his human cells retain certain genetic information that was inevitably and spontaneously passed on? If so, in which of the numerous manifestations of blackness was it clearly but unrecognizedly asserting itself? On the other hand, was the Negro an American? To what degree was he so Americanized or even Westernized that he was in fact only accidentally African and Negroid?[27]

There was also the issue of individual artistic expression. The metaphors and perspectives of the "heritage" seem singularly effective for suggesting death, disease and dislocations. Now, this may be true for the collective racial experience, but to what extent should it be true of the individual response to that experience? Should Phyllis Wheatly have written poems celebrating London in the Graeco-Roman classicism of Alexander Pope when the "heritage" did not acknowledge the existence of London? Should a Harlem Renaissance poet, Claude Mckay, become enamoured of Barcelona and write long poems celebrating that Spanish city? Who or what was at fault here, assuming the question to be relevant? Was the artist or individual guilty of betrayal or at best of an elegant waste of esthetic energies? Or was the "heritage" itself guilty of a distressing betrayal of the scope of human imagination? What kinds of conceptual limitations were inevitable in a heritage born, bred and nurtured on human perversity? Would it be unnatural if these limitations were present in the expressions of the plantation and in those being formed by the city? How then should the individual, artistically or otherwise, align himself with the excellencies and distortions of the "old Negro"?

The polemic issues here, as in the French and Spanish Caribbean, also involved language. How vital and organic was English, a Western and perhaps Westernizing medium, in the expression of that which was intrinsically Negro – however that was defined? How was the artist to relate to the particular rhythms, dialect and dynamism of Negro speech? By the same token, what kinds of conceptual and intellectual limitations were implicitly inseparable from that speech? Two works that may be placed roughly at the beginning and the end of Harlem Renaissence offer the clearest potential in the issue of medium of expression. Paul Laurence Dunbar's *Lyrics of Lowly Life* was published in 1896 and dedicated to showing the potential of the dialect which had up to then primarily functioned in Spirituals and Folktales:

> Dunbar made Negro dialect poetry popular and so founded a school. He was imitated by many writers, both white and black, none of whom quite equaled him in humor, tenderness, and charm, and in the finish with which he generally worked. . . .Dunbar wrought delightful music in the dialect and gained the national ear.[28]

But Dunbar himself was inadequately convinced of the expressive potential of the dialect. "Dunbar thought of Negro dialect as 'broken tongue,' and consequently did not achieve all he was capable of in its use."[29] James Weldon Johnson's *God's Trombones: Seven Negro Sermons in Verse* was published in 1927, two years before the stock market crash would put an end to the exotic negrophilism in Harlem. His primary interest was in transforming what I have called the mythological features of the plantation culture, especially the "organ-toned" majesty in the preacher's exuberance. Significantly, he avoided the use of dialect, but his justification of the choice he made constitutes one of the most literate statements of the case for eclecticism in American Negro literature:

> To place in the mouths of the talented old-time Negro preachers a language that is a literary imitation of Mississippi cotton-field dialect is sheer burlesque. . . .What the colored poet in the United States needs to do is something like what Synge did for the Irish; he needs to find a form that will express the racial spirit by symbols from

within rather than by symbols from without – such as the mere mutilation of English spelling and pronunciation. He needs a form that is freer and larger than dialect, but which will still hold the racial, flavor; a form expressing the imagery, the idioms, the peculiar turns of thought and the distinctive humor and pathos, too, of the Negro, but which will also be capable of voicing the deepest and highest emotions and aspirations and allow the widest range of subjects and widest treatment.[30]

These then were the kinds of intellectual, artistic and social energies that conjoined with the European taste for the exotic to blossom between 1912 and 1929 in the Harlem Renaissance.

This is the background against which *The Weary Blues* (1926) is best read. The title and the title poem are important because they intrude a world of painful reality into the intoxications of Harlem. What we have in the work is a documentation of the excitements *and* the unheard agonies of that Harlem whose seductions are evident in Nicolás Guillén's "Oda a Un Boxeador Negro Cubano," in Leopold Sédar Senghor's "A New York (pour un orchestre de jazz: solo de trumpette)" and in Federico García Lorca's "El Rey de Harlem." That is, the Harlem that attracted black men from the Caribbean, from Africa and, of course, from the American South. In another sense, it is a record of the libidinous irrationality of the European intervention during the same period. In this respect, we observe the primitivism and hedonism that were the guiding forces in this period "when a large and enthusiastic number of people were crazy about Negroes."

The attitude which Langston Hughes demonstrates in the work is quite different from the urgency we find in Césaire's *Cahier d'un Retour au Pays Natal*; there is also none of the polemic power and anger that we see in Guillén's *West Indies Ltd.* These two later works (1938 and 1934, respectively), give evidence of a self-definition born of traumatic disenchantment. The sense of personal despair is muted in *The Weary Blues*. Part of the reason lies in the fact that there are two modes in the work. I would describe the first as Jazz, a major mode, musically speaking. The second, the minor, is the Blues. They correspond to a participatory, celebrative involvement and a lyrically contemplative perception of Harlem. Hughes' own description of his reaction to the period confirms the dual perspective:

> I was there. I had a swell time while it lasted. But I thought it wouldn't last long. . . .For how could a large and enthusiastic number of people be crazy about Negroes forever?[31]

In *The Weary Blues* Hughes had expressed that suspicion about the "jazz rhythm" of the life of Harlem in the quiet premonition that one sees in the last stanza of "Lenox Avenue: Midnight":

> Lenox Avenue,
> Honey.
> Midnight,
> And the gods are laughing at us.

The division of the poems into two modes is also important because of the rhythms in which the respective poems are written. Jazz appears to represent the pathogenic vitality of the period whereas the lyrical observation of catastrophe is done in the style of the Blues. It is thus a lyricism that acknowledges pain and suffering without adopting an *engagé* posture. The poem "To a Black Dancer" shows in its turgid intoxication the Jazz mood. Hughes quite clearly shows his vulnerability to the erotically decadent taste of the time:

> Wine-maiden
> Of jazz-tuned night
> Lips
> Sweet as purple dew,
> Breasts
> Like the pillows of all sweet dreams,
> Who crushed
> The grapes of joy
> And dripped their juice
> On you?[32]

In a similar vein, the Negress in "Nude Young Dancer" belongs to the tradition of Camin's "Elogio a la Negra" discussed in Chapter 4:

> What jungle have you slept under,
> Midnight dancer of the jazzy hour?
> What great forest has hung its perfume
> Like a sweet veil about your bower?
>
> What jungle tree have you slept under,
> Night-dark girl of the swaying hips?
> What star-white moon has been your mother?
> To what clean boy have you offered your lips.[33]

The cloying, even melodramatic sweetness of these jazz moments is soured in "Cabaret" by the intrusion into jazz of the agony of the blues. As yet, it still is merely a suspicion of things incongruous:

> Does a jazz-band ever sob?
> They say a jazz-band's gay.
> Yet as the vulgar dancers whirled
> And the wan night wore away,
> One said she heard the jazz-band sob
> When the little dawn was grey. . . .[34]

The full perception of this vulgarity is expressed with an extraordinary understatement that is in effect quite a shock. The title is explicit enough as the "wine-maiden/of jazz-tuned night" becomes a "Young Prostitute," but the five lines of the poem are as rudely clear-sighted as they are laconic:

> Her dark brown face
> Is like a withered flower
> On a broken stem.
> Those kind come cheap in Harlem
> So they say.[35]

The title poem is significant in many ways. Césaire's awakened and angry disenchantment makes Toussaint Louverture, militant and revolutionary, the prototype or Adam of his *négritude*. In Guillén we find the inarticulate pathos of the *boxeador* buttressed by brute force. There is then in both cases some degree of energetic reaction. In Hughes' title poem, "The Weary Blues," we see neither a revolutionary nor a boxer. There is instead a peculiarly disembodied Orphic voice singing of and with a soul-atrophying weariness. The preacher, Son of Thunder, has been replaced by the blues singer. Vitality and invincible optimism give way to a suicidal awareness of the monotony of suffering:

> I got the Weary Blues
> And I can't be satisfied.
> Got the Weary Blues
> And can't be satisfied —
> I ain't happy no mo'
> And I wish that I had died.

Unlike the Hispanic Negro Orpheus who created a percussive music that was virile and vital, if mindless, the Harlem Orpheus' music is "a drowsy syncopated tune/rocking back and forth to a mellow croon." The kind of intensity the music has is thus a narcotic, self-caressing sweetness. This was indeed an "autobiographical chronicle of catastrophe expressed lyrically." But its very attunement to agony nonetheless served as a powerful opiate, for "while the Weary Blues echoed through his head/ he slept like a rock or a man that's dead." As we shall see in Chapter 7, Regino Pedroso will react violently against the percussive mindlessness in the Afro-Cuban tradition. Small wonder then that James A. Emmanuel shows an angry impatience and disgust in "Get Up, Blues:"

> Blues
> Never climb a hill
> Or sit on a roof
> In starlight.
>
> Blues
> Just bend low
> And moan in the street
> And shake a borrowed cup.
>
> Blues
> Just sit around
> Slipping Hatching yesterdays.
>
> Get up, Blues
> Fly.
> Learn what it means
> To be up high.[36]

And yet the poem is somewhat unjust. It was not so much a case of the Blues rejecting confrontation as it was a case of an overwhelming response to suffering. The Blues were a response to the precarious unfamiliarity of a post-emancipation "Eden." The result was a stultifying atunement of life to pain. This then is the Negro that Langston Hughes singles out in all the vulgar, messianic jubilation of Harlem:

> Droning a drowsy syncopated tune,
> Rocking back and forth to a mellow croon,
>   I heard a Negro play.
> Down on Lenox Avenue the other night
> By the pale dull pallor of an old gas light
>   He did a lazy sway . . .
>   He did a lazy sway . . .
> To the tune o' those Weary Blues.
> With his ebony hands on each ivory key
> He made that poor piano mean with melody.
>   O Blues!
> In a deep song voice with a melancholy tone
> I heard that Negro sing, that old piano moan

"Ain't got nobody but ma self.
I's gwine to quit ma frownin'
And put ma troubles on the shelf."
Thump, thump, thump, went his foot on the floor
He played a few chords then he sang some more —
"I got the Weary Blues
And I can't be satisfied.
Got the Weary Blues
And can't be satisfied —
I ain't happy no mo'
And I wish that I had died."
And far into the night he crooned that tune.
The stars went out and so did the moon.
The singer stopped playing and went to bed
While the Weary Blues echoed through his head.
He slept like a rock or a man that's dead.

But as a final statement, the poem and its lyrical defeatism is unfair to the optimistic expectation of the period. No matter how much the symptoms pointed to the pathogenic, there was undeniably a ferment, a feeling of power generated by the Harlem Renaissance. That power was not necessarily blind. It could and did perceive difficulties when it sought to define its *negritude* in a white world outside the excesses of "jazz cellars:"

My old man died in a fine big house.
My ma died in a shack.
I wonder where I'm gonna die
Being neither white nor black.[37]

This, however, was a "Cross" that could be borne. It simply did not have enough negative energies to cancel the alchemizing drive that the period wished to believe it possessed. Sometimes the enthusiastic optimism would be expressed in terms that were outrageous and bathetic:

I have just seen a most beautiful thing
    Slim and still,
  Against a gold, gold, sky,
    A straight black cypress,
    Sensitive,
    Exquisite,
    A black finger
    Pointing upwards.
Why, beautiful still finger, are you black?
And why are you pointing upwards?[38]

In Langston Hughes' "Epilogue" poem to *The Weary Blues*, the optimism is more restrained, more decorous — even contingent. Hughes develops or perhaps postulates moral and esthetic tolerance as he seeks to establish a "New Negro" identity in terms of a New World Eden. "Epilogue" implicitly rejects definition in terms of the "West African sepia" identity of Wole Soyinka. Walt Whitman, the prophet of the New World, provides the inspiration as the poem turns explicity toward a corrective intervention in America. Whitman had written "I Hear America Singing"; Hughes becomes the "darker brother" singing his American birthright. True, the inconvenience of history and experience must be acknowledged:

> I, too, sing America.
>
> I am the darker brother.
> They send me to eat in the kitchen
> When company comes,
> But I laugh,
> And eat well,
> And grow strong.

But this undignified baptism into a new identity will not destroy the respect and authenticity of the New Negro:

> Tomorrow,
> I'll sit at the table
> When company comes.
> Nobody'll dare
> Say to me,
> "Eat in the kitchen,"
> Then.

The mark of Cain is erased; the Prodigal Son returns home; the Creole finds a resting place:

> Besides,
> They'll see how beautiful I am
> And be ashamed. —
>
> I, too, am America.[39]

In his last book of poems forty-one years later, a work significantly titled *The Panther and The Lash: Poems for Our Times*, identity is once more inseparable from crisis:

> I am the American Heartbreak —
> The rock on which Freedom
> Stumped its toe —
> The great mistake
> That Jamestown made
> Long ago.[40]

By its very nature the cynicism and sense of defeat in this poem would have been strange-sounding during the Harlem Renaissance. It was the period when it was almost universally agreed that the only vital force in an otherwise crumbling world was the Negro. It was a period of contradictory compulsions: creativity and decadence; apotheoses and reductive simplifications. These compulsions had another decade yet to find manifestations in Guillén's and Césaire's works. Then the world would leave the Negro and go about the serious business of preparing the "opulent pause" for the insanity of World War II. But not without a parting shot (1938) from one *assimilé:* "ecoutez le monde blanc/horriblement las de son effort immense." It is also during that "opulent pause" that Nicolás Guillén's Afro-cubanism reached its most dramatic expression in *West Indies Ltd.* (1934).

NOTES

[1] *The Weary Blues*, p. 39.
[2] We may see this as extending into the Jazz Age not so much *a la* Scott-Fitzgerald but rather as in Malcolm X's extraordinary autobiography.
[3] *The Weary Blues*, p. 28.
[4] Langston Hughes, *The Big Sea* (autobiography) in *The Langston Hughes Reader* (New York: George Braziller Inc., 1958), pp. 317-398. Selected item is from p. 371.
[5] *The Weary Blues*, p. 32.
[6] Langston Hughes and Arna Bontemps, *The Book of Negro Folklore* (New York: Dodd, Mead & Company, 1959), p. 384.
[7] See Helen d'Aquin, *Souvenirs d'Amérique et de France par une Creole* (Paris: Bourguet Calas, 1883); James Broussard, *Louisiana Creole Dialect* (Baton Rouge: Louisiana State University, 1942). *Life Magazine*, March 14, 1969 p. 18B, examines the efforts of *Le Conseil pour le Developpement du Francais en Louisiane* in its attempt to prevent the disappearance of French culture among the *Creoles*. The same

movement from Nova Scotia also brought settlers to Freetown.

In the discussion above in text and following on religious influences I have synthesized several Protestant currents into a dominant attitude. For subtler, even contradictory shades see T. Scott Miyakawa, *Protestants and Pioneers: Individualism and Conformity on the American Frontier* (Chicago: University of Chicago Press, 1964), especially the helpful summary of denominational responses to the Negro problem on pp. 159-197. In all studies of Negro religion in the United States, the reader will invariably come across Carter G. Woodson's *The History of the Negro Church.* See also William Sperry, *Religion in America* (Cambridge, England: University Press, 1945). Especially Chapters Five and Six: "The Denominations" and "The Negro Churches."

[8] Richard M. Dorson, *American Negro Folktales* (New York: Fawcett, 1967), p. 12. The most impressive anthology of these tales that I know of.

[9] Some of the lesser-known Spirituals come in dramatically tight rhythms which leads to the possibility that they are not as sentimentally sorrowful as the more celebrated lyrics have been interpreted. See the following from *The Book of Negro Folklore*, p. 88:

> "I got a home in dat rock,
>   don't you see?
> I got a home in dat rock,
>   don't you see?
> Between de earth an' sky,
> Thought I heard my savior cry,
> You got a home in dat rock,
>   don't you see?"

[10] James Weldon Johnson, *God's Trombones: Seven Negro Sermons in Verse* (New York: The Viking Press, 1966), pp. 2-5. The introduction to this work by Johnson himself is a most literate apologia for this aspect of American Negro heritage. For the role of the preacher in Revivalism as a whole the following may prove contrastively interesting: Charles Coleman Sellers, *Lorenzo Dow, The Bearer of the Word*; as also studies and writings from Puritan New England, Cotton Mather, Jonathan Edwards and of course the aberrant drama of Salem.

[11] It is for this reason that I choose to illustrate from Ellison below, *The Book of Negro Folklore* and other studies have preserved early sermons, e.g. "De Sun Do Move" and "Dry Bones." But it is distortive to leave out the congregation's antiphonal responses which are of course unrecorded.

[12] Ralph Ellison, *Invisible Man* (New York: The New American Library, 1952), pp. 12-13. Compare the following from Herman Melville, *Moby Dick*, p. 8:

> "...this, then must needs be the sign of 'The Trap.' However, I picked myself up and hearing a loud voice within, pushed on and opened a second, interior door.
>
> It seemed the great Black Parliament sitting in Tophet. A hundred black faces turned round in their rows to peer; and beyond, a black Angel of Doom was beating a book in a pulpit. It was a negro church; and the preacher's text was about the blackness of darkness, and the weeping and wailing and teeth-gnashing there. Ha, Ishmael, muttered I backing out, Wretched entertainment at the sight of 'The Trap!'"

It is not insignificant that Ellison places the ceremony at a *lower level*. For discussions of the antiphonal drama as a trap and a wretched entertainment see illustrations from Rudolph Fisher in text following.

[13] *American Negro Poetry*, ed. Arna Bontemps, p. 38.

[14] William Sperry, *op. cit.*, p. 195.

[15] Dorson, *op. cit.*, pp. 48-49. I have avoided, because the arguments are tendentiously tiresome to me, the whole argument about the African or European origins of these tales. But see, in addition to Dorson's good introduction, Melville Herskovits' *The Myth of the Negro Past*; Stith Thompson, *Motif-Index of Folk Literature*; Zora Neale Hurston, *Men and Mules*; Arthur Huff Fauset, "American Negro Folk Literature," in *The New Negro*, pp. 238-247. And of course the unfortunate benefits of Joel Chandler Harris' Uncle Remus stories.

[16] *American Negro Poetry*, p. 65.

[17] Rudolph Fisher, "Vestiges: Harlem Sketches, IV" in *The New Negro*, pp. 83-84.

[18] *The Langston Hughes Reader*, p. 382.

[19] *Ibid.*, p. 371.

[20]. William C. Blades, *Negro Poems, Melodies, Plantation Pieces, Camp Meeting Songs* (Boston: The Gorham Press, 1921), p. 162. Work songs of this nature formed part of the secular music of the plantation heritage. The non-work songs show exactly the same triumph by wit or mockery as is seen in the folktales. See the following from *The Book of Negro Folklore*, p. 88:

> "My ole mistress promise me,
> W'en she died, she'd set me free,
> She lived so long dat 'er head got bal',
> An' she give out'n de notion a-dying at al."

[21] *Negro Folklore*, p. 399. In addition, for discussion following see *ibid.*, pp. 371-397, "The Blues as Folk Poetry", Samuel Charters, *The Poetry of the Blues* (New York: Oak Publications, 1963); W. E. B. Dubois, *The Souls of Black Folk*. Also *Bawdy Blues*, Bluesville Records, Bluesville 1055 (Bergenfield, New Jersey); *The Blues Box*, FTS 3011-3, Verve Folkways, Metro-Goldwyn-Mayer Inc.

[22] *Negro Folklore*, p. 393.

[23] *Ibid.*, p. 385.

[24] *Ibid.*, quoted by Arna Bontemps, p. xiv.

[25] *Ibid.*, p. 393.

[26] Rudolph Fisher, *op. cit.*, p. 82.

[27] There are numerous poems in the Harlem Renaissance anthology, *The New Negro*, which confront this crisis, but the most effective – perhaps the best Creole poem given the nature of the period – is Countee Cullen's "Heritage," from which the following, pp. 250-252:

> "What is Africa to me:
> . . . .
> *One three centuries removed*
> *From the scenes his fathers loved*
> *Spicy grove and banyan tree,*
> *What is Africa to me?*
>
> Africa? A book one thumbs
> Listlessly, till slumber comes.
> . . . .
> *Stubborn heart and rebel head.*
> *Have you not yet realized*
> *You and I are civilized?*
>
> So I lie and all day long

Want no sound except the song
Sung by wild barbaric birds
Goading massive jungle herds,
Juggernauts of flesh that pass
Trampling tall defiant grass
Where young forest lovers lie
Plighting troth beneath the sky.

So I lie, who always hear
Though I cram against my ear
Both my thumbs, and keep them there.
Great drums beating through the air.
So I lie, whose fount of pride,
Dear distress, and joy allied,
Is my somber flesh and skin
With the dark blood dammed within.
Thus I lie, and find no peace
Night or day, no slight release
From the unremittent beat
Made by cruel padded feet,
Walking through my body's street.

. . . .

In an old remembered way
Rain works on me night and day.
Though three centuries removed
From the scenes my fathers loved.

My conversion came high-priced.
I belong to Jesus Christ,

. . . .

"*Father, Son and Holy Ghost*"
Do I make an idle boast,
Jesus of the twice turned cheek,
Lamb of God, although I speak
With my mouth thus, in my heart
Do I not play a double part?

. . . .

Moreover, the Harlem of the twenties was a city of blackness from Africa,
the South, Latin America, the Caribbean; as Fisher puts it in "City of Refuge" (*The New Negro*, p. 57) there were "big lanky Negroes, short squat Negroes; black ones, brown ones, yellow ones. . . .This was Negro Harlem."

[28] Arna Bontemps, introduction to *American Negro Poetry*.

[29] Gerald W. Haslam, *Forgotten Pages of American Literature* (Boston, 1970), p. 272.

[30] Introductory remarks to *God's Trombones*. See also Juan Marinello's expectations of the Afrocuban culture in the next chapter.

[31] *The Langston Hughes Reader*, p. 371.

[32] *The Weary Blues*, p. 35.

[33] *Ibid.*, p. 33.

[34] *Ibid.*, p. 29.

[35] *Ibid.*, p. 34
[36] *American Negro Poetry*, pp. 175-176.
[37] *The Weary Blues*, p. 52
[38] *The New Negro*, p. 148 for Angelina Grimke's "The Black Finger."
[39] *The Weary Blues*, p. 109.
[40] *The Panther and The Lash* (New York: Alfred Knopf, 1967), p. 25.

CHAPTER 7

NICOLÁS GUILLÉN AND AFRO-CUBANISM

To follow the interests of Nicolás Guillén's poetry from 1929 to 1934 is in a sense to follow the development of the West and its negrophilism through two stages, from the vulgar tourisms of the Twenties to the fullness of Marxist interest in the Negro during the Thirties. For this reason, the title of Guillén's 1934 work, *West Indies Ltd.*, carries a double implication. First, the limitations of a pathological, caricatured Caribbean and second, the exploitative vulgarity of a capitalist, essentially United States, intrusion into that world:

> El negro
> junto al cañaveral.

> El yanqui
> sobre el cañaveral.

> La tierra
> bajo el cañaveral.

> ¡Sangre
> que se nos va!

The Negro/in the sugar plantation/the Yankee/above the sugar plantation/the earth/under the sugar plantation/God/how we bleed! "Caña" is a 1931 poem from *Songoro Consongo*. In the tight-lipped, barely controlled violence of the poem we have an important expression of the times. It marked the conjunction of the Caribbean Negro's search for identity with the United States' contribution to the apocalyptic sense of the end of the nineteenth century and the beginnings of the twentieth.

We can, by way of the decadent, bohemian excitement of Paris, diagnose Europe's *fin-de siècle malaise* as feverish anemia. The United States' by way of Sandburg's "hog-butcher capital of the world, Chicago," appeared to have been a hyper-dynamic charge of energies leading to a gluttonous constipation. At least, so it seemed to those American artists who chose to rage in Zenith rather than despair on the Left Bank. This was in part a consequence of the conversion of Walt Whitman's trans-cendental visions into enthusiastically unapologetic greed.[1] Writing some six years before Darwin, Herbert Spencer coined the expression "sur-vival of the fittest" – a most strategic expression for the concerns of the

West in the nineteenth century. The intent of nature was to weed out the unfit. In the United States, Darwin's *Origin of Species* (1859) and Spencer's views combined to justify the "fact" that "the growth of large business is merely a survival of the fittest." "The contrast between the palace of the millionaire and the cottage of the laborer with us today measures the change that has come with civilization. This change, however, is not to be deplored, but welcomed as highly beneficial:"

> The millionaires are a product of natural selection. . .the naturally selected agents for certain work. They get high wages and live in luxury, but the bargain is a good one for society.

To the millionaires themselves, this manifestation of natural, scientific truth was overwhelmingly educative: "Not only had I got rid of theology and the supernatural, but I had found the truth of evolution." And so according to the Gospel of Wealth this was the best of all possible worlds:

> Thus Jefferson's yeoman became industry's suppliers, Franklin's mechanics its hirelings, and his tradesmen the distributors of its products; and all were degraded from the economic self-sufficiency and independence which gave them dignity. American opportunity no longer meant the right to be a man in a society of equals, independent because economically self-sufficient; it meant the chance to get rich by exploiting the physical resources of the country and the labor of other men. America's destiny was not to be God's commonwealth as the Puritans imagined, nor a republic wherein ordinary men could rise to their full and equal worth as Paine and Jefferson supposed, but an economic empire run by captains of industry.[2]

And so too in the metaphors of the Twenties was created Babbitt, that personification of materialistic, self-satisfied mediocrity. He joined the pathetically decent and anemic J. Alfred Prufrock as the twin personalities of a "botched-civilization."

To the European and American artistic elite there was much in this conjoined energy of "erring barbarians" and "philistines" that pointed toward the Apocalypse. That much we have already seen. Insofar as the "superior wisdom" of the millionaire could not be trusted to take care of his "poorer brethren" the writings of Karl Marx and the Russian Revolution became pivots around which much of the intellectual disaffection of the period was organized. Socialism or communism would be embraced with a passion that indicated not so much an intelligent awareness of the proposed remedy as a profound disgust with the disease.[3] It is against this background the Guillén combines racial awareness, socialist inclinations and a violent disgust for the Unites States into *West Indies*

Ltd. (1934). The work is certainly one of the most artistically brilliant creations of the period. Broadway, insofar as it symbolized the thickening center of vulgar and exploitative Babbittry, will provoke Guillén to mordant and yet exquisite poetry. The final impression is, however, that Guillén is concerned not so much with economic exploitation as with the banality that inevitably precedes and results from exploitation. His unsparing description of the Caribbean is comparable to Graham Greene's fascination with the banal caricature that the Sierra Leone Creole illustrates. The difference, was that the African Jacobin was a mongrel aristocrat, whereas insofar as it was possible and insofar as the United States was the intrusive force the West Indies became a mongrel Babbitt.

Just as Langston Hughes brought a Negro subculture to bear on his chronicle of the Harlem Renaissance, so, too, we cannot ignore the peculiar configurations of native impulses in Guillén's work. As with Hughes, their influences are inseparable from the dynamics of Guillén's works. Moreover, they determine the trajectory which caricature and re-definition follow. Juan Marinello has written of Guillén:

> Nicolás Guillén es una integración sorprendente de naturaleza y cultura: de la naturaleza en su impulso primario, indefectible, vencedor; de la cultura como sabio ursufructo del ímpetu natural. Ello la nace del tesoro de sus sangres: grito irrestricto, músculo gigante de su Africa ancestral; dominio de técnicas y virtuosismos del abuelo europeo. Sus sangres han salvado a Guillén y logrado en él uno de los momentos más plenos de nuestra lírica actual.[4]

Guillén's electic brilliance was thus the happy synthesis of two dominant allegiances, to Africa and to Europe. He was biologically a Creole, born in 1904 in Camagüey, Cuba, of Spanish-Criollo and Negro parentage. Artistically, he fused the European concerns of the time with his Afro-Cuban literary heritage into his own peculiar conception of things. The opening lines of his most impressive statement of this dualism in his personality, "Balada de los Dos Abuelos," put it well:

> Sombras que sólo yo veo
> me escoltan mis dos abuelos.
>
> . . . .
> Pie desnudo, torso petreo
> los de mi negro;
> pupilas de vidrio antártico,
> las de mi blanco.[5]

Much in the tone of the period, Guillén, like Countee Cullen in the Harlem Renaissance, will equate the dynamic with his black blood and the analytic with his white blood. The major intent then is to arrive at a balanced syncretism between "ansia negra" and "ansia blanca." The identity of the Cuban Negro is, of course, not separable from the influence exerted on what I called the Atlantic-Forest Axis (Chapter 2). Roman Catholicism and the nature of the hispanic response to the Negro and to the New World all played significant roles in the kind of culture the Negro created in Cuba.

The first group of Negro slaves, some 300 in number, arrived in Santiago, Cuba, about 1521. They were, as is to be presumed, a heterogenous representation of several African tribes. At that early date it would have been an even more seriously fragmented group since, as indicated in Chapter 2, efforts toward expansion and consolidation did not really begin in the Atlantic-Forest Axis until well past the eighteenth century. Nonetheless, it will become evident that a cultural symbiosis was created out of several individual African residuals. The fact that the Negro was then not completely defined outside an organic union with African tribalism can be attributed in part to the Roman Catholic Church. By and large, it displayed a less reactionary attitude toward the Negro and that which made him religiously different. This can be seen as both a fortuitous and opportunistic combination of forces. The fundamentally polytheistic drama of Roman Catholicism did not violently clash with the religious impulses which the Negro brought with him. Moreover, to the theologically uninitiated and to the educationally ignored, there was much that was attractive and theatrically immediate in Roman Catholicism. The arid landscapes of Protestantism were here replaced by the celebrative clutter of the Catholic's response to a multitude of beatified ancestral spirits, sacraments and requiems. To fortuitously find much that was sensible and organic in all this was of course contrary to the intentions of St. Augustine or St. Thomas Aquinas. But the fact was that the Negro slave found it easier and less repugnant to convert by way of misinterpretation and symbiosis. The African residuals were therefore not subjected to the same kind of traumatic disruptions that they suffered under Protestantism.

The ethnographic studies of Fernando Ortiz, Romulo Lacatañere's *O mio Yemayá* and the stories of Lydia Cabrera suggest, among others, the complexity and variety of African influences at work in the Afro-Cuban culture.[6] Nonetheless, it can be condensed and related to the culture discussed in Chapter 2. We are, in general, dealing with the culture created by the *bembón* and the *bozal*. All the African impulses were organized into a religious and social organization called *Ñañiguismo*. Significantly, the adherrent did not see himself as a *bozal* but as a *ñañigo, a custodio de los antepasados*, a custodian of the ancestors. He was a *cuidadoso del culto ancestral*, a guardian of the ancestral cult. It was and is, a cult that shows the same belief in some kind of Cosmic Mana both related to and independent of pantheistic manifestations. There was a force, a *ñanga*, which infused and animated all visible phenomena. There is thus a *ñanga* of trees, of rocks and the like. This all-pervading force could be harnessed for good or for evil. There are charms, *embo* or *mayumba*, which determine how to use and direct that force. The belief in this all-pervasive energy in the cosmos does not cancel a polytheistic hierarchy in *Ñañiguismo*. Abasi the Creator formed the universe by removing the component parts from a tree. He is the father of Ecúe who, naturally, is sometimes identified with Jesus. The Supreme Deity, different from Abasi, the Prime Mover, is Eribo. Under him are a host of divinities: Obatala, Chango and Babayu-ayé, god of poverty. There is also Guije, a protean divinity with the head of a Negro and the tail of a fish. He could appear as male or female and each appearance presaged serious public calamities. Closely allied with Babayu-ayé is Echu (Eshu Elegba in Yoruba, who also appears as Atibô Legba, an intercessory divinity in Haitian Voodoo). In *Ñañiguismo* Echu provides the satanic and dionysian dimension. His color is red and his rituals are associated with blood and rum. *Ñañiguismo* also offers sacrifices and rituals. To that extent there are totemic and fetish animals. The snake, as in Haiti and Dahomey, is the most important totemic animal. The sacred serpent is called *itongo*. The cock is the fetish animal called *enkiko*. Its meat is the most important element in the sacred food. The organization of *Ñañiguismo* suggests its religious and social nature. The *cabildo* is not only a temple; it is also a social unit. Thus *ñañigos* belong religiously and socially to *cabildos* which are further subdivided into *juegos*, the members of which are *ecobios*, friends. The altars in the *cabildos* on which are placed fetish or totemic items are called *famba* and the guardian *famballén*. The social leader and indeed the high priest of the cult is the *Iyamba*. The call to worship, best translated as *te deum laudamus*, is *yamba-ô*.

　　But there is also a non-mythological dimension to the Afro-Cuban culture. There is thus a corpus of stories and dances which will influence Afro-Cuban poetry. The rumba as it became popular in the Twenties is really a ballroom simplification of the *rumba guaguanco*. The ballroom version which thrilled tourists from Havana to Harlem differs from the *guaganco* in several ways. It is thematically and rhythmically monotonous, and deliberately so to function as a dance rhythm rather than as a rite musically narrated. It thus derives its value as a ballroom piece by the elimination of vital but now extraneous complexities. The rumba *sui generis* was a symbolic representation of the courtship of a hen by a cock with the hen gracefully and elegantly defending herself against the cock's aggressive attacks.

Thus in the guaganco version the rumba is slower and less rapidly synthesized into a sustained rhythmic structure. It may, for example, start with a melancholic, Blues-like flute solo with a slow set of drum beats gradually building up an animated background. This background is further emphasized by the insertion of high-pitched *quinto* drums and deeper *tumba* drums, to which are added *conga* drums and the sharp, dry sounds of *palitos*—cylindrical sticks struck against the sides of the drums. In addition to the *guaganco* there is also the *yambo* rumba and other songs and dances independent of the rumba cycle. The *comparsa*, for example, is, properly speaking, the *conga* as danced during the carnival. This accounts for the fast, stringent, climactic way in which it ends with a full sound blending whistles, voices and *cencerros* or cow bells. The *comparsa* is really a dancing procession, the long line of dancers appropriately referred to as a *cola* or tail. In its earliest form, the *conga* was more simply a march with a strongly accented syncopation in alternate measures. These are the most common rhythms from this cycle of dances which also offers the *meringue*, the *candombe*, the *son*. Out of *Ñañiguismo* there came too a body of legends, fables and songs or hymns. Among the last, the most influential are *cantos de cabildos, cantos funerales* and the dramatic *cantos para matar culebras*—songs that celebrate the killing of serpents.[7]

These details are relevant to this chapter for two reasons. First, they suggest the continuity of the African elements in the Caribbean Negro thus linking him organically with the African continent and contrasting him with the United States Negro. But more important, they show why the Negrophilism of the Twenties and Thirties assumes the dimensions it does in Chapter 4. The words that describe the Afro-Cuban cult have much about them that is exotically strange to the Western ear. Just as the Indian had supplied tropical, hispanic romanticism with incantatory New World sounds, so these Afro-cuban sounds came to serve as the basis for elaborate *jitanjáforas* such as Luis Pales Matos orchestrated in his *poesía negra*. We may see this as the genesis of that bongo-beating Orpheus mentioned in Chapter 4. It is also the basis for the formalism in Arturo Torres-Rioseco's assessment of hispanic Negro poetry. Just as the rhythms of Jazz and the Blues forced imitative poetry into prosodic architectures excitingly alien to English literature, so too the configurations of *cantos, sones, comparsas* and rumbas worked changes in Spanish poetry. But all this came to fruition during the Twenties and resulted much too frequently in what Emilio Ballagas has called an expression "turístico en el tiempo y el espacio, sin dimensión histórica"—an expression that was essentially tourism in time and space, lacking historical dimensions.

Much like Langston Hughes, there is evidence in Guillén's early works that he was also seduced by the facile, folkloric dilettantism that produced *sones para turistas*—and this in spite of the ever-present sarcasm and irony in his entire expression.[8] These early works, much like the temper of the folktales in the United States, treat the Negro with a kind of tolerant mockery from which sympathy and concern are not absent. The poetic world here is narrow; it is a world that does not really seek to define itself outside the limitations of the *bembón's* horizon. It is therefore a world of *mulatas*, the cries of fruit sellers and of the American tourist seen from the attenuated perspective of the *bembón*. Almost all of these are written in the broken dialect, *disfraces negros* of the *bozal* and also show evidences of other exotic inclinations:

> Ya yo me enteré, mulata,
> mulata, ya sé que dice
> que tengo la narice
> como nudo de corbata
> . . . .[9]

Mulata, Ah found out, mulata/you'se been sayin' things 'bout me/lak how I'se got a nose/like the knot in a necktie. Seduced doubtless by the tropical fecundity of Cuba and in the tradition of "fruitismo" Guillén breaks out with the cries of a fruit peddler—ah/what a piece of the sun/the flesh of the mango/watermelons/bananas:

> ¡Ah
> qué pedazo de sol,
> carne de mango!
> Melones de agua,
> plátanos.

The intoxication erupts into *jitanjáforas:*

> ¡Quencuyere, quencuyere,
> quencuyere!
> ¡Quencuyere, que la casera
> salga otra vez!

And the last stanza onomatopoeically rolls like wheels on cobbled pavement to its conclusion:

> ¡Triqueña de carne amarga,
> ven a ver mi carretón;
> carretón de palmas verdes
> carretón;
> carretón de cuatro ruedas,
> carretón;

> carretón de sol y tierra
> ¡carretón! [10]

In the sheer exuberance of poems like "Canto Negro" there is really little, if anything, to suggest more than a dilettante's familiarity with the exotic names in *Ñañguismo:*

> ¡Yambambó, yambambé!
> Repica el congo solongo,
> repica el negro bien negro:
> congo solongo del Songo
> baila yambo sobre un pie.
>
> Mamatomba
> serembé cuseremba.
>
> El negro canta y se ajuma,
> el negro se ajuma y canta,
> el negro canta y se va.
>
> Acuememe serembó,
>   aé
> Yambó
>   aé.
>
> Tamba, tamba, tamba, tamba,
> ¡tamba del negro que tumba!
> tumba del negro, caramba,
> caramba, qué el negro tumba:
> ¡yamba, yambó, yambambé! [11]

Small wonder, given the proliferation of this kind of expression, that Regino Pedroso vents his indignation in a long, passionate appeal: Brother, black brother, Negro/muffle your bongo a little bit/aren't we more than negroes? /...aren't we more than rumbas, lusts and comparsas? /are we no more than grimaces and color/grimaces and color

> To satisfy their tastes
> the rich turn you into a toy ...
> ...and in Paris and in New York and in Madrid and in Havana
> . . . .
> there are men who reward your hunger with laughter;
> ride on your sweat
> trade with your pain,
> and you laugh, you give in, you dance. [12]
> . . . .

What was called for was not imitation Negroes, "negros de pajas," but what Césaire and *Negritude* will call some four years later a *Noir Nègre*, a black Negro. Esthetically and artistically, what was required, as much as the social reaction which Pedroso demanded, was a profound plumbing of the Afro-Cuban soul. What was not required was the exhibition of elements which white, European artists had turned into a caricature. That was the way Juan Marinello put it:

> Se inquiere del alma negra, no lo que el blanco ha deformado en el forcejo secular por someterla, ni lo que el poco cultivo da en algun caso de caricaturesco y desmesurado. Se marcha a la conquista de lo inédito, de lo que ante el cerco pertinaz se recogió en el rincon más recoleto del almario afrocubano.[13]

It would be unjust to imply that Nicolás Guillén shows no awareness of these needs in his early writings. There are glimpses, occasionally light, occasionally savage, of the dominant concerns of *West Indies Ltd*. Again we have that tightlipped suggestion of impending explosion in the dialect poem to a female *bozal:*

> ¡Hay que tener voluntá,
> que la salasion no é
> pa toa la vida!
>
> Camina y no llore, negra,
> ve p'alla;
> camina, negra, y no llore,
> ven p'aca;
> camina, negra, camina,
> ¡que hay que tener voluntá! [14]

The most unrestrained expression by Guillén as polemicist-lyricist before *West Indies Ltd.* is the poem "Oda a un Negro Boxeador Cubano" written in 1929 and published in *Songoro Cosongo* (1931). In a sense, it marks the culmination of Guillén's use of the *bembón*. Many of the concerns of this ode will appear in *West Indies Ltd.*, with this difference—that there Guillén himself becomes polemicist, artist and *protagonist*. There appears no persona or mask between the poet and his concerns. The "Oda" raises the *bembón* to his most pathetic, even tragically deformed height, he is in a sense trapped like a modern elastic monkey in the boxing ring

> . . .los rings
> en que tu saltas como un moderno mono elástico.

He is initially described in these pathetic terms, but then is urged as the
ode ends to emerge from this undignified baptism like a strong, finely
finished club with the aggressive powers of a black jack:

> . . .es bueno, al fin y al cabo,
> hallar un *punching bag*,
> eliminar la grasa bajo el sol,
> saltar,
> sudar,
> nadar,
> y de la suiza al *shadow boxing*,
> de la ducha al comedor,
> salir pulido, fino, fuerte
> como un baston recién labrado
> con agresividades de *black jack*

This becomes necessary because of the slack decadence of a Europe,
stripping itself naked/to toast its flesh in the sun/searching in Harlem and
in Havana/for jazz and rumba. But the force of the poem lies in the violent
insistence on "ese mismo Broadway," which becomes symbolic of the
rampaging beast with insatiate tongue. The boxer appears trapped in the
ring surrounded by . . .that same Broadway/which opens its melon-shaped
mouth in awe/before your exploding fists. . ./that same Broadway/which
opens its snout with an enormous, wet tongue/to gluttonously lick up/all
the blood from our canefields:

> El Norte es fiero y rudo, boxeador.
> Ese mismo Broadway
> . . . .
> ese mismo Broadway
> que unta de asombra su boca de melón
> ante tus puños explosivos
> . . . .
> ese mismo Broadway,
> es el que estira su hocico con una enorme lengua húmeda,
> para lamer glotonamente
> toda la sangre de nuestra cañaveral.

The style is an effective fusion of boxing slang and virulently quiet
Spanish. The Negro's mission in this world of European decadence and
American greed is to "shine in black while the boulevards applaud/and in
the face of the envy of the whites/speak of truth in black:"

> lucirse negro mientras aplaude el bulevar,
> y frente a la envidia de los blancos
> hablar en negro de verdad.

The entire work nonetheless is infused with an element of bitterness, pathos and frustration in spite of the defiant optimism with which the poem ends. The "Pequeña Oda a un Negro Boxeador Cubano" is a long poem but it bears full quotation:

Tus guantes
puestos en la punta de tu cuerpo de ardilla,
e el *punch* de tu sonrisa!

El Norte es fiero y rudo, boxeador.
Ese mismo Broadway,
que en actitud de vena se desangra
para chillar junto a los rings
en que tu saltas como un moderno mono elástico,
sin el resorte de las sogas,
ni los almohadones del *clinch*;
ese mismo Broadway
que unta de asombra su boca de melón
ante tus puños explosivos
y tus actuales zapatos de charol;
ese mismo Broadway,
es él que estira su hocico con una enorme lengua húmeda,
para lamer glotonamente
toda la sangre de nuestra cañaveral.
De seguro que tú
no vivirás al tanto de ciertas cosas nuestras,
ni ciertas cosas de allá,
porque el *training* es duro y el músculo traidor,
y hay que estar *hecho un toro,*
como dices alegremente, para que el golpe duela más.
Tu inglés;
un poco mas precario que tu endeble español,
solo te he de servir para entender sobre la loma
cuanto en su verde slang
mascan las mandibulas de los que tú derrumbas
jab a *jab.*
En realidad acaso no necesitas, otra cosa,
porque como seguramente pensarás,
ya tienes tu lugar.
Es bueno, al fin y al cabo,
hallar un *punching bag*,
eliminar la grasa bajo el sol,
saltar,
sudar,
nadar,

y de la suiza al *shadow boxing*,
de la ducha al comedor,
como un bastón recién labrado
con agresividades de *black jack*.
Y ahora que Europa se desnuda
para tostar su carne al sol,
y busca en Harlem y en La Habana
jazz y son,
lucirse negro mientras aplaude el bulevar,
y frente a la envidia de los blancos
hablar en negro de verdad.[15]

The angry *agresividades* which Guillén shows in this poem will in *West Indies Ltd.* be directed to a broader enquiry into the meaning of blackness on a personal and racial scale. The dispossessed of the earth, the mongrelization of identity and the banality of exploitation become the subjects of great import.

There are contradictory voices in *West Indies Ltd.*, which are resolved in two ways. We may divide the work into two modes much as in Hughes' *The Weary Blues*. Two poems serve as the definitive statement in each mode. "Balada de los dos Abuelos" finds Guillén striving for a sense of equilibrium in his allegiance and identity. The pull of the blue-eyed antarctic North and that of the tropical South demand resolution. Federico of Europe and Facundo of Africa and their antithetical effects are to be resolved in the identity of Guillén, their descendant. The poetic temperament here is lyrical; it is, in a sense, also celebrative. The title poem, "West Indies Ltd.," is the culmination of the other mode. It is poetically combative, polemic and profoundly anti-American vulgarity. We may call it the *canción de los hombres perdidos*, the song of the dispossessed, in two manifestations. "West Indies Ltd.," is motivated by disgust and sustained by contempt. Another poem, "Canción de los Hombres Perdidos," is sustained by anger and rendered dramatic by the promise of violent retribution from the exploited and dehumanized victims.

The entire work opens somewhat deceptively. The tropics that Guillén celebrates in "Palabras en el Trópico" give no hint of the agonies and incongruities that highlight *West Indies Ltd.* In much the same way that Wordsworth celebrates Northern pastoralism in "Tintern Abbey," Guillén revels in the luxurious tropicalism of the "Antillas:"

Aquí,
en medio del mar,
retozando en las aguas con mis Antillas desnudas,
yo te saludo, Trópico!

Here in the middle of the ocean/. . .I salute the Tropics/. . .To you I owe my black body/my agile feet and kinky hair/from you. . .these intense days in whose blue skies are stamped/round and smiling suns/from you these wet lips/the tail of the jaguar and the saliva of snakes. . . .

> Te debo el cuerpo oscuro,
> las piernas ágiles y la cabeza crespa;
> mi amor hacía las hembras elementales
> y esta sangre imborrable.
> Te debo los dias altos en cuya azul estan pegados
> soles redondos y risueños;
> te debo los labios húmedos,
> la cola del jaguar y saliva de las culebras;
> te debo el charco donde beben las fieras sedientas;
> te debo, Trópico,
> este entusiasmo niño
> de correr en la pista
> de tu profundo cinturón lleno de rosas amarillas,
> riendo las montañas y las nubes,
> mientras un cielo marítimo,
> se destroza en interminables olas de estrellas a mis
> pies! [16]

It would be naïve to say that Guillén was completely seduced by the somewhat exotic paradise we find in the opening poem. Insofar as he was descended from Facundo, his black, African ancestor, that paradise carried its own negation. This is what we find in "Balada de los Dos Abuelos." There had been an earlier tropical paradise of sorts in the origins of Facundo-Guillén. The "pure, burnished sun/trapped in the arc of the tropics/the moon, shining round and clean/on the sleep of monkeys." That paradise had been disrupted by "ships, Lord, the ships/and Negroes, Lord, the Negroes." There had been a cacophonous confusion of cries in canefields, black whiplashes, tears and blood, veins and eyes opening into empty mornings. And a strong voice, a voice loud/splitting silences/the ships, lord, the ships/and Negroes!

> ¡Qué de barcos, qué de barcos!
> ¡Qué de negros, qué de negros!
> ¡Qué largo fulgor de cañas!
> ¡Qué látigo el del negrero!
> ¡Piedra de llanto y de sangre,
> venas y ojos entreabiertos,
> y madrugas vacias
> y atardeceres de ingenio,

y una gran voz, fuerte voz
despedezando el silencio.
¡Qué de barcos, qué de barcos,
¡Qué de negros!

Quite obviously, Facundo's misfortunes could never be separated from the appearance of Federico's eyes, "eyes of blue antarctic glass." But in Nicolás Guillén, *mulato*, Creole, an equilibrium is necessary. And so "I unite them in an embrace/Federico! Facundo! /...two strong heads raised/to the same height/under distant stars/...I unite them in/shouts, dreams, tears, songs/in dreams, cries, songs/in tears, songs/singing:

Yo los junto. ·
   ¡Federico!
¡Facundo! Los dos se abrazan.
Los dos suspiran. Los dos
las fuertes cabezas alzan;
los dos del mismo tamaño
bajo las estrellas altas;
los dos del mismo tamaño
gritan, sueñan, lloran, cantan.
Sueñan, lloran, cantan.
Lloran, cantan.
¡Cantan! [17]

The equilibrium is arrived at by this peculiar hysteria and harmony that one sees in the staccato, uncertain lines, the stuttering caesuras and conflicting trochees that end the poem.

"Palabras en el Trópico" in its optimistic sweep over the Caribbean appears to suggest that the same harmony pervades the area, but this proves to be untrue. Guillén had earlier written in "Palabras:" "Jamaica says/she is content to be black/and Cuba already knows she is mulata."[18] This would perfectly match the *négritude* spirit of the period. Césaire would complete the coordinated cry of black pride in the Caribbean when he writes of "Haiti, où la négritude se mit debout pour la premiére fois et dit qu'elle croyais à son humanité." The general impression then is one of an awakened Caribbean and Harlem where blackness raises its head and for the first time asserts the value of its black humanness. The odd thing about Guillén's *West Indies Ltd.* is that he begins in a tropical paradise, which he then proceeds to negate. Indeed, the title poem ends with the polemicist's raucous laughter of disdain floating over a botched, mongrel Eden. The poem thus develops the concerns already expressed in the "Oda" of 1929. But there are other expressions of this disenchantment which progressively lead to the mockery and the disgust in "West Indies Ltd." An earlier poem,

"La Canción del Bongó" had negated the idea that Cuba was content to be mulatto. The song of the bongo there had mockingly suggested that she was instead compulsively Criollo, that is, she preferred to deny the blackness in her blood. The style of "La Canción del Bongó" is not loud or percussively dramatic as the title would lead one to expect. It is instead curiously flat, demolishing the pretentious by way of colloquial rhythms and laconic mockery. The bongo is Cuban and African and cannot be wished away. This is the song of the bongo/.... In this country, mulatto/African and Spanish/(Santa Barbara on the one hand/on the other hand, Chango)/there's always some grandfather missing/or else an extra Don in the family/and there are Castilian earls/with relatives in Bondoh/look, friends, we'd better keep quiet/and not push the matter too far. . .:

> Esta es la canción del bongó
> . . . .
> En esta tierra, mulata
> de africano y español
> (Santa Bárbara de un lado,
> del otro lado, Changó)
> Siempre falta algún abuelo,
> cuando no sobra algún Don,
> y hay titulos de Castilla
> con parientes de Bondó:
> vale más callarse, amigos,
> y no menear la cuestión,
> porque venimos de lejos,
> y andamos de dos en dos.
> . . . .[19]

On the other hand, this tropical Eden was also the victim of exploitation. We have seen as much implied in "Oda" and in "Caña." Two poems pick up the thread in *West Indies Ltd.* before the explosion in the title poem. In "Caminando," Guillén assumes the role of a voice compulsively, hypnotically driven by anger, poverty and pain. The tight rhythms of the poem and the compelling return to the word *caminando* almost as a *jitanjáfora* sequence, make for a poem that radiates obsessive and impending menace:

> ¡Caminando, caminando,
> caminando!
> Voy sin rumbo caminando,
> caminando;
> voy sin plata caminando,

caminando;
voy muy triste caminando,
¡caminando!
Ay,
las piernas se ponen duras,
caminando;
. . . .
la mano agarra y no suelta,
caminando
. . . .
y aunque me pida perdón,
me lo como y me lo bebo,
me lo bebo y me lo como,
¡caminando,
caminando,
caminando! [20]

The menace is transformed into a more direct threat of violence in the song of the dispossessed, "Canción de los Hombres Perdidos," with its twenty stanzas of ferocious tercets:

. . . .
Somos asmáticos, diabéticos,
herpéticos y paralíticos,
mas sin regimenes dietéticos.

. . . .
¡Saltemos sobre la ciudad,
como perros abandonados
en medio de una tempestad! [21]

We are asthmatics, diabetics/herpetics and paralytics/but without dietetic prescriptions. . . .We'll jump on the city/like dogs abandoned/in a storm.

The United States has become the center of an angry storm by the time we get to "West Indies Ltd." The mainland was not content to sink in its own thickening vulgarity; it had been exported to the Caribbean. The America of Babbittry had gone international. The decadent, juvenile world of negrophilist inclinations had gone syphillitic compounding its slack absurdities in the smoke of opium and marijuana. The harmony of identity attributed to Jamaica and Cuba and Haiti is negated. Here are "imitation negroes, whose eyes bulge open at the cars of the rich/who are ashamed to look at their negro hair." Here, too, is the white Caribbean who speaks of "pure aristocracies." The tropical *paradiso* has become an *inferno*. Harmony becomes a discordant jangle of bastardized and bastardizing American slogans leaving a trail of vulgarity from Port-au-Prince (Haiti) to Kingston to Havana. Here was the land of "all right" where everybody was diseased:

> Esté es el pueblo del *all right*,
> donde todo se encuentra muy mal;
> esté es el pueblo del *very well*,
> donde nadie está bien.

> Aqui estan los servidores de *Mr. Babbit*.
> Los que educan sus hijos en *West Point*.
> Aqui estan los que chillan: *hello baby*,
> y fuman *"Chesterfield"* y *"Lucky Strike"*
> Aqui estan los bailadores de *fox trots*
> los *boys* del *jazz band*
> y los veraneantes de *Miami* y de *Palm Beach*.
> Aqui estan los que piden *bread* and *butter*
> y *coffee* and *milk*.
> Aqui estan los absurdos jóvenes sifilíticos,
> fumadores de opio y de mariguana.
> exhibiendo en vitrinas sus espiroquetas
> y cortandose un traje cada semana.
> Aqui esta lo mejor de Port-au-Prince,
> lo mas puro de Kingston, la *high life* de La Habana. . .
> Pero aqui estan tambien los que reman en lagrimas,
> galeotes dramáticos, galeotes dramáticos.

"A low dishonest decade" was coming to a close with a vengeance. Guillén faced with this world in which the worst was filled with passionate intensity and "with political parties/and speakers who say: 'In these critical moments. . . .'" His reaction is in a sense psychologically understandable given the barely controlled restraint and violence in his anger up to this publication. It is an all-inclusive, nihilistic mockery motivated by bitter indignation. One suspects behind all this a sense of frustration and a feeling of impotence in the face of a world gone vulgar and apparently headed for insanity. To hell with you, white "noble" of the Tropics/. . . .I laugh at you and the obscene blood you try so much to hide/with your talk of pure aristocracies/. . . .To hell with you, aping Negro/. . .ashamed of your kinky hair/when your fist is so powerful/To hell with everybody: the police and the drunk/father and son/the President and the fireman/I laugh at you all: to hell with the whole world:

> ¡Me rio de ti, noble de las Antillas,
> mono que andas saltando de mata en mata,
> payaso que sudas por no meter la pata,
> y siempre la metes hasta las rodillas.
> Me rio de ti, blanco de verdes venas,

–bien se te ven aunque ocultarles procuras!
me rio de ti porque hablas de aristocracias puras,
de ingenios florecientes y arcas llenas.
¡Me rio de ti, negro imitámicos,
que abres los ojos ante el auto de los ricos,
y que te averguenzas de mirarte el pellejo oscuro,
cuando tienes el puño tan duro!
¡Me rio de tódos: del policía y del borracho,
del padre y de su muchacho,
del Presidente y del bombero.
Me rio de todos: me rio del mundo entero.
Del mundo entero que se emociona frente a cuatro peludos,
erguidos muy orondos detras de sus chillones escudos,
como cuatro salvajes al pie de un cocotero.[22]

The final poem in *West Indies Ltd*. lacks the intensity of the title poem. It is actually a quietly and deliberately etched tableau. But there is in that quietness and succinctness a suggestion of profound emotional exhaustion and even bitter resignation. The poem is titled "Guadalupe W. I. (West Indies):"

Los negros, trabajando
junto al vapor. Los árabes, vendiendo,
los franceses, paseaudo y descansando,
e el sol ardiendo.
. . . . [23]

Negroes, working/on the ship. Arabs, selling/the French, strolling and resting/and the sun burning down. Bitterness, the banal excesses of Americanism and the Jazz Age combine to make Guillén's *West Indies Ltd*. the most disenchanted of the three works selected for assessment in this section. Langston Hughes postulates an Eden; we shall see Aimé Césaire making a return to his native land in *Cahier d'un Retour au Pays Natal*. There is therefore some degree of optimism, no matter how facile and misguided, in Hughes and Césaire. For Nicolás Guillén in *West Indies Ltd*. the *pays natal* was a tropical Eden into which the Serpent had already entered.

NOTES

[1] To the extent in which Walt Whitman's transcendental, optimistic Romanticism encompassed earlier and more decorous statements of the same, as from Jefferson, Paine, Franklin *et al.* See following. Much of the discussion in this chapter's first paragraphs has been shaped by studies of America's "Gilded Age" such as Merle Curti's *The Growth of American Thought;* also John W. Aldridge, *After the Lost Generation;* Sinclair Lewis, "The American Fear of Literature" (Nobel Prize Acceptance Speech); *The Autobiography of Malcolm X* in its effective chronicling of the latter day Jazz Age. For the selections immediately following in text on the millionaires and comments from Carnegie see "The Gilded Age" in *Masterworks of American Realism: Twain, Howells, James,* (Volume Three of American Literature Series) by Darrel Abel, pp. 1-9.

[2] Abel, *op. cit.,* p. 3. See also, Barbara Tuchman, *The Proud Tower* for United States' indelicate search for *Lebensraum* in the Caribbean and Latin America during the nineteenth and early twentieth centuries.

[3] See the later confessional essays in *Communism, the God that failed,* ed. by Richard Crossman (New York: Bantam Books, 1965).

[4] From the prefatory remark to Nicolás Guillén, *El Son Entero: Suma Poética, 1929-1946* (Buenos Aires: Editorial Pleamar, 1947). *El Son Entero* contains the following works by Guillén: *Motivos de Son* (1930), *Songoro Cosongo* (1931), *West Indies Ltd.* (1934) *Cantos para Soldados y Sones para Turistas* (1937), *España* (1937), *El Son Entero* (Inédito).

[5] From *West Indies Ltd.* See later paragraphs for full treatment of the "Balada."

[6] See also for discussion following: Vincente Rossi, *Cosas de Negros: los orígenes del tango y otros aportes al folklore rioplatense: Rectificaciones históricas* (Rio de Plata, Cordoba: Imprenta argentina); Paulo de Neto Carvalho, *El negro uruguayo hasta la abolición* (Quito: Editorial *Universitaria, 1965*); Fernando Ortiz, *Glosario de Afronegrismos* (La Habana: El Siglo XX, 1924).

[7] The *cantos para matar culebras* are the inspiration for Guillén's most effective and popular use of the folklore in *West Indies Ltd.* I refer to "Sensemayá." For the discussion of secular music in text above see, in addition to Rossi, *op. cit.,* Otiz, etc, *Cuban Festival: Traditional Dance Music of Cuba,* Washington Records WLP 728, album notes by Odilio Orfe (recorded in Havana by Urfe and the *Instituto de Investigaciones Folklóricas*).

[8] As will be noticed in note 4 above, there is a coincidence between the expression "sones para turistas" and the 1937 publication by Guillén. The equation exists only insofar as the expression suggests works written for tourists. The 1937 publication is a deliberate sarcasm.

[9] *El Son Entero,* p. 16, "La mulata."

[10] *Ibid.,* p. 43, for "Pregon."

[11] *Ibid.,* p. 33.

[12] See Chapter 4, note 26.

"....................

Negro, hermano negro,
enluta un poco tu bongó.

¿No somos más que negros?
¿No somos más que jacara?
¿No somos más que rumba, lujuriás y comparsas?

¿No somos más que mueca y color,
mueca y color?

. . . .
Para sus goces
el rico hace de ti un juguete,
y en Paris, y en Nueva York, y en Madrid, y en la Habana,
igual que bibelotes
se fabrican negros de paja para in exportación;
hay hombres que to pagan con hambre la risa;
trafican con tu dolor,
y tu riés, te entregas y danzas."

[13] Emilio Ballagas quotes Marinello in *Antolgiá de Poesiá Negra Hispono-Americana* (Madrid: Aguilar, 1935), p. 17.

[14] *El Son Entero*, p. 18.

[15] *Ibid.*, p. 30.

[16] *Ibid.*, pp. 47-49.

[17] The poem begins as quoted earlier. It bears comparison with Hughes' admittedly less ambitious "Cross."

[18] From "Palabras del Trópico!"
"Dice Jamaica
que ella está contenta de ser negra,
y Cuba ya sabe que es mulata."

[19] *El Son Entero*, pp. 28-30. The Bondoh, as extant in many African tribes, is a female initiation secret society.

[20] *El Son Entero*, p. 62.

[21] *Ibid.*, p. 67.

[22] *Ibid.*, p. 70ff.

[23] *Ibid.*, p. 81.

CHAPTER 8

AIMÉ CÉSAIRE AND HAITIAN VOODOO

Aimé Césaire's *Cahier d'un Retour au Pays Natal* can be seen as a symphonic re-orchestration of the concerns in the last two chapters. However, it differs from *The Weary Blues* and *West Indies Ltd.* in significant ways. Stylistically, it is the most complex in its surrealist eclecticism. It is also the most agonized and paradoxically the most rarefied of the expressions of exile and return in this part of the study. Its pulsations are dramatically personal, more so than Guillén, present as that Cuban is as protagonist in *West Indies Ltd.* By comparison, we can say that Hughes functions primarily as the artistic-poetic historian of the impulses of the period. *West Indies Ltd.* elucidates by way of polemical lucidity, and *The Weary Blues* by way of precise, even laconic observation. The imagination at work in *Cahier* is firmly grounded in the esthetics of Western, especially French, *fin-de-siècle* inspiration. This is somewhat of a paradox that in this most insistent of all returns to a native identity we should have the least evidence of Negro-Caribbean impulses. But the crisis of the *assimilé*, as may be gathered from Chapter 5, involved far more corrosive stimuli than are apparent elsewhere. The process by which the *assimilé* would attempt a transformation from *nègre généreux* to *noir nègre* by way of the *nègre révolté* illustrates the processes of assimilation and de-similation. We have already seen the philosophical parable of that trajectory in Senghor.

We can see the *Cahier* as the poetic parable of the prodigal Son who had suffered a moral atrophy and a spiritual and cultural death in the *pays des richesses*. Numerous and even conflicting identities are evoked in the process of regeneration: Prodigal Son, Judas, *Noir Negre, Messiah.* The note insistently sounded as the *Cahier* opens is *partir des blancs* to leave the white world: "Je force la membrane vitalline qui me separe de moi-même/... Je force les grands eaux qui me ceinturent de sang." The title is therefore spiritually, emotionally and geographically declarative: return to my native land, *Cahier d'un Retour au Pays Natal*. Since Toussaint

156

Louverture, the prototype of the *nègre révolté*, will become the *assimilé's* Adam, we can see Haiti and its intense African residuals as the new Eden:

> Haïti, où la négritude se mit debout pour la première fois et dit qu'elle croyais à son humanité.

The choice was logical. J.C. Dorsainvil's *Manuel d'Histoire d'Haiti*, among other studies, gives evidence that these residuals, as coordinated into Voodoo, played a significant role in the beginnings of the Haitian revolution. Voodoo, like *Ñañiguismo*, was not only an ancestral cult but also the organic extension of a protective social identity. This in part explains the very intensity of Voodoo and its hypnotic, compulsive celebrations:

> A religion such as Voudoun (*sic*), whose function is to impart to the individual of the community a system of mental and emotional convictions upon which the very survival of the community is dependent, does not, and could not require of them that they perceive and understand its principles on an abstract, metaphysical level in order that they be inspired to participate in it.[1]

But as we shall soon see, the Voodoo impulses to which the *assimilé* returns owe much to the exquisite elegance of Parisian finesse than they do to any violently non-European, atavistic energy. The *tam-tam* of Voodoo's dark union with elemental forces becomes the elaborate *tam-tam verbal* of Senghor's exegesis and the delicate, arabesque mystery of *assimilé* poetry such as we find in Leon G. Damas' "Ils sont venus ce soir:"

> Ils sont venus ce soir où le
>> tam
>>> tam
>>>> roulait de
>>>>> rythme
>>>>>> la frénésie
> des yeux
> la frénésie des mains la frénésie
> des pieds de statues
> DEPUIS
> combien de MOI
> sont morts
> Depuis qu'ils sont venus ce soir où le
> tam
>> tam
>>> roulait de

rythme en
rythme
la frénésie
des yeux
la frénésie des mains la frénésie
des pieds de statues.[2]

To this extent, therefore, we find here the same exotically inclined transformation to which jazz and the blues in Harlem and *Ñañiguismo* in Cuba were subjected.

The nature of the transformation is naturally inseparable from the nature of French intervention such as we have seen in Chapter 5. Equally important is the nature of that which was transformed. We therefore have different consequences from the instrusion of Jazz and Blues, *Ñañiguismo* and now Voodoo into the period under study. What follows is a summary presentation of what is the most inviolate, non-European culture which defines the Negro in the Americas.[3]

Properly speaking, the term "voodoo" or "Vodu" or "Voudoun" is a generic one which encompasses at least two denominations of an African-Haitian-Indian culture. Within these two denominations, Rada and Petro, are several cults, *nanchons*, and cult divinities. The *nanchons*, like the *cabildos* of Afrocubanism, are social and religious groups. These representative groupings are determined by tribal origins and tribal divinities as they have acquired identities in isolation from the African continent. The Rada is the voodoo of songs and dances. Its *nanchons* and *loas* (gods) are African and generally Dahomean in origin. The Petro is the voodoo of the blood-sacrificial ceremonial cults. These cults are generally traced to Carib indian origins. To a large extent, much of the atavistic energies as popularly associated with Voodoo appear to have their origin in the Petro. The important *culte des morts*, cult of the dead, and its chief "divinity" Baron Samedi, Guardian of the Dead and Lord of the Cemetery, constitute perhaps the most vital manifestation of the Petro. But it would be inaccurate to insist on a rigidly neat categorization of the cults of voodoo, just as it would be inadequate to ignore its shades of complexity.

The snake plays an important role in Voodoo as in *Ñañiguismo*. The supreme being of all Voodoo is the Serpent-God, Dambalia Oueddo, of Dahomean origin. But there are other tribal gods too. Among the most frequently encountered prayers and songs in Voodoo (Rada) are those to Legba. No longer a dionysiac or satanic force as in Cuba or an evil, even if essentially mischievous god as in Yoruba, Legba is in Haiti the Guardian of the Gate to the *loas*, to the gods. He is thus a most important intercessory force, the key to the deeper mysteries and forces of voodoo:

> Atibô Legba, l'ouvri bayé pou mwe
> Papa Legba, l'ouvri bayé pou mwe
> Pou mwe pasé
> Lo m'a touné, m'a salié loa-yo
> Voodoo Legba, l'ouvri bayé pou mwe
> Lo m'a touné, m'a remesyé loa-yo
>
> Atibô Legba, open the gate for me
> Papa Legba, open the gate for me
> Let me pass;
> When I return, I'll salute the loa
> Voodoo Legba, open the barrier for me
> When I return, I'll thank the loa.[4]

The ceremonies that celebrate these mysteries are coordinated by the chief of spirits, *houngan*, by priest, *papaloi* or priestess, *mamaloi*. The *houngan* presides over the ceremonial, ritualistic performances of the faithful or of *hounsis*, initiates. He is assisted by a musical (vocal) leader, *houngenikon*, and the *la-place* whose duties involve the proper deployment of materials required during worship. The snake, *couleuvre*, the goat, *cabrit*, and the cock, *poule*, are fetish animals. It is rather more accurate to describe the snake as totemic and the goat and cock as fetish, sacrificial animals. Thus when a voodoo man is conceived of sacrificially he becomes a "goat without horns," *cabrit sans cor.*

Worship in Voodoo is not exclusively Rada or Petro; nor is it ever exclusively determined, in time and space, by the individual *nanchons* or *nanchon* of *loa* (group of spirits). There is instead a hierarchical, sequential celebration of and by *nanchons*. The following hypnotic, liturgical "roll-call" is recorded by Louis Maximilien:

> En Hen madioment en hen
> Doumbouquelle – en hen madioment en hen
> Wanquinan Wannime
> Tous les saints congo. En hen mandioment en hen
> Tout Nanchon petro. En hen mandioment en hen
> Tout Nanchon caplaou. En hen mandioment en hen
> Tout Nanchon amine, En hen mandioment en hen
> Tout Nanchon Ibo. En hen mandioment en hen
> Tout Nanchon Mondongue. En hen mandioment en hen.
> Tout Nanchon Cangale. En hen mandioment en hen
> Tout Nanchon Simby. En hen mandioment en hen.

> Tout Nanchon Quitta. En han mandioment en hen.
> Tout Nanchon Sinigal. En hen mandioment en hen
> Tout Nanchon Tibritus. En hen mandioment en hen
> Paternel. Maternelle. En hen mandioment en hen
> Sur la terre dans le Ciel. En hen mandioment en hen[5]

Each *nanchon* has a peculiar rhythm and chant which identifies it. A slow rhythmic pattern would, for example, generally identify a Rada station, while a more intense configuration would indicate a Petro. It is thus a worship that is phasal in nature. It is the sum total of these liturgical moments which constitutes voodoo worship.

Responsibility for anticipating, leading and sustaining these liturgical stations falls on the *houngenikon* and on the drums. Three drums are responsible for illustrating and indeed provoking the phasal architecture. The first, *ountogni* or *boula*, represents in its beat the fixed, rhythmic center of worship. Its beat is stable and unchanging. In a psychological sense, that rhythmic center provides the percussive equilibrium on which trance-inducing intensity depends. Artistically, it explains the structural, even tonal similarity in any given corpus of voodoo chants. The second drum, *ountogui* or *second*, identifies the phase of worship. The rhythms it develops or syncopates from the pulsations of the *boula* indicate the *nanchon* or *loa* being addressed. The third drum, *ountor* or *manman*, is responsible for developing both the *boula* and the *second* rhythms to their climactic moments. Maximilien interpretatively summarizes:

> On pourrait donc ainsi les classer:
> Le 1er tambour (ountogni ou boula) est le tambour abstrait.
> Le 2e tambour (ountogui ou second) est le rite.
> Le 3e tambour (ountor ou manman) est le sang ou l'homme lui-même.[6]

Each drum thus plays a different beat at each phase, but there is always a specific rhythmic combination demanded for every liturgical station. As may well be imagined, a slip or a missed beat involves the risk of toppling the whole ritual architecture. It is to these compelling rhythms above that Voodoo chants its prayers, from pleas to Atibô Legba to the more atavistic fears expressed to Maîtresse Ezilée:

> Maîtresse Ezilée, vini 'gider nous
> Si ou mander poule, me bai ou.
> Si ou mander cabrit, me bai ou.
> Si ou mander bef, me bai ou.
> Se ou mander *cabrit san cor* (my emphasis)

Coté me pren' pr bai ou

Maîtresse Ezilée, come, help us.
If a cock is called for, I'll give it.
If a goat is called for, I'll give it.
If a bull is called for, I'll give it.
If a goat without horns is called for
Where do I go to get one? [7]

The most intrusive outside influence at work in Voodoo is Roman Catholicism. But as in the case of *Ñañiguismo*, its effects are not as reactionary and disruptive on the cult as Protestantism would have been. It would seem that the structural, visible drama of Catholicism afforded a convenient background for *les saints de Congo*, much to the ineffective exasperation of a Church that was really more tolerant than its Protestant counterpart. In spite of observations such as William Seabrook offers below, Voodoo and Roman Catholicism resulted in a union that was harmonious enough for the Voodoo adherent and not violently uncomfortable for the Church:

> Les nègres font sans scrupule ce que faissaient les Philistins; ils joignent l'arche avec Dagon et conservent secret toutes les superstitions de leur ancien culte idolâtre, avec lea cérémonies de la religion chrétienne. [8]

In spite of that instrusion, indeed because it was essentially superficial, it could not work the same kind of vital changes that we see in the culture of the Negro in the United States. It is not Jerusalem or Calvary which commands the attention of the Voodoo adherent. The ancestral home is *Guinée* for, paradoxical as it may seem since Guinea is to the east, that is where the sun rises and returns home:

Coté solei leve?
Li leve nans l'est.

Coté solei couche?
Li couche nans Guinée. [9]

Thus, a man undergoing the most visible manifestation of the influence of the *loa*, the trance, has in a sense returned to the ancestral home: "Li nans Guinée," he is in Guinea. Heaven is not Timbuktu as in the hispanic tradition, nor is it a Protestant berth in Abraham's bosom. As quoted earlier from Moore and Beier:

The black man in Haiti. . .without even knowing, in the vast majority of cases, from which part of Africa his ancestors came, was obliged to build up a romantic, idealized vision of "Guinea," a kind of heaven to which all good negroes go when they die.

But Moore and Beier are rather unjust, insofar as this is applied to the Voodoo adherent and somewhat simplistic insofar as it is meant to capture the *assimilé's* dilemma and Voodoo. One must accept the existence of a vital culture and language in the French Caribbean as created above by Voodoo. As with *Ñañiguismo* in Cuba, Voodoo with its gods, drums, African words and French patois represents the bridge by which the *assimilé* would attempt the return to a spiritual and cultural *pays natal*. But the history of the *assimilé* is not without its incongruities.

Articles 409 and 249 of the *Code Penal d'Haiti* comprehensively but ineffectively forbid the practice of Voodoo. Article 249 concerns itself with the *culte des morts*, primarily then with Petro. Article 409 applies generally to Voodoo as a whole:

> Tous faiseurs de ouanges, caprelats, vaudoux dompedres, mascandals et autres sortilèges seront punis de trois a six mois d'emprisonnement par le tribunal de simple police; et en cas de récidive, d'un emprisonnement de six mois a deux ans par le tribunal correctional, sans prejudice des peines plus fortes qu'ils encourrant a raison des délits ou crimes par eux commis pour préparer ou accomplir leurs malefices.
>
> Toutes danses et autres pratiques quelconques qui sont de natures à entretenir dans la population l'esprit de fetichisme et de superstition seront considerées comme sortileges et puniées des mêmes peins.[10]

Implicit in these articles are the *assimilé's* estrangement from the *pays natal* and his francophilist inclinations. The *mission civilisatrice* to which the elitist world of Port-au-Prince willingly subjected itself was incompatible with the energies and identities generated by Voodoo. But the contrary negrophilist tendencies and the eschatological concerns of the beginnings of the twentieth century provoked the crisis we have partly examined in Chapter 5. It was Paris-based in origin, but it also had intense manifestations in the French Caribbean, particularly in Haiti.

In 1918, Dr. Arthur C. Holly had prefaced his study, *Les Daimons de Culte Vodu*, with the following pertinent observation:

> We are Latin-Africans. But our civilization is all on the surface; the old African heritage prolongs itself in us and dominates us to such an extent that in many circumstances we feel ourselves moved by

mysterious forces. Thus, our sensibility and our will undergo strange emotions when the unequal rhythms of the sacred dances of Voodoo, now melancholy, now passionate, always full of magic effects, are heard in the silent night.

By a sort of dilettantism, the cultured Haitian possesses the elegant art of deceiving himself. By constantly counterfeiting his ideas and sentiments, and feigning to adapt himself with facility to a borrowed estheticism, the Haitian has lost his personality as a human type.[11]

In 1925, there appeared the most elaborate manifestation of Haitian elegant dilettantism. The publication of Louis Morpeau's *Anthologie d'un Siècle de Poésie háitienne: 1817-1925* was both timely and unfortunate for the "borrowed estheticism" of its elitist elegance. The conflict between the delicately *precieux* memories of Africa and the harshness of the Haitian's origins is captured with an incongruous lack of self-consciousness in the preface to the anthology:

> Torturés, suppliciés, vivant à l'état de bêtes de somme, Sénégalais, Congolais, Dahoméens, natifs de la Guinée, de la Cote-d'or, Mandigues, etc., gardaient le souvenir des nuits claires ruisselantes d'astres et des jours où le soleil deroule ses happes d'or en des éblouissements.

The sensibility that insists on these memories of sparkling, starlit nights and days of golden streams of sunlight is quite obviously contrary to the atavistic dynamism in Voodoo. And this, in spite of the fact that adherent and *assimilé* have the same genesis: "Senegalese, Congolese, Dahomeans, natives of Guinea, of the Gold Coast, Madingos, etc., tortured, whipped, forced to live the lives of beasts of burden etc." The then President of Haiti, Louis Borno, was appropriately represented in the Morpeau anthology. He contributed "metaphysical love lyrics" and other poems in the exquisite lyrics of which romantic nights were illuminated by blackness in a display of effete oxymoron and paradox, such as we find in "Claire de lune."

> Calme divinité trônant sur son pilastre,
> Sur mon coeur asservi règne sa beauté brune.
> Elle a de grands yeux deux, noirs comme un ciel sans astre
> Elle a de grands yeux noirs, doux comme un clair de lune,
> Toujours sombres, toujours doux. Et c'est comme un clair
> De lune qui serait noir.[12]

The incongruous and unclear relationship between these aristocratic rarefications and Haitian *négritude* was best expressed in Leon Laleau's poem significantly titled "Trahison" (Betrayal). In essence, it asks, is there suffering and despair comparable to this: to encompass in French this heart which comes to me from Senegal?

> . . . sentez-vous cette souffrance
> Et ce désespoir à nul autre égal
> D'apprivoiser, avec des mots de France
> Ce coeur qui m'est venu de Sénégal? [13]

The conflict can be further illustrated by the following examples. To the pulsations of *nanchon* drums a voice expresses fear to a Voodoo spirit:

> Ogoun Badagris
> Are you going to eat my flesh?
> Are you going to leave the bones for tomorrow?

> I ask, what are you going to do with me?
> My life is yours.

> Ogoun Badagris
> Ou a manger viandes moins,
> Ou a quitter zos pour demain?

> Me mander ca ou fais moins?
> La vie moins est la. [14]

And yet another voice, in splendidly romantic and French alexandrines, laments the depopulation of heaven: "Et j'ai compris enfin, O cieux, la chose amère/Que tous les dieux sont morts, vous ayant désertés. . . . [15]

A polemic issue was involved here and the crisis of definition and allegiance would coincide with the Paris-based *assimilé* dilemma. The literary polarities were "la muse haïtienne d'expression française" and "la muse haitienne d'expression créole." In what way could and should *l'ndigénisme, l'haïtianisme* or *l'africanisme* best be captured and expressed? Where lay the peculiar genius of the Haitian spirit? The poets of the Midi had reached their greatest heights in Provençale. Would the same be applicable to the poets of Haiti if they used the créole du peuple? There was also the matter of inspiration. Was the Haitian artist to seek inspiration in the classic French tradition or in Negro, African stimuli? A literary polemic war would be waged as to "whether cypress trees, marble columns, and weeping-willows had any legitimate place in Haitian poetry." [16] In all of this some kind of a return was implicitly called for to that set of non-European, non-French energies which Articles 409 and 249 had declared to be less than conducive to the public health.

By 1927, Jacques Roumain had founded the *Revue Indigène* dedicated to the expression of Haiti's *négritude*. In his novel, *Gouverneurs de la Rosée*, Roumain uses Voodoo to provide the framework of the action. The tone of his *négritude* was essentially activist and *révolté* as the following lines from *Bois d'Ebène* attest: "que les nègres/n'acceptent plus/n'acceptent puls/d'être vos niggers/vos sales nègres." For his efforts, Roumain was repeatedly jailed by Borno. He was prudently exiled to Mexico City as *chargé d'affaires* by the Lescot government[17]. There was to this extent more optimistic prophecy than accuracy to Césaire's "Haiti où la négritude se mit debout por la première fois et dit q'elle croyait à son humanité." But it is accurate to the degree that it relates a ferment of Negro-Creole activity in Haiti to similar manifestations during the period in Harlem, Cuba and Paris. The purpose of that activity was clarification of identity and allegiance. This clarification would lead to the emergence of a rejuvenated personality. In the complex associations of Césaire's metaphors and similes, Lazarus would rise from the dead; the cadaver becomes living flesh; the messiah is resurrected. Petar Gubinera's preface to the *Cahier* summarizes the involved expectations of the *Noir Nègre* effectively:

> . . .tout ce qui dormait et était cadavre, peut se réveiller . . . .Le cadavre se "decadaverisera". . . .le symbole des Noirs eduqués par des Européens lui rend l'âme de ses ancêtres. Car les morts vivent en Afrique et veillent sur les-vivants. Leur âme, lorsqu'elle rentre dans un cadavre qui est devenu un cadavre sous la domination des Blancs, animera le cadavre et lui donnera une vie libre qui luttera aussi pour la liberté des Blancs eux-mêmes.[18]

Since the living and the dead exist in symbiotic union in Africa, a corpse, mummified under white domination, can be resurrected by the ancestral spirits and refined into a force that will liberate the whites also.

The concern with death in the *Cahier* is not in terms of biological disintegration. It is instead, moral blindness, esthetic treachery and intellectual and emotional counterfeiting, the results of assimilationism, which constitute death or mummification. The *assimilé* is seduced into an acceptance of the conglomerate *clichés* with which malice and prejudice condemn his Negro origins. (Niggers are all the same/they have all the vices in the world/niggers smell — they smell so much/it makes the cane grow/. . .you know, beat a nigger and you feed him. . . .)

> (Les nègres-sont-tous-les-mêmes, je-vous-le-dis
> les vices-tous-les-vices. C'est-moi-qui-vous-le-dis

l'odeur-du-nègre, ça'fait-pousser-la-canne
rappelez-vous-le-vieux diction:
battre-un-nègre, c'est le nourir)[19]

Or else the *assimilé* falls victim to the exotic silliness of irresponsible negrophilism:

Ou bien tout simplement comme on nous aime!
Obscenes gaiment, très doudous de jazz sur leur
exces d'ennui.
Je sais le tracking, le Lindy-hop et les claquettes.
Pour les bonnes bouches la sourdine de nos
plaintes enrobées de oua-oua.[20]

The lucid and unsparing confessions of an ex-colored *assimilé* become intense as Césaire illustrates by way of self-analysis. He, as an *assimilé*, had believed in the caricatures above and had proceeded to define himself *outside* their scope. His blackness and reflections of his Negroidness in others had led to confused embarrassment. An uncompromisingly negroid Negro, pathetically and grotesquely out of place in a Paris subway provokes Césaire to treachery. He looks at the Negro not as the victim of aberrant malice but through the mocking eyes and uncomfortable snicker of a disgraced mongrel Parisian. The subway Negro was grotesque, his nose like a peninsula: "un nègre hideux, un nègre grognon, un nègre melancholique, un nègre affalé, ses mains reunies un prière sur un baton noueux. Un nègre enseveli dans une vielle veste eliminé. Un nègre comique et laid." Behind this pathetically ugly creature some women were snickering. "El des femmes derrière mai ricansaient en le regardant." And Césaire blessed the good fortune that had diluted his Negro blood:

Il était COMIQUE ET LAID,
COMIQUE ET LAID pour sur. . . .

Je salue les trois siècles qui soutiennent mes droits
civiques et mon sang minimisé.[21]

As the *Cahier* unflatteringly states the case, "I hid behind a stupid vanity" in a disintegrating world:

Je me cachais derrière une vanité stupide le destin m'appelait j'étais caché derrière et voici l'homme par terre, sa très fragile défense dispersée, ses maximes sacrées foulées aux pieds, ses declamations pédantesques rendant du vent par chaque blessure voici l'homme par terre. . . .[22]

Given this kind of spiritual and moral atrophy, the watchword as the Cahier begins is *partir des blancs,* to leave the world of white civilization and its atrophied and atrophying energies. A return to the self, defined independently of *les blancs,* was imperative. Hence *Cahier d'un Retour au Pays Natal.* The work thus has two impulses; the first is exilic and agonistic and the second, integrative and messianic.

The return demands more than mere confessional disemboweling. The Prodigal Son turns to ancestral forces. He returns in a delicate, refined manner to the face of a god in a voodoo shrine:

> voum rooh oh
> voum rooh oh
> à charmer les serpents à conjurer
> les morts
> voum rooh oh
> à contraindre la pluie à contrarier
> les raz de marée
> voum rooh oh
> à empêcher que no tourne l'ombre
> voum rooh oh que mas cieux à moi
> s'ouvrent.[23]

The *nègre généreux*, as he leaves "l'Europe toute révulsée de cris. . .peureuse," undertakes an argosy symbolized by Toussaint Louverture and his revolt in a universe of white death.

> Thus he writes of the imprisoned hero Toussaint Louverture, dying in the Jura mountains amid the snows the Northern winter:
> What I am
> is a man alone imprisoned in
> white
> is a man alone who defies
> the white cries of white death
> (TOUSSAINT, TOUSSAINT
> LOUVERTURE)
> Is a man who fascinates the white hawk of white death
> is a man alone in the eternal sea of white sand
> is an old darky braced against
> the waters of the sky.[24]

The Prodigal Son arrives rejuvenated, supple and the enlightened mouthpiece of the *pays natal.* "Et voici soudain que force et vie m'assaillent comme un taureau."

Mon coeur bruissait de génerosité emphatiques. . . j'arriverais lisse et
jeune dans ce pays mien et je dirais à ce pays dont le limon entre dans
la composition de ma chair: "J'ai longtemps erré et je reviens vers la
hideur desertée de vos plaies"

Je viendrais à ce pays mien et je lui dirais.
"Embrassez-moi sans crainte. . .Et si je ne sais que parler, c'est pour
vous que je parlerai"
Et je lui dirais encore:
"Ma bouche sera la bouche des malheurs qui n'ont point de bouche,
ma voix, la liberté de celles qui s'affaissent au cachot du désespoir"

Et venant je me dirais à moi-même:

"Et surtout mon corps aussi bien que mon âme, gardez-vous de vous
croiser les bras en l'attitude sterile du spectateur, car la vie n'est pas
un spectacle, car une mer de douleurs n'est pas un proscenium, car un
homme qui crie n'est pas un ours qui danse."[25]

The *Noir Nègre* in effect becomes symbolic of a universal pariah – a Man
of Sorrows who elevates "DE PROFUNDIS," a song of the dispossessed:

. . .je serais un homme-juif
un homme-cafre
un homme-hindou-de-Calcutta
un homme-de-Harlem-qui-ne-vote-pas

L'homme-famine, l'homme-insulte, l'homme-
torture on pouvait à n'importe quel moment le
saisir le rouer de coups, le tuer. . .sans avoir de compte
à rendre à personne. . . .[26]

The crowning achievement then in the *Cahier* was to invert the very
means of denigration and insult in a poetic alchemy that stamps Man of
Sorrows on the *assimilé* and then to make that Sorrow an icon. The
difficulty, however, lies in the fact that the *assimilé*'s history makes a
definition of health hard to conceive. The dimensions of self-definition are
never separable from crisis and confrontation. It is therefore not surprising
that the quality of *assimilé-Creole* health should be aligned with that of the
creolizing power. It was Césaire's good fortune – and mistake – that he
was writing in a frame of mind passionately sensitive to "the
unmentionable odor of death" of the period. It made the messianic
inclination easy at the same time that it prevented any intelligent
assessment of the kind of syncretistic culture by which the *assimilé* should

be re-defined in health. The impulses for the magnificent optimism of the *Cahier* as it ends have much more to do with the nature of disease than with the nature of recuperative medicine. This aggravated awareness of disease results in two different evaluations. There were Caucasian Europe's convulsions, which were presumably terminal, or at least pathological:

Ecoutez le monde blanc
horriblement las de son effort immense
ses articulations rebelles craquer sous les étoiles dures
ses raideurs d'acier bleu transperçant la chair mystiques
ses victoires proditoires trompeter ses défaites
écoute aux alibis grandioses son piètre trébuchement.[27]

Given the above, it is apparently easier to accept and alchemize a less pathological identity and to postulate an illogical belief in a regenerative disease:

J'accepte.. .j'accepte. . .entierement, sans reserve. . .
ma race qu'aucune ablution d'hysope et de lys
mêlés ne pourrait purifier
. . . . [28]

But there is a problem involved here. To what extent can that same race be defined in terms of what it positively offers? The problem is perhaps unfair to Césaire. The *Cahier* may best be seen as an intensely therapeutic performance. It moves from the agony and exile of a confused *assimilé* through the rash indignations of revolt to a final mood that is in a sense Whitmanesque. The magnanimity is transcendental: "je ne suis plus qu'un homme qui accepte n'ayant plus de colère/(il n'a plus dans le coeur que de l'amour immense, et qui brûle.") There is perhaps something of a monumental conceit here which has transformed a sycophant francophile into a brilliantly, surrealistically resurrected cliché. He becomes a Noble Savage at one with spontaneous nature and correctively antithetical to the sterile constipation of European intellect:

ma négritude n'est pas un pierre, sa surdité ruée
contre la clameur du jour
ma négritude n'est pas une taie d'eau morte sur
l'oeil mort de la terre
ma négritude n'est ni une tour ni une cathédrale

elle plonge dans la chair rouge du sol
elle plonge dans la chair ardente du ciel
elle troue l'accablement opaque de sa droite patience.[29]

The Negro race becomes the ultimate symbol of victimized innocence whose chief virtue does not lie in exploratory intellect or conquistadorial domination. It lies instead in *négritude's* unbroken relationship with primordial and quintessencial forces in nature and in its keen senstivity to the quietest whispers of the wind:

> Eia pour le Kaïlcédrat royal!
> Eia pour ceux qui n'ont jamias rien inventé
> pour ceux qui n'ont jamais exploré
> pour ceux qui n'ont jamais rien dompté
>
> mais ils s'abandonnent, saisis, à l'essence de toute chose
> ignorants des surface mais saisis par le mouve-
> ment de toute chose
> insoucieux de dompter, mais jouant le jeu du monde
>
> véritablement les fils aînés du monde
> poreux à tous les souffles du monde
> aire fraternelle de tous les souffles du monde.[30]

It is then appropriate that the work should end with a celebrative dance, "la danse il-est-beau-et-bon-et-legitime-d'être-nègre." And it is fitting that that dance should make the poet one with the elements, that *negritude* should literally cast its fate to the winds and so be re-integrated in its *"noire vibration au nombril du monde,"* in its black vibrations into the world.

> A moi mes danses et saute le soleil sur la raquette
> de mes mains
> mais non l'inégal soleil ne me suffit plus
> enroule-toi, vent, autour de ma nouvelle croissance
> pose-toi sur mes doigts mesurés
> je te livre ma conscience et son rythme de chair
> je te livre les feux où brasille ma faiblesse
> je te livre le chain-gang
> je te livre le marais
> . . . .
> je te livre mes paroles abruptes
> dévore tout et enroule-toi
> et t'enroulant embrasse-moi d'un plus vaste frisson
> embrasse-moi jusq'au nous furieux
> embrasse, embrasse NOUS.[31]

All these reservations are perhaps unfair to the impression the *Cahier* leaves. It is the exquisite lucidity of uncompromising integrity and the sheer music of an exilic *tam-tam verbal* that most impress. Conceptually, the *Cahier* does not stray far from the excellence and limitations of the trajectory that gave it impetus. It is familiar enough ground on which Langston Hughes and Nicolás Guillén had traced the agony and the exile of the Creole's attempt at self-assessment. It was, moreover, an assessment in a world that constrained him to define himself as Negro and thereby imposed upon him an unfair burden.

NOTES

[1] Maya Deren, *Divine Horsemen, The Living Gods of Haiti* (London & New York: Thames and Hudson, 1953), p. 91.

[2] In *Mapa de la Poesía Negra*, p. 203.

[3] For the discussion of Voodoo following, see in addition to Deren above, Louis Maximilien, *Le Voudou haitien: Rite Rada-Canzo* (Port-au-Prince; Imprimerie de l'Etat, 1945); J.C. Dorsainvil, *Manuel d'Histoire d'Haiti* (Port-au-Prince, 1925); Alfred Metraux *Haiti: Black Peasants and Voodoo*, trans. by Peter Lengyel (New York: Universe Books, 1960); William Seabrook, *The Magic Island* (New York: Harcourt, Brace and Co., 1929) and J. Price-Mars, "Transatlantic African Survivals and the Dynamism of Negro Culture," *Presence Africaine*, Nos. 8-8-10, Special Issue, pp. 276-284.

[4] *Metrauz op, cit.,* p. 62. See also for language, Robert Hall, Jr., *Haitian Creole: grammar, texts, vocabulary* (Philadelphia: American Folklore Society, 1953): also *Pidgin and Creole Languages* (Ithaca, New York: Cornell University Press, 1966) by the same author.

[5] Maximilien, *op. cit.*, p. 105. He speculates that the *language* of the rhythmic sequences, being neither French nor creole, constitutes a special priestly language.

[6] *Ibid.*, p. 213.

[7] Seabrook, *op, cit.*, pp. 38-39.

[8] *Ibid.*, p. 292.

[9] *Ibid.*, p. 36.

[10] *Ibid.*, p. 294. The French is as quoted. See also p. 335 for article 249.

[11] Dr. Arthur C. Holly, *Les Daimons du Culte Vodu* (Port-au-Prince, Haiti: Edward Chênet, 1918). Quoted here as in the translation in Seabrook, *op. cit.*, pp. 313-314.

[12] This is a much anthologized poem. See any of the Hispanic-Caribbean anthologies in bibliography in addition to Morpeau, *Anthologie d'un Siècle de Poesie haitienne, 1817-1925* (Paris: Bossard, 1925).

[13] Leon Laleau, "Trahison" in *Du Saint-Domingue à Haiti: Essai sur la Culture, les Arts et la Literature* by Dr. Jean Price-Mars (Paris: Presence Africaine,

1959), pp. 46-47.

[14] William Seabrook, *op. cit.*, p. 38.

[15] "Le Pelerin" by Damocles Vieux in *De Saint-Domingue à Haiti*, p. 35.

[16] For the range of this polemic see in addition to Price-Mars, and Seabrook, J. Alexis, "Of the Marvellous Realism of the Haitians" in *Presence Africaine*, Special Issue, pp. 249-275. See also, Lilyan Kesteloot, *op. cit.* for perhaps the best summary treatment.

[17] See a most helpful preface to *Masters of the Dew*, Langston Hughes' translation of *Governeurs de la Rosée*. Roumain died in Mexico City in 1944.

[18] *Cahier*, pp. 22-23.

[19] *Ibid.*, p. 58.

[20] *Ibid.*, p. 58.

[21] *Ibid.*, pp. 64-65.

[22] *Ibid.*, pp. 66-67.

[23] *Ibid.*, p. 51.

[24] Moore and Beier, *op. cit.*, pp. 16-17.

[25] *Cahier*, pp. 41-42.

[26] *Ibid.*, p. 39. Compare the last clause with Vautrin's, Chapter Five, text and note 2. The suspicion is that Césaire is quoting sarcastically.

[27] *Ibid.*, pp. 72-73.

[28] *Ibid.*, p.77.

[29] *Ibid.*, pp. 71.

[30] *Ibid.*, pp. 71-72.

[31] *Ibid.*, p. 90.

CONCLUSION

The selection from Lewis Nkosi, which opens Part III of this study, has exerted both a benign and a malignant effect on the Negro-Creole. To repeat the quotation: "Black consciousness really begins with the shock of discovery that one is not only black but also *non-white*." To the extent that it defines the Creole in relation to blackness, its influence is benign. To the extent that it denies the eclectic or syncretistic origins of the Creole, it poses what should be a needless and yet is a painful dilemma to the Creole exiled in Western civilization. Clarification may be needed here in reference to Nkosi. I do not imply a direct influence. I suggest instead that there is a process of self-definition encompassed by the statement with which Hughes, Guillén and Césaire, wrestle somewhat agonizingly. How can one define blackness acceptably in a world that insists on exiling the Creole in racial *purgatorios?* A most relevant statement about the Creole would be that in *The Weary Blues, West Indies Ltd.* and in *Cahier d'un Retour au Pays Natal* he awakens to the shock of discovery that he is not only *non-white* but also *non-black*. His non-blackness by and large accounts for the romantic excesses of the protestations of blackness in these authors. By the same token, the unresolved symbiotic identification with his ineradicable whiteness would seem to account for the other half of his exilic exasperations. Langston Hughes inadvertently states half of the truth in the autobiographical *The Big Sea:*

> You see, unfortunately, I am not black. There are lots of different kinds of blood in our family. But here in the United States, the word "Negro" is used to mean anyone who has *any* Negro blood at all in his veins. In Africa, the word is more pure. It means *all* Negro, therefore black.
>
> I am brown. My father was a darker brown. My mother an olive yellow.

It is the Creole's peculiar difficulty that the aberrant nonsense of racial malice forces him into a chronic and pathogenic blackness from which he has been permanently exiled. By the same token, a necessity not to remain undefined or ill-defined forces on him the exotic and inorganic display of *négritude* such as the works studied compulsively flaunt.

173

Blackness is insistently defined not in terms of value and validity inviolate to itself but in opposition or contradistinction to whiteness. One looks in vain in all the drama of the three Creole voices of Part III for a literate statement about what blackness consists in, independent of the Romanticism of the Noble Savage, the presumed moral or esthetic superiority of Rhythm or the uplifting pathology of a Man of Sorrows. But these figures should really be mere traumatic *stations* in the Creole's development. To see them as unevolving and permanent or even preferable identities is to display a fancy for the romantic pose. That is not to say, however, that one denies the profound miseries and brilliant enough energies expended in that pose. I have chosen to study and illustrate that misery and brilliance in its manifestations in the Americas between 1926 and 1940.

The compulsion to make prognostications about the future and to illustrate by way of the present is almost unavoidable, especially as one witnesses the "new" convulsions of the New Negro in American society. But I envision a different study that would develop a similar trajectory from the start of World War II to the Seventies. I have established three subcultures in Negro America and the Caribbean. Much of my discussion of them holds true for their manifestations during the Twenties and Thirties. I am not sure that the changes worked by history since then have not rendered different analyses imperative. In Cuba, we have a political but even more fascinating human experiment—the influence of Communism on the Latin-American temperament and on blackness. It is not at all certain therefore that the neanderthal restrictions of "Soviet Realism" or of "Diamat" in the arts as they have been discussed by Czeslaw Milosz' *Captive Mind* can apply on the island. Equally important, the nature of the revolution in Cuba caused disaffection among the upper and middle classes. It perforce focuses its energies on the lower classes, in the traditional rung of the Negro or Creole. Subcultures like *Ñañiguismo* generally develop in isolation and thrive on neglect or voluntary and involuntary ostracism. It cannot suffer the same ostracism under the premises from which the present Cuban society must operate. What kind of identity will thus be created for the Negro and the racial impulses behind it await fruition. A first generation has yet to come to maturity in Cuba at this writing.

The situation in Haiti again awaits development. To a certain extent, there has been a continuation of circumstances that favor the intensification of Voodoo and the elitist estrangement of the ruling class. The dictatorship of Duvalier is certainly more crudely fascinating but hardly a profoundly different thing from the political abilities or intentions of Borno or Lescot. One must presume some kind of change, however, when Duvalier leaves the scene. The conjunction of that departure and the definition of Haiti's *négritude* may offer interesting sequels to Césaire and Senghor.

There are contradictory impulses in the Negro activity in the United States. On the one hand, there is the movement toward an assertion of black pride, of manifestations of *absolute* and therefore suspect *négritude*. At the same time, there is the systematic and exploitative neutralization of that *négritude* in the obsessive commercialization of the society. All the important attributes of the 'new' *négritude* can be synthetically reproduced in gestures, styles and postures functional to any other identity. The same Afro haircut, for example, functions in terms of race glorification and also as a most necessary extension, presumably, of television saleswomen ecstatically satisfied with clean toilet bowls. The same dynamism manifests itself in the sensationally virulent autobiographies that constitute a corpus of Negro creativity and energy. It may be no coincidence that creativity manifests itself as literate and illiterate, spectacular disembowelings much amenable to profitable reproduction in the paragraphs of popular magazines. The conflict between therapeutic hari-kiri and therapeutic profiteering should make interesting study at a later date. We have seen a somewhat less abrasive coinicidence of such contradictory impulses in the period under study—slack exoticism and crises of racial allegiance and definition. This, however, was before the Blues Orpheus went on television to moan about the ambrosial purity of beers, whiskies and colas. In the meantime, and in conclusion to this study of what may be called a *danse macabre* between whiteness and blackness in human forms, I look upon the aberrant ingenuity and speculative perplexity of "Yacub's History" as the extreme pulsation of that *danse*. It would be simplistic to dismiss the parable as merely aberrant, however. In its surrealist inventiveness, it illustrates the perplexing and inspired madness or unreality that lies at the heart of the caricatures that populate this study:

> Original Man was black, in the continent called Africa where the human race had emerged on the Earth. The black man, original man, built great empires and civilisations and cultures, while the white man was still living on all fours in caves. . . . .First the moon separated from the earth. Then, the first humans, Original Man, were a black people. They founded the Holy City Mecca.
>
> Among this black race were twenty-four wise scientists. One of the scientists, at odds with the rest, created the especially strong black tribe of Shebazz, from which America's Negroes, so-called, descend.
>
> About sixty-six hundred years ago, when seventy percent of the

people were satisfied, and thirty percent were dissatisfied, among the dissatisfied was born a Mr. Yacub. He was born to create trouble, to break the peace, and to kill. *His head was unusually large. When he was four years old, he began school. At eighteen, Yacub had finished all of his nation's colleges and universities. He was known as "big-head scientist."* Among other things, he had learned how to breed races scientifically.

This big-head scientist, Mr. Yacub, began preaching in the streets of Mecca, making such hosts of converts that the authorities increasingly concerned, finally exiled him with 59,999 followers to the island of Patmos. . . .

Though he was a black man, Mr. Yacub, embittered toward Allah now decided, as revenge, to create upon the earth a devil race—a bleached-out, white race of people. . . .

Two hundred years later—the white race had at last been created.

On the island of Patmos was nothing but blond, pale-skinned, cold-blue-eyed devils—savages, nude, and shameless, many like animals, they walked on all fours and they lived in trees. . . .

When this devil race had spent two thousand years in the caves, Allah raised up Moses to civilize them, and bring them out of the caves. It was written that this devil white race would rule the world for six thousand years.

It was written that some of the original black people should be brought as slaves to North America - to learn to better understand, at first hand, the white devil's true nature.

And so the Negro-Creole and Creoledom.

NOTES

[1] This remarkable fable forms the "theological" basis of the Black Muslims, "The Lost-Found Nation of Islam in the wilderness of North America." See Malcolm X and Alex Haley, *Autobiography of Malcolm X* (New York: Grove Press, Inc., 1966), pp. 162-167. The emphasis (mine) is of course true to the tradition that defines whiteness in Faustian terms.

BIBLIOGRAPHY

Alberes, R. M. *L'Aventure intellectuelle de XXe Siècle: Panorama des littératures européenes*. Paris: Albin Michel, 1959.

Andrade, Mario. *Antologia de Poesía negra de Expressao portuguesa, precedida de Cultura negro-africana e assimilacao*. Paris: P.J. Oswald, 1959.

Auden, W.H. "The Alienated City." *Encounter*. Vol. XVII, No. 2 (August 1961).

Ballagas, Emilio, *Antologia de Poesía negra hispano-americana*. Madrid: M. Aguilar, 1935.

——————. *Mapa de la Poesía negra americana*. Buenos Aires: Editorial Pleamar, 1946.

Balzac, Honoré. *Le Père Goriot*. Paris: Gallimard, 1965.

Baudelaire, Charles. *Les Fleurs du Mal*. Edited by Antoine Adam. Paris: Garnier Frères, 1959.

Baudin, Paul Noel, Reverend. *Fetichism and Fetich Worshipers*. Translated by Miss M. McMahan. New York: Benziger Brothers, 1885.

Beaumont, Francis and Fletcher, John. *The Works*. Vol. VII. Cambridge, England: Cambridge English Classics, 1909.

Beckford, William. *Italy; with Sketches of Spain and Portugal*. Vol. II. Paris: Baudry's European Library.

Behn, Aphra. *The Novels*. Edited by Ernest A. Baker. London: G. Rutledge and Sons Ltd., 1905.

Béraud, Louis Francis and Joseph de Rosny, *Adonis ou le bon Nègre*. Paris: Clisau, 1798.

Bernth, Lindfors. "Amos Tutuola's *The Palm-Wine Drinkard and Oral Tradition*." *Critique*. Vol. XI, No. 1, pp. 42-50.

Blades, William C. *Negro Poems, Melodies, Plantation Pieces, Camp Meeting Songs*. Boston: Gorham Press. 1921.

Blake, William. *The Complete Writings*. Edited by Geoffrey Keynes. London: Oxford University Press, 1966.

Bontemps, Arna, ed. *American Negro Poetry*. New York: Hill and Wang, 1965.

Bovill, E.W. *The Battle of Alcazar*. London: Batchworth Press, 1952.

Broussard, James. *Louisiana Creole Dialect*. Baton Rouge: Louisiana State University, 1942.

Ca da Mosto; Usodimare, Antoniotto; Niccoloso de Recco. *Le Navigazione Atlantiche, XIII-XVI* in *Viaggi e Scoperte di Navigatori ed Esploratori Italiani*. Vol. I. Edited by Rinaldo Caddeo: Milano: Edizioni "Alpes," 1929.

Campbell, John. *Negro-Mania: being an Examination of the Falsely Assumed Equality of the Various Races of Men*. Philiadelphia: Campbell and Power, 1851.

Cendrars, Blaise. *Petits Contes nègres pour les Enfants des Blancs*. Toulouse: Imprimerie Regionale. 1946.

——————. *Comment les Blancs sont d' anciens Noirs*. Argenteuil: R. Coulouma, 1930.

Cervantes, Miguel, Saavedra de. *Don Quijote de la Mancha*. Madrid: Ediciones Castilla, no date.

Cesaire, Aime. *Cahier d'un Retour au Pays Natal*. 2nd edition. Introduction by Petar Guberina. Paris: Presence Africaine, 1956.

Connestagio, Girolamo Franchi. *D'ell 'Unione del Regno di Portogallo alla Corona di Castiglia*. Edited by F. Maria Rodreiquez. S. Domingo: Instituto Escholar, 1878.

——————. *The Historie of the Uniting of the Kingdom of Portugall to the Crowne of Castill*. Translated by Edward Blount. London: A Hatfield, 1600.

Couffon, Claude. *Nicolás Guillén*. Poètes d'Aujourd'hui. Vienna: Pierres Sighers, 1964.

Damas, Leon G. *Black Label, poèmes*. Paris: Gallimard, 1956.

Davidson, Basil. *Africa: History of a Continent*. New York: Macmillan. 1966.

Deren, Maya. *Divine Horsemen: The Living Gods of Haiti*. London and New York: Thames and Hudson, 1960.

Doob, Leonard. *Ants Will Not Eat Your Fingers: A Selection of Traditional African Poems*. New York: Walker and Company, 1966.

Dorson, Richard M. ed. *American Negro Folktales*. New York: Fawcett World Library, 1967.

Ellison, Ralph. *Invisible Man*. New York: The New American Library, 1952.

Ellman, Richard and Charles Feidelson, Jr., eds. *The Modern Tradition: Backgrounds of Modern Literature*. New York: Oxford University Press, 1965.

Embil-Rodriques, Luis. *La Poesía negra en Cuba*. La Universidad de Chile,1939.

Etienne, Servais. *Les Sources de Bug-Jargal.* Bruxelles: Academie de Langue et de Litterature francaise, 1923.

Fage, J.D. *An Introduction to the History of West Africa.* Cambridge, England: Cambridge University Press, 1962.

Fanon, Frantz. *Peau noir Masques blancs.* Paris: Seuil, 1952.

Freyre, Gilberto. *Casa Granda & Senzala.* 2 vols. Rio de Janeiro: Livraria Jose Olympio Editora S.A., 1964.

Fyfe, Christopher. *Sierra Leone Inheritance.* London: Oxford University Press. 1964.

Gautier, Theophile. *Poésie Complete. 3 vols. Edited by Rene Jasuisko. Paris: Firmin-Didot, 1932.*

Giraldi Cintio, Giovanni Battista. *Hecatommithi.* Venice: Deuchino & Gio. Battista Pulciani, 1608.

Góngora, Luis de. *Obras Poeticas.* Vol. II. New York: Hispanic Society of America, no date.

Green, Graham. *Journey Without Maps.* London: William Heineman, 1953.

——————. *The Heart of the Matter.* Compass Books. New York: The Viking Press, 1966.

Guillén, Nicolas. *El Son Entero.* Buenos Aires: Editorial Pleamar, 1947.

Guirao, Ramon, ed. *Orbita de la Poesía Afrocubana, 1928-37.* Havana: Ugar, Garcia y Cia., 1938

Hall, Robert Jr. *Haitian Creole grammar, texts, vocabulary.* Philadelphia: American Folklore Society, 1953.

——————. *Hands off Pidgin English.* Sydney, Australia: Pacific Publications, 1955.

——————. *Melanesiam Pidgin English: grammar, texts, vocabulary.* Baltimore, Maryland: Waverly Press, Inc., 1943.

——————*Pidgin and Creole Languages.* Ithaca, New York: Cornell University Press, 1966.

Herskovits, Melville J. *The Human Factor in Changing Africa.* New York: Alfred Knopf, 1962.

——————."The Role of Culture-Pattern in the African Acculturative Experience." *Presence Africaine*, Vols. VI-VII, Nos. 34-35, pp. 7-17.

Heywood, Thomas. *The Dramatic Works.* Vol II. New York: Russell and Russell, 1964.

Hughes, Langston. *The Panther and the Lash: Poems of our Times.* New York: Alfred A. Knopf, 1967.

——————. *Selected Poems.* New York: Knopf, 1959.

——————. *The Langston Hughes Reader.* New York: George Braziller, Inc., 1958.

——————. *The Weary Blues*. New York: Knopf, 1959.

——————, and Arna Bontemps. *The Book of Negro Folklore*, New York: Dodd, Mead and Company, 1959.

Hugo, Victor. *Oeuvres Romanesques Complètes*. Edited by Francis Bouvet. Paris: Jean-Jacques Pervert, 1962.

Johnson, James Weldon. *God's Trombones: Seven Negro Sermons in Verse*. New York The Viking Press, 1966.

Jones, Eldred. *Othello's Countrymen*. London: Oxford University Press, 1965.

Kesteloot, Lilyan. *Aimé Césaire*. Poete d'Aujourd'hui. Vienna: Pierre Seghers, 1962.

——————. *Les Ecrivains noirs de Langue francaise*. Belgium: Universite Libre de Bruxelles, 1963.

Landes, Ruth. *City of Women*. New York: Macmillan Company, 1947.

Lasebikan, E.L. "The Tonal Structure of Yoruba Poetry." *Presence Africaine*, Nos. 8-9-10 (June-November, 1956). Full Acount of the 1st. International Conference of Negro Writers and Artists, Paris, 1956, pp. 43-50.

Little, Kenneth, *Negroes in Britain, A Study of Racial Relations in English Society*. London: Kegan Paul, Trench, Trubner and Company, Ltd., 1947.

Longfellow, Henry Wadsworth, *The Complete Poetical Works.* Boston and New York: Houghton-Mifflin and Company, 1922.

Lorca, Federico García. *Obras Completas*. Madrid: Aguilar, 1954.

Mandelbaum, Maurice; Francis W. Gramlich; and Alan Ross Anderson, eds, *Philosophic Problems*. New York:The Macmillan Company, 1964.

Marlowe, Christopher. *Plays and Poems*. Edited by M. R. Ridley. New York: E.P. Dutton, 1963.

Mars, Jean Price. *De Saint-Domingue a Haiti*. Paris: Presence Africaine, 1959.

——————. "Transatlantic African Survivals and the Dynamism of Negro Culture." *Presence Africaine*. Nos. 8-9-10, pp. 276-84.

Marston, John. *The Plays*. Vol. II. Edited by H. Harvey Wood. London: Oliver and Boyd, 1938.

Maurois, André. *Les Trois Dumas*. Paris Hachette, 1957,

Maximilien, Louis. *Le Vodou Haitien: Rite Radas-Canzo*. Port-au-Prince, Haiti: Imprimerie de l'Etat, 1945.

Melville, Herman. *Moby Dick*. Modern Library. New York: Random House, 1950.

Métraux, Alfred. *Haiti, Black Peasants and Voodoo*. Translated by Peter Lengyel. New York: Universe Books, 1960.

Middleton, Thomas. *The Works*. Vol. VII. Edited by A.H. Bullen. Boston: Houghton, Mifflin and Company, 1886.

Milosz, Czeslaw. *The Captive Mind*. Translated from the Polish by Jane Zielonko. New York: Vintage Books, 1955.

Miyakawa, T. Scott. *Protestants and Pioneers: Individualism and Conformity on the American Frontier*. Chicago University of Chicago Press, 1964.

Moore, Gerald and Beier, Ulli. *Modern Poetry from Africa*. Baltimore, Maryland: Penguin Books, 1966.

Morpeau, Louis. *Anthologie d'un Siècle de Poesie haitienne, 1817-1925*. Paris: Editions Bossard, 1925.

Nilon, Charles H. *Faulkner and the Negro*. Boulder: University of Colorado Press, 1962.

Peele, George. *The Dramatic Works*. Edited by Hook and Yorklavich. New Haven: Yale University Press, 1961.

Quevedo y Villegas, Francisco Gomez de. *Obras Completas*. Barcelona: Editorial Planete. No date.

Quinones, Luis Benavente de. *Entremeses*. Vol. II, Edited by Don Cayetano Rosell. Madrid: Libros de Antano, 1874.

Randeynes et Fils. *Debarquement de la Flotte française a Saint-Domingue*. Paris: Tiger, 1820.

Sackille-West, V. *Aphra Behn the Incomparable Astrea*. London: G. Howe Ltd., 1927.

Sartre, Jean Paul. *la Nausée*. Paris: Gallimard, 1938.

Seabrook, W.B. *The Magic Island*. New York: Harcourt, Brace and Company, 1929.

Senghor, Léopold Sédar. *Anthologie de la nouvelle Poésie negre et malgache de langue francaise*. With an introduction "Orphee Noir" by J.P. Sartre. Paris: Collection Colonies et Empire, 1948.

——————. *Poèmes*. Paris: Seuil, 1964.

——————. "The Spirit of Civilization or the Laws of African Negro Culture." *Présence Africaine*, Nos. 8-9-10.

Shakespeare, William. *The Complete Works*. 2 Vols. Edited by W.G. Clark and Aldis Wright. Garden City, New York: Nelson Doubleday, Inc. No date.

Sperry, William. *Religion in America*. Cambridge, England: University Press. 1945.

Thackeray, William Makepiece. *Vanity Fair, A Novel without a Hero*. Introduction by Whitelaw Reid. New York: E.P. Dutton and Co., 1930.

Trend J.B. *The Language and History of Spain*. London: Hutchison House, 1964.

Tuchman, Barbara. *The Proud Tower: A Portrait of the World before the War: 1890-1914*. New York: Bantam Books, Inc., 1967.

Valdes, Ildefonso Pereda. *El Negro rioplatense*. Montevideo: C. Garcia y Cia., 1937.

Valle-Inclán Ramon del. *Sonatas: Memorias del Marqués de Bradomin*. Mexico, D.F.: Populibros "La Prensa," 1959.

Wescott, Joan, "The Sculpture and Myths of Eshu Elegba the Yoruba Trickster." *Africa* Vol. XXXII, 1962.

Whitfield, Irene Therese. *Louisiana French Folk Songs*. University, Louisiana: Louisiana State University Press, 1939.

Whitman, Walt. *Leaves of Grass and Selected Prose*. Edited by John Kouwenhoven. New York: The Modern Library, 1950.

INDEX

Wheatley, Phyllis, 89, 123
Whitman, Walt, 13, 130, 136; "Ethiopia
   Saluting the Colors", 55
Williams, William Carlos, "A Negro
   Woman", 59

Wordsworth, William, on Toussaint
   Louverture, 55

Work Songs: (American Negro), 120-21
Yoruba, 14, 22, 25, 140